D1796447

Edinburgh German Yearbook

Edinburgh German Yearbook

General Editor: Peter Davies

Edinburgh German Yearbook

Volume 8

New Literary and Linguistic
Perspectives on the German Language,
National Socialism, and the Shoah

Edited by
Peter Davies
and
Andrea Hammel

 CAMDEN HOUSE
Rochester, New York

Copyright © 2014 by the Editors and Contributors

All Rights Reserved. Except as permitted under current legislation,
no part of this work may be photocopied, stored in a retrieval system,
published, performed in public, adapted, broadcast, transmitted,
recorded, or reproduced in any form or by any means,
without the prior permission of the copyright owner.

First published 2014
by Camden House

Camden House is an imprint of Boydell & Brewer Inc.
668 Mt. Hope Avenue, Rochester, NY 14620, USA
www.camden-house.com
and of Boydell & Brewer Limited
PO Box 9, Woodbridge, Suffolk IP12 3DF, UK
www.boydellandbrewer.com

ISSN: 1937-0857
ISBN-13: 978-1-57113-597-1
ISBN-10: 1-57113-597-9

This publication is printed on acid-free paper.
Printed in the United States of America.

Edinburgh German Yearbook appears annually.
Please send orders and inquiries to Boydell & Brewer at the above address.

Edinburgh German Yearbook does not accept unsolicited submissions: a
Call for Papers for each volume is circulated widely in advance of publication.
For editorial correspondence, please contact either the General Editor,
Professor Peter Davies, or the editor(s) of individual volumes, by post at:

Edinburgh German Yearbook
German Section
Division of European Languages and Cultures
59 George Square, Edinburgh, EH8 3JX
United Kingdom

or by email at: egyb@ed.ac.uk.

Contents

Words and Music

Translation

Introduction: The German Language, National Socialism, and the Shoah

Peter Davies, University of Edinburgh
Andrea Hammel, Aberystwyth University

THERE IS SEEMINGLY NO ESCAPING the association of the language of Goethe with the language of Hitler. Whatever one may feel about the rather leaden cliché that juxtaposes Buchenwald and Weimar, the disciplines of cultural history, literary criticism, discourse analysis, "Sprachkritik," and memory studies have all, in their various ways, contributed to a rich field of concepts ("Tätersprache," "Sprache *des* Nationalsozialismus" vs. "Sprache *im* Nationalsozialismus,"[1] "unheimliche Heimat,"[2] and many others) that both describe and embody the ambivalent, uneasy status of the German language and its traditions after the Shoah.

"Sprachkritiker" such as Victor Klemperer suggested that the *Lingua Tertii Imperii* was a perversion of German that needed to be purged from the language in order to restore its healthy traditions. However, does the notion of "Nazi language" as an identifiably separate entity really hold water, or is it simply a form of linguistic purism analogous to the desire to construct a clear demarcation line between "Germans" and "Nazis"? Is the German language really so fraught with history and violence that constant vigilance and self-reflexivity are necessary, or is neutral or even innocent speech in German still possible in the post-Holocaust world? And do the descendants of victims and of perpetrators have comparable attitudes and responsibilities regarding language, or radically different ones?

The poet Gerschon Ben-David, who had survived the Holocaust as a child with non-Jewish foster parents, and continued to write in German in Israel after his emigration in 1947, wrote strikingly in the 1960s about a longing for authentic communication with non-Jewish Germans and a fear that this communication can only take place in a social context in which language is characterized by cliché and the legacy of the Nazi assault on truth. How possible is it to break old habits and start anew?

Du sagst ich schreibe für tote
aber wie du bin ich
ein versuch
am geläufigen wahn
neue schritte zu bemessen
doch der enteilende
schritt in das jetzt
findet sich nur im verbrauchten
text und mit anderen[3]

For Ben-David, Jewish and non-Jewish speakers of German have similar longings, but the language is both that which connects them and that which divides them. By contrast, Ruth Klüger demonstrates a very different understanding of language. Clear, courageous naming of the crimes of the Shoah, and in particular of the concrete places in which they were carried out, is possible, and indeed vital for honest communication and to honor the dead:

Sprich die Namen der Orte:
Theresienstadt, Auschwitz, Groß-Rosen.
Sprich sie deutlich und ohne zu stammeln,
wie man ein Streichholz entzündet
(kräftig, dem Zitternden bricht es),
um den Toten die Kerze zu weihn.[4]

German literary traditions are subject to questioning or rescue, depending on the perspective of the writer. In her poem "Früher Mittag" (1952), Ingeborg Bachmann exposes in echoes of the literary canon (here, Goethe's "Der König in Thule" and Wilhelm Müller's "Der Lindenbaum") the complicity of the German tradition in Nazism, expressing fears about the return of the repressed National Socialist past:

Sieben Jahre später
fällt es dir wieder ein,
am Brunnen vor dem Tore,
blick nicht zu tief hinein,
die Augen gehen dir über.

Sieben Jahre später,
in einem Totenhaus,
trinken die Henker von gestern
den goldenen Becher aus.
Die Augen täten dir sinken.[5]

Here, even the poetic forms of Romanticism seem complicit. However, such anxiety is foreign to a writer like Wolf Biermann, whose Marxist view of literary history allows him to construct a divide between progressive and regressive traditions, in order to create a space in which to work:

> Mein Deutsch ist das von Hölderlin und Büchner und Heine und Rosa Luxemburg, es ist meine Muttersprache von Emma Biermann, es ist unsere Vatersprache von Bertolt Brecht und kein Schweinefraß, zusammengemanscht aus Abfällen von Bismarck, Hitler, Honecker, Blödel-Otto, Leni Riefenstahl, Mielke und Stolpe.[6]

The tension between a perceived need for hyper-reflexivity in language and a perceived imperative for plain naming and clear communication forms a starting point for this collection. Literary language, with its hypersensitivity to nuance, connotation, ambivalence, and the weight of its own history, is a subtle instrument in the hands of a writer committed to the ethical project of sensitizing us as readers to the consequences of unthinking speech, and critical writing—as the essays collected in this volume show—can contribute to this ethics of reflection and sensitivity.

Further contributions to the present volume show that other kinds of text—for example, private letters or life writing in various forms—can provide valuable insights into individuals' attitudes and experiences, and into how they interpret them. Discourse analysis and critical readings of autobiographical texts can expose the determining role of language in constructing an individual's social and private identities, as well as showing how both victims and perpetrators have employed the linguistic resources available to them to understand their identities within or outside the Third Reich, or in the post-Holocaust world.

The volume begins with two contributions that seek to intervene directly—polemically, and from very different positions—in current discussions about the legacy of National Socialism. Marko Pajević takes on negative stereotypes about German in the English-speaking world and, via a discussion of theories of language and "national character," addresses the question of the role of German Studies scholars in counteracting such stereotypes. Next, Sylvia Degen explores critically the controversial politics of naming in the establishment of concentration camp memorials, arguing against the euphemistic nature of some standard labels.

These essays are followed by four pieces that explore, from various perspectives, the idea of German as "Tätersprache." In their essays, Simone Schroth and Andrea Hammel discuss the attitudes of German-speaking refugees (in the Netherlands and the UK, respectively) towards their native German, while Geraldine Horan and Arvi Sepp reflect on the question of "Nazi language" from the perspective of private citizens' letters and of Victor Klemperer's language-critical work, respectively.

The next group of essays explores the anxious politics of representation in German literary language after the Shoah. Mary Cosgrove reflects on writers' employment of the literature of melancholy in the tradition of literary *Vergangenheitsbewältigung*, while Teresa Ludden, Jenny Watson, and Dora Osborne assess questions of language and representation in the work of Anne Duden, Herta Müller, and Reinhard Jirgl, respectively. This group is followed by two essays on words and music: James Parsons's piece on Hanns Eisler's critical re-workings of the German Romantic tradition in his *Hollywooder Liederbuch*, and Beate Müller and Ian Biddle's piece on multilingual strategies in Arnold Schoenberg's text for his cantata, *A Survivor from Warsaw*.

Finally, two pieces on translation round off the collection, demonstrating how the processes of translating and editing a text by a victim (Simon Ward on Jakob Littner) and a text by a perpetrator (Peter Davies on Rudolf Höß) involve compromises with the agendas of translators, editors, and intended readers.

There are many points of connection between the essays, as well as radically different views of similar questions: for example, questions of identity, exile, multilingualism, and the language of Romanticism are raised by several authors, and Victor Klemperer's work is discussed from a number of different angles. Some of the essays celebrate the German language, while others take up a more critical position. Several authors warn of the dangers of appropriating victims' voices for one's own purposes, while others explore ways of understanding the language of the perpetrators and their descendants. These essays are ultimately about the possibilities and limitations of communication, about self-reflexive and naïve language, and this collection participates in an ethical project that is the real responsibility of scholarship: that of speaking clearly, critically, and self-critically about the legacy of the Shoah, not only in the German language, and of clearing a space for the voices of the silenced to be heard.

We leave the last word to Gerschon Ben-David, whose work explores the tension between the desire for perfect communication between Jews and non-Jews who think and speak the same language, and an awareness of the pitfalls that await the unwary:

> Du—ich wollte eine brücke bauen
> richtungslos
> über versengte seelen
> schritt haltend
>   stolpere ich[7]

Notes

[1] See the contribution by Geraldine Horan in this volume.

[2] W. G. Sebald, *Unheimliche Heimat: Essays zur österreichischen Literatur* (Frankfurt am Main: Fischer, 1995).

[3] Gerschon Ben-David, "An meine deutschen Freunde," in *In den Wind werfen: Versuche um Metabarbarisches,* ed. Renate Birkenhauer and Otto Dov Kulka (Jerusalem: Straehlener Manuskripte Verlag, 1995), 47–49, here 48–49.

[4] Ruth Klüger, "Im Käfig," in *Zerreißproben: Kommentierte Gedichte* (Vienna: Paul Zsolnay Verlag, 2013), 51.

[5] Ingeborg Bachmann, "Früher Mittag," in *Werke* I, ed. Christine Koschel, Inge von Weidenbaum, and Clemens Münster (Munich: Piper, 1983), 44.

[6] Wolf Biermann, "Jizchak Katzenelson, ein Jude," in Itzhak Katzenelson and Wolf Biermann, *Dos lied vunem ojsgehargetn jidischn volk / Großer Gesang vom ausgerotteten jüdischen Volk* (Cologne: Kiepenheuer & Witsch, 1994), 7–29, here 9.

[7] Gerschon Ben-David, "An meine deutschen Freunde," 49.

German Language and National Socialism Today: Still a German "Sonderweg"?

Marko Pajević, Royal Holloway, University of London

GERMAN IS OFTEN CONSIDERED TO BE less a language, and more an assault, maybe particularly so in the United Kingdom. John Cleese gave evidence of this attitude in an interview with the *Frankfurter Allgemeine Zeitung* on 26 May 2006 by saying that many English people, including him, think that German is a language that is barked, after having been conditioned by movies about English people escaping from German concentration camps.[1] Most European countries formed this impression of German as a barked, rather than spoken language, if not already from Wilhelmine Germany, at the latest during the Second World War, and the media have since perpetuated this stereotype, particularly the tabloid press, but also many films. The "barbaric German language" has become a stereotype that is difficult to get rid of, and I intend to show that this damages not only the German reputation globally but also German society itself, and indirectly other nations as well. Additionally, it is based on a generally false conception of language.

"Normalization" has been the key term for German politics and society over the past fifteen years: should we Germanists apply it to the German language as well or will we continue in our discourse, more or less consciously, to promote a German "Sonderweg"? What role should we adopt in a situation in which our student numbers are dwindling, our departments are threatened with closure, and German language and German history are largely negatively perceived?[2]

In this context, we cannot bypass the thorny issue of National Socialism and the effect it had and still has on German culture and language, or common ideas about them. I will first discuss the relation between language and society by drawing on the concepts developed by Wilhelm von Humboldt and Émile Benveniste, which are very useful for *thinking language*. By this unusual term, in analogy to the French "pensée du langage" or the German "Sprachdenken," I want to stress the fact that thinking is done in language and that language is not only a tool. This will provide the foundation for the subsequent analyses of National Socialist language as well as a discussion of the consequences of preconceptions about German language after National Socialism, abroad (denigration) and in Germany ("Sprachscham"). The results will shed some light on the mechanisms at stake and the role we play in them.

Language and Society: Thinking Language

First of all, we should ask ourselves what we refer to when we speak of the German language. Does it exist as such? Is it the German spoken in Germany, in Austria, in Switzerland, or in northern Italy? If in Germany, do we refer to the German spoken in Hamburg, or in Bavaria? Is there no difference between the language spoken in the new *Länder* compared to the old Federal Republic, after forty years of separate history and very different conceptions of society? And even more so, can we compare the German of a professor of German literature to that of a construction worker, for instance? Are we referring to the official standard language, or dialect; and are we referring to written language, or spoken? There are probably also different attitudes concerning sociolects and dialects in different countries. In Germany, for instance, due to the long history of relative political independence of the different *Länder*, the dialect often transports positive associations of identity, regardless of class and social prestige; whereas in Great Britain, dialect can be more indicative of social class. Sociolects and dialects aside, what about history? Are we talking about the German of today or of 1940 or 1820? Is it the language of Goethe or of Hitler? There is obviously not one German language. What is a national language, then? How does it work? What does it do? And what is the individual's relationship with the language community?

At least since the early nineteenth century and Wilhelm von Humboldt (1767–1835), we know that different languages are not simply different signs to communicate the same ideas, as Aristotle believed, but that they are also the means of cognition, of thinking itself. We cannot think outside of language.[3] Today this is an acknowledged fact, not accepted by all but by most. Humboldt wanted to find "in der Eigenthümlichkeit ihres [der Sprache] Baues Hülfsmittel zur Erforschung und Erkennung der Wahrheit, und Bildung der Gesinnung, und des Charakters"[4] (IV:33). The way language is *articulated*—articulation is Humboldt's key concept—shapes our mind, our being, and our world. Language is hence the "bildende Organ des Gedankens"; thinking is inherently inscribed in sound. Moreover, each language represents its own "Weltansicht," its own realization of thinking, which is consequently manifest in the diversity of languages. According to Humboldt, the content of thinking is largely dependent on the form of language, inseparable from it ("Ein sehr bedeutender Theil des Inhalts jeder Sprache steht daher in so unbezweifelter Abhängigkeit von ihr, dass ihr Ausdruck für ihn nicht mehr gleichgültig bleiben kann," IV:21–22). Each language is therefore a different worldview; a language is not only a means to represent a known truth, but a means to discover truth (IV:27). Each language shapes the perception of the world in different ways. And this can only function dialogically, in an essential dualism—it is inherently social (VI:26; cf. Trabant, "Die gebellte Sprache," 69–71).

Even if theoretically most people would nowadays agree that we cannot separate thought and linguistic form, the consequences of this do not always seem to be taken into account. The French linguist Émile Benveniste (1902–76) convincingly demonstrated the absurdity of the separation of form and content in language. Outside of language it is impossible to define the content of thought; thought cannot exist but in language.[5] National Socialism was conceived of in the German language—is the German language therefore National Socialist? Well, the German of the National Socialists was, but this cannot be generalized to German language more broadly.

The categories of a language, then, define the framework of thought. This poses a problem, however: if different languages have different qualities, are perhaps some languages more suitable for thinking, or possibly more inclined towards inhuman thought than others? Both have been said stereotypically about German. Benveniste's answer to this is clear: it is not the language itself that favors or hinders the activity of the mind, but rather the capacities of the individual, and the general cultural conditions (Benveniste, "Catégories de Pensée," 74). The French poet, translator and linguist Henri Meschonnic (1932–2009) denies the interaction between language and individual to be determining, but considers it to be "the action of discourse on language [*langue*], and of language on discourse; of literature on language, and of language on literature; of culture on language, and of language on culture."[6] This implies that national languages (langue) as such simply do not exist in life; language always becomes manifest as used language (langage), spoken by one person in a particular historical situation. It is always in *interaction*—Humboldt used this term, "Wechselwirkung," as a key concept—and consequently language is a continuous process, constantly subject to change.

Admittedly, in every moment of speech we take part in a battle between the force of the conventions of language and the force of the speaking subject who can counter these conventions and indeed becomes subject of her or his speech exactly in this act, in speaking his or her own individual language. As Jürgen Trabant has written, we should not consider this process as being full of constraints, but as being rich in possibilities.[7] It keeps the future open.

Benveniste's notion of *discourse* is key, if we want to understand what happens in language: he defines discourse as "language as it is appropriated by the person speaking, and in the condition of *intersubjectivity*."[8] This implies that language only manifests itself in the form of discourse. He thereby places himself in the tradition of Humboldt, who said "Die Sprache liegt nur in der verbundenen Rede, Grammatik und Wörterbuch sind kaum ihrem todten Geripppe vergleichbar" (VI.1:147). Consequently, there can be no national language (langue)—that is an abstraction. There is always and only the language spoken by the individual and manifest in discourse.

The identity of language and thinking has to be considered as such: our thinking is identical with our language, but with "langage," not "langue"—it all depends on what we make of our national language in each moment of speech, "parole," and here we have infinite options. It is an error to attribute certain qualities to a language. These qualities are always in the subject that is speaking—even though of course a tradition of thought in a culture facilitates certain ideas and obstructs others. But these things are only to a very small degree linguistic issues in a narrow sense. Even if different languages might have concepts that allow for thinking property or subjectivity in different ways and therefore for developing different conceptions, this can still always be countered and changed. Language has to be considered historically and culturally.

This *thinking language* is the foundation of our profession: teaching Modern Languages, we have to keep in mind what it means to develop an additional worldview and we have to pass this on to our students and to society as a whole. If that were more widely acknowledged, nobody would ask for any further justification of our existence.

Stereotypes of the German Language

Everything depends on the meaning we give to it. We can continue to stress the putatively anal character of the Germans and of German language by pointing at the Germans' focus on scatology in cursing, but we can also interpret this fact as a reluctance to use sexual metaphors in a negative way.[9] In English, something unpleasant provokes the swearword "fuck," yet nobody accuses all English-speakers of being sexually perverted. And does it not seem rather healthy to connect the unpleasant to shit rather than to sex?[10] As so many thinkers—such as Humboldt and, following him, Wittgenstein and Jaspers—have pointed out, it is not language but its use that is decisive. Our conception of a language is determined by the historical context.

The problem of ignoring this becomes obvious in the sketch of the comedian Tim Allen, who mocks German by first sarcastically calling it a beautiful poetic language, and then offering unflattering comparisons: he gently pronounces "butterfly," "papillon," and "mariposa," then suddenly delivers an aggressively screamed "Schmetterling." He comments that in German, even butterflies are afraid of their name.[11] People find that funny; it serves all the clichés. Germans are an easy target for such jokes. But obviously, when the German word "Schmetterling" is perceived as aggressive as opposed to the gentle "butterfly" or "papillon" or "mariposa," that is not for inherent, objective linguistic or acoustic reasons, but the result of the audience's conditioning. It is in the perception, not in the language, and is related to associations and representation. Of course, in the imagined mouth of the inhumane SS-officer, "Schmetterling" becomes a threatening sound, but it does not in the mouth of a joyful German child. Of course, the world does not hear many joyful German children speak German, but they do hear the SS-officers, or the standardized representation of them, in films. The English word "butterfly" would be just as frightful in the mouth of the cliché-Nazi. The character of a language is not in the language but in the person who speaks that language.

It is interesting to note that in recent films by Quentin Tarantino the cliché receives another twist. The SS-officer in *Inglourious Basterds*, played by the Austrian Christopher Waltz, speaks not only an extremely elaborate and gentle German, he masters French, English, and Italian to the same degree of finesse. Of course, this multilingual, cultivated German is defeated by the American soldier chasing down the evil Nazis, an American who is not only incapable of speaking any word in any other language, but also exhibits poor language skills in American English. But Tarantino makes up for this in his following film *Django Unchained* by having the same Christopher Waltz playing, in the same cultivated manner, this time a good German appalled by the brutal racism in the south of the United States of America at the time before the Civil War.

What these Tarantino films render evident to a mass public is that stereotypes about nations depend very much on the historical situation, and that no nation should forget about their own crimes. There is no doubt that each time period develops certain speech patterns and a certain dominant character of speech. In the case of Germany, this character was certainly very different in the thirties and forties from nowadays. In spite of comparisons made in the recent economic crisis and Germany's unpopular role in it in some countries, there is simply no common ground between Merkel's way of speaking and Hitler's.

It is also telling that the world always complains about the Germans having no sense of humor because they do not laugh at jokes made at their own expense. After having been repeatedly associated with inhumane SS-men when abroad—as has happened more or less jokingly many times even to me, and I am not of a very German "breed"—it is difficult not to be tired of it. Robin Williams makes of this lack of humor a typical German feature, relating the humorless reaction of a German interviewer when he told her that there are probably no funny people in Germany since "you" have all killed them.[12] Sure, one could react by making another joke, but would Robin Williams himself be amused placed in that position? Would he deem it funny to be accused of having killed the American Indians?

In previous times, the image of Germany was very different. The most famous example would be Madame de Staël's very influential book *De l'Allemagne* at the start of the nineteenth century, where the Romantic Germany is presented as the counterpart to Napoleonic France.[13] At the time, France was characterized by action and lack of thought, as opposed to a Germany full of thought, but with a lack of action. Cultural stereotypes, then, are related to the political situation. The status of a language and the political power of its country are always connected. The dominant role of English in our times is not a result of the inherent qualities of the English language, but of the British Empire, and of American hegemony. Such an awareness of the historicity of our ideas, as well as an outside perspective on ourselves, can be passed on in Modern Languages—this is also part of our task as Germanists.

Nazi German and Its Analysis

Since language is a historical phenomenon, political systems do leave their imprint on a language. It is worthwhile to read Victor Klemperer's famous book *Lingua Tertii Imperii* (*LTI*),[14] instead of simply using the title as a buzzword. Klemperer singles out interesting linguistic transformations of German that resulted from National Socialist usage, for instance the proliferation of acronyms for organizations (such as BDM, HJ, DAF, etc: *LTI*, 15), and the transformative use of certain adjectives, such as "fanatisch," which in its frequent repetition in the meaning of "heroic" or "virtuous" finally led people to believe in the identity of heroism and fanaticism (*LTI*, 21). Klemperer also points at the mechanisms at play, the general standardization of every written word so that they entered the minds of the people and their way of speaking and therefore thinking (*LTI*, 18). This was done to such an extent that he predicted some characteristic Nazi expressions would remain part of the German language for a long time, such as "charakterlich," or "kämpferisch" (*LTI*, 20). Even the Germans who cursed Nazism at the end of the war did so using its language, which shows how much the LTI, the Language of the Third Reich, penetrated German society (*LTI*, 296). According to Klemperer, it was not the individual use of language that had an effect but this constant repetition. Through the unconscious perception of those terms, phrases, and constructions, "der Nazismus glitt in Fleisch und Blut der Menge über" (*LTI*, 21). He concludes: "Aber Sprache dichtet und denkt nicht nur für mich, sie lenkt auch mein Gefühl, sie steuert mein ganzes seelisches Wesen, je selbstverständlicher, je unbewußter ich mich ihr überlasse" (*LTI*, 21). By transforming the associations of words and by incorporating them into their ideology, the Nazis used language to serve their goals (*LTI*, 22). Klemperer demonstrates various forms of language transformation used by the Nazis in pursuit of their goals: next to adoption and inversion, we can name for instance conceptual clusters, binary definitions, essentialization and exclusion, as well as contradiction.[15]

Referring to Talleyrand's aphorism that language is a means to conceal one's thoughts, Klemperer argues the contrary: "Was jemand willentlich verbergen will, sei es nur vor andern, sei es vor sich selber, auch was er unbewußt in sich trägt: die Sprache bringt es an den Tag" (*LTI*, 16). Whereas a statement might be a lie, the style of language discloses the real meaning. Unfortunately, we cannot rely on this either, but there is some truth to Klemperer's point. As the subtitle *Notizbuch eines Philologen* explicitly indicates, *LTI* is written by a philologist: a lover of language. Similarly, the motto, taken from Franz Rosenzweig, "Sprache ist mehr als Blut" demonstrates Klemperer's belief in the power of language, as well as in the possibilities and blessings of a conscious use of language. He sees his task in rendering people conscious of the poisonous effects of the LTI. He claims that German needs to be purified of this kind of language, that some words will have to be buried for a long time, some even forever (*LTI*, 22). The criticism of language is indeed a necessary and noble task and we should all, always and everywhere, pursue it.

Klemperer is of course not completely free of contamination; he makes, for instance, an unconscious use of the biological metaphor of the German "Volkskörper" (*LTI*, 61) that certainly belongs to the LTI, and later on, in his life in the GDR, against his convictions, he gave in to some of the linguistic norms of the new system by applauding Stalin and the FDJ (Freie Deutsche Jugend—Free German Youth, the youth organization of the GDR).[16] But this does not invalidate his point. More problematic and misleading is the idea of the *perversion of a language*, since this term of perversion implies a core or a natural state of the language that would be pure and innocent, and could be perverted for base goals. No language has such an essence. Language can be cultivated in order to develop certain traditions of thought so that these ideas are more easily thought in this specific cultural environment—that is all. Our judgment of these things, too, is always rooted in our own historical position.

All studies of Nazi German are in agreement that its specificity cannot be found in German linguistic structures, but in a particular use of the German language, in its application to certain situations and thus in conveying certain ideas. This becomes very clear in the other famous early study of the issue: *Aus dem Wörterbuch eines Unmenschen*.[17] Here too, the philologist's point of view becomes immediately manifest in Dolf Sternberger's preface of 1945:

Soviel und welche Sprache einer spricht, soviel und solche Sache, Welt oder Natur ist ihm erschlossen. Und jedes Wort, das er redet, wandelt die Welt, worin er sich bewegt, wandelt ihn selbst und seinen Ort in dieser Welt. Darum ist nichts gleichgültig an der Sprache, und nichts so wesentlich wie die façon de parler. Der Verderb der Sprache ist der Verderb des Menschen. (Sternberger, *Wörterbuch*, 7)

Sternberger says that we live in a world made of language and that we are ourselves constituted by language—this grants the philologist the outstandingly important role of keeping watch over its use. The destiny of humankind depends on it. This sounds melodramatic, but the point is correct. Human beings' access to the world—that is, the human, meaningful world—is through language. Sternberger formulates it this way: "Es gibt keine vorsprachliche Menschenwelt" (Sternberger, *Wörterbuch*, 286). We do not have any other access to the world apart from through language, and we should therefore be careful of how we use it since this determines our world. Sternberger also notices in the prefaces to the later editions (of 1957 and 1967) that the inhumane use of language persists, and he claims that the "Unmensch" has always existed, even before 1933, and always will. His dictionary treats terms such as "Anliegen," "Herausstellen," "Intellektuell," "Problem," "Schulung," etc.; what is at stake is clearly not the words as such but their use in a specific historical situation.

Sternberger, a professor of political science, positions himself in the tradition of Humboldt's theory of language, which was at the time probably better known in Germany than it is now, and he refers explicitly to Humboldt at several points. He echoes what Humboldt says about nations: "Ihre Sprache ist ihr Geist, und ihr Geist ist ihre Sprache—man kann sich beide nie identisch genug denken!" (Sternberger, *Wörterbuch*, 286) In this context, he tells the anecdote about Carl von Ossietzky conceiving of the following punishment for the Nazis: "Deutsch müssen sie lernen!" (285) This is supposed to mean that this would stop them being Nazis—which is not true, of course. The Nazis spoke German, their German. Yet Ossietzky had a point, even if his view of the German language is clearly idealized. Nonetheless, the language we speak represents our being. Sternberger also states: "Obgleich der Mensch die Sprache nicht geschaffen hat, hat er doch seine jeweilige Sprache zu verantworten" (312). As Jaspers said: "Sprache ist im Sprechen."[18]

Sternberger also sees very clearly that language is not only an expression of something but also forms the situation; he stresses the creative aspect of language:

Und die Sprache ist nicht bloß ein Erzeugnis der Gesellschaft, sondern ebensosehr eine gesellschaftliche Bilde-Kraft. Sie hinkt nicht hinter den "Verhältnissen" her, als wären diese ihr unweigerlich vorgegeben, sondern sie wirkt fortwährend auf die "Verhältnisse" ein. Diese Dialektik gibt uns auch eine Chance. (334)

There is reason for hope, then. The Germans are not doomed as a result of the Nazis' use of the German language. Changing people's minds and their language is not an easy process; it takes time as well as cultural and political measures. The Germans also renounced certain expressions and formulations after the Allies forced them to.[19] There is an immense variety of reasons why and how a society changes.

The German "Sprachscham" and Its Consequences

Literature is one of these reasons. Reading and writing, of course, hugely influences people. It shapes their language and therefore their thinking, their outlook on life and the world, their being. It is debatable who shapes the world more—politicians or writers. People like Kafka are still shaping the universe of many readers all around the world. Even though undoubtedly literature has lost its role as a "Leitmedium," it is still important, and always will be, due to its creative work on language.

Paul Celan is often named as one of the authors who tried to purify German after 1945. He stated in his 1958 speech upon accepting the Bremen Literature Prize that the German language passed through "die tausend Finsternisse todbringender Rede," and reappeared "angereichert" by all of this, that is, by the "tausendjährige Reich" (he put "angereichert" in quotation marks himself).[20] Yes, German language and society are burdened by this experience; they consist of many layers and it is crucial to be aware of what we refer to with the words we use. Celan achieved much in this respect. Even though he could barely stand being in Germany, he continued to write in German and insisted on the uniqueness of the mother tongue.

The often-evoked dilemma of the identity of "Muttersprache" and "Mördersprache" fits his situation.[21] His mother, who taught him the love of the German language and literary tradition, was killed by the Nazis. Maybe it needs to be said explicitly: German is also the idiom of a major portion of the victims of National Socialism. It is not only the language of the perpetrators; it is also the language of many of the victims.

Thomas Mann insisted on "the other Germany." The two sides of Germany's Faustian aspiration were also the topic of his *Doktor Faustus*.[22] During the war, he appealed to the Germans to refer to other strands of tradition. That is possible; our identity depends on our choices, and in any culture there are options. And, finally, culture is a matter of *discourse* in Michel Foucault's sense of the term—the result of the way a community talks about things.[23]

But, indeed, many dissociated themselves from the German language, even from German names. Jean Améry, formerly Hanns Chaim Mayer, is the best example; he wrote: "Das Kartoffelacker- und Ruinen-Deutschland war für mich eine versunkene Weltregion. Ich vermied es, seine, meine Sprache zu sprechen, und wählte ein Pseudonym romanischer Resonanz."[24] Améry was a victim, a Jew tortured by the Nazis, a man with the intellectual resources to go abroad and live in another language. However, he chose to write in German afterwards.

But how about the large number of Germans who lived through the time of National Socialism, more or less involved, not necessarily followers or at least not active perpetrators, but also not victims of this ideology? How were they able to position themselves, once the enormous responsibility had been acknowledged?

It is maybe a unique case that a society aspires to dissociate from its tradition and language to such an extent, as if to free itself from the burden of history and gain an innocence impossible for the German language. As a result, the Germans are certainly inclined to use English more than many other nations, English being not only the language of the victors and of modern life, but also a language that is not guilt-ridden, a language that clears and cleanses German speakers of the national catastrophe and internationalizes them. Another reason why Germans embraced English so willingly is that they simply did not know how to define a German identity. There was a vacuum after 1945, when the version of German identity that had been dominant became unacceptable and all traditions seemed tainted by National Socialism. Since the Nazis were so good at incorporating all cultural movements, virtually no aspect of German culture remained untouched.

At the start of the twentieth century, 44% of all publications worldwide in the sciences were in German. From this leading position, the percentage was reduced by 1996 to only 1.2%. The First World War started the decline of German as an international language of academia because the international research community boycotted German until 1926, due to German academics' support of the war. The Second World War and the Nazi atrocities then completely destroyed the German language on an international level. Nowadays, most German academics, if they want to get international recognition, are obliged to publish in English.[25] But it is not only German academia that is increasingly renouncing the German language; even on an educational level the Germans seem keen to free themselves of their language. More and more schools teach, or intend to teach, some subjects in English; universities even more so. Many German enterprises in Germany opt to use English in their offices. English is omnipresent in German advertisements, often with quite comic effects: many Germans do not understand these messages correctly and believe, for instance, that the publicity slogan for Parfümerie Douglas, "Come in and find out," means that you need to find your way out of the shop again. In addition, German is often shunned in Germany for public signposting. Instead of "Stadtmitte," or at least "Zentrum," in many cities one finds "City Center" on street signs. The discredit German has fallen into after the Second World War made Germans particularly willing to give up their language in favor of the global English. Jürgen Trabant speaks of a "spezifische deutsche Sprachscham"; the Germans are traumatized by their crime, which was mediated by the German language.[26] Before National Socialism, says Trabant, Germans were proud to speak the language of Goethe; after it, they are aware that they are speakers of the "barked" language of the concentration camps. This, Trabant asserts, still influences language policies. He cites the example of German politicians speaking English at a conference of German language teachers outside of Germany, even answering questions in English despite the fact that they are posed in German by a public that speaks little English. This indicates identity issues even if we keep in mind that German never developed a tradition as a language of diplomacy; it was only Bismarck, for instance, who asked his ambassadors to write their reports in German and even the peace treaty with defeated France in 1871 was exclusively written in French.

This "Sprachscham," however complex its reasons might be, has considerable consequences. If Germans are taught at schools and universities in English, they do not learn certain discourses in their mother tongue. To talk for instance about National Socialism in English would have the side effect that the Germans would not have to identify too much with it; they would gain some distance from German history. But it also weakens the capacities of expression in German if high discourses, academic research and education first and foremost, no longer take place in German anymore. Future generations will not be able to accurately express in German those things they only learned in English—and it remains doubtful whether many of them will be able to express them well in English.

German as a standard and high-level language loses significance, warns Trabant, when English takes over these discourses. Consequently, there will be, on the one hand, a strengthening of dialects as the familiar language, which implies a regionalization and, on the other hand, a strengthening of English as the language of work and the high-level language. For German as a national standard language, fewer and fewer tasks and functions remain—it risks getting lost between dialects and English. As Karl-Heinz Göttert indicates, most linguists in recent years have concluded that due to national media and mobility, dialects are declining.[27] Yet, at the same time, there is also a renaissance of dialects, mostly in the south, because in a globalized world, the desire for a feeling of home and belonging is growing. However, as Göttert suggests, it seems to be less the dialects and more the colloquial language that is on the rise.

Whatever the power relations between dialect, high, and colloquial German might be, the situation may lead to an intellectual impoverishment for many, since those students who do not do very well in English will have less access to higher discourses. As a result, the gap between the well-educated and the less well-educated will widen. A small elite will distinguish itself by good knowledge of English—but even they will always have a disadvantage on the international level compared to native speakers of English.

The common German-language area will disappear—we can observe this already in Switzerland, for instance, where Swiss German is taking over many discourses that were formerly held in standard German. Other high-level discourses are dealt with in English. The same phenomenon exists within Germany: in Baden-Württemberg, an extremely successful publicity campaign for the "Ländle" from 1999 to 2010 claimed: "Wir können alles außer Hochdeutsch."[28] In addition, the prime minister at the time, Günther Oettinger, wanted to introduce English as the language of the office. That means that in Baden-Württemberg the people would speak Swabian, possibly colloquial German, with family and friends, and English at work. Standard German would not be spoken anywhere; the German-language community would cease to exist.

These tendencies are characteristic of a country where identity was traditionally built not on political structures, but on the common language area. Consequently, without this common language area, there is no need for common political structures, nor even for Germany itself. "Nie wieder Deutschland" seems finally realized, as Trabant comments sarcastically. At least, the space for high German seems to be shrinking.

This weakening of the national language also creates problems for the integration of immigrants, a process that is increasingly important. In Germany these groups have until relatively recently not been offered sufficient opportunities to learn German, even after it became obvious that these immigrants were going to stay. One reason for this might be that, after National Socialism, the German state does not want ever again to force its culture upon anyone. As opposed to France, for example, which has no inhibitions in this respect, Germany does not aggressively promote the teaching of the German language.

But the intended multicultural plurilingualism in Germany requires real cultivation from all sides of both languages, German and the family language. However, in spite of some initiatives, institutions do not provide sufficient support for either language, and the necessary interaction and cultural exchange often remain limited, leading to discontent or indifference.[29] The weakening of the status of German worsens the situation: if immigrants are supposed to speak English at work, their exposure to German is diminished even further. Furthermore, they would not be able to learn good English at a German school if they do not speak good German.

In an effort to gain political and historical innocence, the consequences of German language policies are an impoverishment of culture, social tensions on various levels, and the cessation of cultural cohesion and cultural identity. This attitude towards German language is not only a problem for Germany, but can become one also for other nations. Germany, a handy scapegoat, can serve to keep them from facing their own issues. Compared to Nazi Germany, any nation is a paragon of virtuousness. The roles are distributed; we all know who the bad guys were, so "we," the others, are by default the good ones. No need for further reflection or even self-criticism.

If this then translates into neglecting the study of German language and culture, the world as a whole also loses out. It is hardly even possible to think of the contemporary western world without German traditions. German traditions of thought and of all the arts shaped our world to a considerable degree. Without German, that is, without access to these sources in the original, people outside the German-speaking world are deprived of these sources. Translations do not exist sufficiently and are always to a certain degree adaptations into another system of thought and into another worldview, as we have seen at the start. They are not the same as the originals.

German used to be the international language of philosophy and many of the sciences; this should still be the major motivation for learning German. The economy will always be a factor, of course; in moments of crisis, people would even consider learning German if that means getting a job. But generally, everybody believes that you can do business with Germans in English. This is not necessarily true, not only because of what Chancellor Willy Brandt once famously said: "If I'm selling to you, I speak your language. If I'm buying, dann müssen Sie Deutsch sprechen."[30] Nobody wants to learn German for Germany's beaches and relaxed lifestyle in the sun (even though Germany does also offer beautiful beaches and a relaxed lifestyle, albeit less often in the sun). The idea of language learning as part of cultural enrichment and intellectual expansion needs to be promoted; the general public, politicians, students and often even university senior management do not seem to be much aware of this dimension of language learning. So if we do not want more Modern Languages Departments to be closed, or possibly replaced by Language Centers, we have to bring this message across.

Conclusions

After the Third Reich, it was indeed necessary and beneficial for German culture to be obliged to put itself under scrutiny to a degree that might be unequalled in history. Germany developed a considerable culture of self-awareness. Of course, this is a never-ending process, and there is also the risk of this introspection becoming one-sided. By focusing too much on one aspect of history, a society might be considered under too narrow a perspective and other important elements might be neglected.

Yes, writing a poem after Auschwitz can only be done on the basis of Auschwitz, as Adorno said in revising his initial dictum asserting that the writing of poetry after Auschwitz would be barbaric;[31] but reducing German culture to Auschwitz is neither a solution nor is it justified.

It is time to break up patterns of thinking that have become convenient, in Germany and abroad, to allow for a better flow in the exchange of ideas. German, as every language, is always the language its speakers make of it; it is always historical and individual. In Germany, the situation has been changing rapidly for many years now. Famously, the 2006 Football World Cup contributed significantly to creating a new image of Germany, both outside and within. It helped the Germans to cultivate a new identity. If we want to consider the issue of German culture and language today, we should work on changing the perception around the world.

Germanists have a great responsibility in these processes. We have to present Germany in a more varied way. A critical point of view is necessary and we want to pass on this critical capacity; it might even be that it is this self-reflection and self-criticism that some of us particularly appreciate about German culture. But generally speaking, there must be something about German culture that we find attractive or intriguing, and fascination with evil alone won't do.

Germans used to pride themselves with reason on being "das Land der Dichter und Denker." This dates back to the early nineteenth century when literary production in German was enormously influential. It is also commonly acknowledged worldwide that the contribution of the German-speaking countries to the fields of classical music and philosophy is second to none. We must transmit those ideas and cultural values to convince society that studying German is worthwhile. German is evidently the language of the Holocaust, it became the language of the "Richter und Henker" (Karl Kraus), yet it is also the language of an extremely enlightening reflection on totalitarian mechanisms (i.e., Adorno, Arendt, Anders) and the functioning of memory and society (i.e., Aleida and Jan Assmann), as well as of much complex and fascinating literature on these topics (i.e., Celan, Bachmann, Aichinger, Sebald, and many others). But beyond this field, German is also a language with a hugely rich register of inwardness and sensitivity. We should not neglect other great writers, epochs like Romanticism and Expressionism with their diverse forms, music and painting, as well as various philosophical, sociological, and psychological traditions. In most disciplines, in the sciences and in the humanities as well as in the arts, Germans have contributed greatly to human knowledge and perception—this point should also be put forward and cultivated, for the benefit of all.

The Germany of today, its problems and preoccupations, has changed. Over the course of its history, Germany has pursued several "Sonderwege," and this is engraved in our minds. But the time has come to step out of this pathway. The world actually holds Germany in high esteem in many ways; particularly outside of Europe, it is one of the most popular countries worldwide. Due to the economic crisis and the comparatively strong economic situation in Germany, many people currently want to learn German to find employment; at the time of this writing there are runs on the Goethe-Institutes in Spain, Greece, and other countries. Another reason is that many young people cannot afford the high university fees in Great Britain anymore, which makes Germany an affordable alternative. Politics and the economy are driving forces for people's attitudes and decisions. But the main motivation for anyone to learn a language should be an interest in the culture; if this is not the case from the start, it should become so. Cultural performances are also what will keep the German language in demand internationally in the long run. Next to economic power, cultural prestige counts. Promoting this culture—literature, film, music, etc.—and passing it on in an appealing manner will have an effect.

It was not that long ago, in the 1980s, that the Argentinian Jorge Luis Borges wrote an *Ode an die deutsche Sprache*:[32]

> Die kastilische Sprache ward mir zum Schicksal [. . .]
> Dich aber, süße Sprache Deutschlands,
> Dich habe ich erwählt und gesucht, ganz von mir aus.
> In Nachtwachen und mit Grammatiken,
> aus dem Dschungel der Deklinationen,
> das Wörterbuch zur Hand, das nie den präzisen Beiklang trifft,
> näherte ich mich Dir.
> Meine Nächte sind mit Virgil ausgefüllt:
> so sagte ich einmal.
> Ich könnte aber auch gesagt haben:
> mit Hölderlin und Angelus Silesius.
> Heine gab mir seine Nachtigallenpracht;
> Goethe die Schickung einer späten Liebe,
> gelassen sowohl wie bereichernd;
> Keller die Rose, gelegt von der Hand
> in die eines Toten, der die Blume liebte
> und der nie wissen wird, ob sie weiß oder rot ist.
> Du, Sprache Deutschlands, bist Dein Hauptwerk:
> die verschränkte Liebe der Wortverbindungen,
> die offenen Vokale, die Klänge,
> angemessen dem griechischen Hexameter,
> und Deine Wald- und Nachtgeräusche.

This "Hauptwerk," which any language represents for the nation it belongs to, is a never-completed *chef d'œuvre*; we all participate in the process. Everybody is responsible and is part of it: language is a *res publica*, as Jutta Limbach states.[33] Jürgen Trabant calls languages "cathedrals"

(2008, 80) just as worthy to be visited as the cathedrals built of stone; travel guides should pay them the deserved attention. It is us, the Germanists, who have to explain the fascinating richness of the German language, this cathedral of thought, initiating others to and guiding them through the great adventure of another worldview.

After having passed through "die tausend Finsternisse todbringender Rede," as Celan formulated,[34] German continues to develop. This long process of change and criticism of language will always be necessary, everywhere. We take part in this process, also by interfering with and participating in the constant process of image-building. Germanists should be aware of the major role they play in this discourse on German language and culture, and allow for a more productive and more realistic representation of contemporary Germany.

Notes

[1] Jürgen Trabant gives this reference in his chapter, "Die gebellte Sprache: Über das Deutsche," in *Was ist Sprache?* (Munich: Beck, 2008), 205–28, here 205. In future references in the text as Trabant 2008.

[2] The Guardian blog "World Cup 2010: Tabloids go on putting das boot into the Germans. British red-tops build up to big World Cup match with Germany with string of punning headlines" offers a panorama of British headlines on June 25, 2010 exposing unflattering clichés about Germany still current and regularly published in the UK: http://www.theguardian.com/media/greenslade/2010/jun/25/world-cup-2010-england-germany-papers1 (accessed August 5, 2014). For the situation of modern languages in the UK see the following Guardian article, dating already from 2010 but summarizing well the situation: http://www.theguardian.com/education/2010/aug/24/who-still-wants-learn-languages?guni=Article:in%20body%20link (accessed June 9, 2014).

[3] However, to a certain extent, this idea was put forward much earlier, by Bacon, Locke and Leibniz. For the history of "thinking language," see Jürgen Trabant, *Mithridates im Paradies: Kleine Geschichte des Sprachdenkens* (Munich: Beck, 2003).

[4] All quotations of Wilhelm von Humboldt are taken from the following edition: Wilhelm von Humboldt, *Gesammelte Schriften, 17 Bände*, ed. A. Leitzmann et al. (Berlin: Behr, 1903–36). References will be by volume and page number.

[5] Émile Benveniste, "Catégories de pensée et catégories de langue," in *Problèmes de linguistique générale 1* (Paris: Gallimard, 1966), 62–74, here 62–63. Future references in the text as Benveniste and page number. Translation by the editors of the current volume.

[6] Henri Meschonnic, *De la langue française. Essai sur une clarté obscure* (Paris: Hachette, 1997), 355. Translation by the editors of the current volume.

[7] Jürgen Trabant, "Du génie aux gènes des langues," in *Et le génie des langues?*, sous la direction d'Henri Meschonnic (Saint-Denis: Presses Universitaires de Vincennes, 2000), 79–102, here 93.

[8] Émile Benveniste, "De la subjectivité dans le langage," in *Problèmes de linguistique générale 1* (Paris: Gallimard, 1966), 258–66, here 266 (first published in *Journal de Psychologie*, juillet–septembre, 1958).

[9] Philipp Oltermann demonstrated this on July 3, 2013, in the Guardian, http://www.guardian.co.uk/commentisfree/2013/jul/03/shitstorm-german-dictionary-angela-merkel (accessed June 9, 2014).

[10] However, deducing anything about national character or culture from cursing practices seems almost impossible; cf. the complexity of attaching a coherent interpretation to the cursing habits of a nation: Damaris Nübling and Marianne Vogel, "Fluchen und Schimpfen kontrastiv. Zur sexuellen, krankheitsbasierten, skatologischen und religiösen Fluch- und Schimpfwortprototypik im Niederländischen, Deutschen und Schwedischen," *Germanistische Mitteilungen* 59 (2004): 19–33, also online: http://bgdv.be/Dokumente /GM-Texte/gm59_nuebling_vogel.pdf (accessed June 9, 2014).

[11] http://www.youtube.com/watch?v=s9ehI6nyZNM (accessed June 9, 2014).

[12] http://www.youtube.com/watch?v=GwwJw849HWc (accessed June 9, 2014).

[13] Madame de Staël, *De l'Allemagne* (Paris: Flammarion, 1980 [1810]).

[14] Victor Klemperer, *LTI. Notizbuch eines Philologen* (Leipzig: Reclam, 1980 [1946]). Further references in the text.

[15] James W. Underhill recently gave an insightful comment on Klemperer's analysis in a chapter of his book, *Creating Wordviews: Metaphor, Ideology and Language* (Edinburgh: Edinburgh University Press, 2011), 128–71.

[16] Cf. Kristine Fischer-Hupe, *Victor Klemperers "LTI. Notizbuch eines Philologen": Ein Kommentar* (Hildesheim: Olms, 2001).

[17] Dolf Sternberger, Gerhard Storz, Wilhelm E. Süskind, *Aus dem Wörterbuch eines Unmenschen: Neue erweiterte Ausgabe mit Zeugnissen des Streites über die Sprachkritik* (Hamburg: Claassen, 3. Auflage, 1968 [1957, as individual articles since 1945]).

[18] Karl Jaspers, *Von der Wahrheit* (Munich: Piper, 1991 [1947]), 409, quoted by Sternberger, 315.

[19] Cf. Dirk Deissler, *Die entnazifizierte Sprache* (Frankfurt am Main: Peter Lang, 2004).

[20] Paul Celan, *Gesammelte Werke, Dritter Band* (Frankfurt am Main: Suhrkamp, 1986), 186.

[21] Cf. Theo Buck, who applies it to Celan in his *Muttersprache, Mördersprache: Celan-Studien* (Aachen: Rimbaud-Verlag, 1993).

[22] Thomas Mann, *Doktor Faustus: Das Leben des deutschen Tonsetzers Adrian Leverkühn erzählt von einem Freunde* (Frankfurt am Main: Fischer, 1947).

[23] Michel Foucault, *L'Archéologie du savoir* (Paris: Gallimard, 1969).

[24] Jean Améry, *Jenseits von Schuld und Sühne: Bewältigungsversuche eines Überwältigten*, in *Werke*, ed. Gerhard Scheit (Stuttgart: Klett-Cotta, 2002 [1966]), 123.

[25] Ulrich Ammon analyzed the decline of German for academic discourse in *Die internationale Stellung der deutschen Sprache* (Berlin: de Gruyter, 1991), and *Ist Deutsch noch eine internationale Wissenschaftssprache? Englisch auch für die Lehre an den deutschsprachigen Hochschulen* (Berlin: de Gruyter, 1998). More recently, he confirmed his thesis of the decline of German as an international language of science in "Deutsch als Wissenschaftssprache: Wie lange noch?," in *Englisch in Academia: Catalyst or Barrier?*, ed. Claus Gnutzmann (Tübingen: Narr, 2008), 25–43. But it is difficult to find concrete figures for German's decline as a language of science after 1990; even the following recent article does not give them: Zsuzsa Mezei, "Deutsch als Wissenschaftssprache—Geschichtliche Übersicht," *Argumentum* 8 (2012): 277–305.

[26] The following observations are based on Jürgen Trabant's reflections on this "Sprachscham" and its consequences in *Was ist Sprache?* (Munich: Beck, 2008), chapter 10: 205–28.

[27] Cf. for instance the conclusion of Karl-Heinz Göttert in *Alles außer Hochdeutsch: Ein Streifzug durch unsere Dialekte* (Berlin: Ullstein, 2011).

[28] The German publicity company with the name Scholz & Friends, thus combining the German name with the English international "friends," developed the slogan and offered it first to the Land of Saxony, which declined. The contract with Baden-Württemberg ended officially in 2010.

[29] For an analysis of the institutional situation and the role of language in migrant families, see Anna Schnitzer, "Sprich mit mir—zur Rolle der Sprache für die Integration von Familien mit Migrationshintergrund," in *Migration, Familie und soziale Lage. Beiträge zu Bildung, Gender und Care*, ed. Thomas Geisen, Tobias Studer, and Erol Yıldız (Wiesbaden: Springer, 2013), 125–44.

[30] Quoted for instance by the British Academy: https://www.britac.ac.uk/policy/Talk_the_Talk.cfm (accessed June 9, 2014).

[31] For the evolution of Adorno's position on literature and National Socialism, cf. Peter Stein, "'Darum mag falsch gewesen sein, nach Auschwitz ließe sich kein Gedicht mehr schreiben' (Adorno). Widerruf eines Verdikts? Ein Zitat und seine Verkürzung," *Weimarer Beiträge* (1996, Heft 4), 485–508. Also Sven Kramer, "'Wahr sind die Sätze als Impuls . . .' Begriffsarbeit und sprachliche Darstellung in Adornos Reflexion auf Auschwitz," in *DVfLG* (1996, Heft 3), 501–23.

[32] Jorge Luis Borges, *Die zwei Labyrinthe* (Munich: dtv, 1986), 201.

[33] Jutta Limbach, *Hat Deutsch eine Zukunft? Unsere Sprache in der globalisierten Welt* (Munich: Beck, 2008), 11. Limbach also quotes the Borges poem.

[34] Paul Celan, "Ansprache anlässlich der Entgegennahme des Literaturpreises der Freien Hansestadt Bremen," in *Gesammelte Werke*, III (Frankfurt am Main: Suhrkamp, 1986 [1958]), 186.

Clear Wording or "Historical" Euphemisms? Conceptual Controversies Surrounding the Naming of National Socialist Memorial Sites in Germany

Sylvia Degen, University of Aberystwyth (UK)/transmute Network Berlin

Introduction

THIS ARTICLE ADDRESSES QUESTIONS about the words used in Germany today to negotiate the National Socialist past. The principal focus of this discussion will be the memorial sites and places of remembrance that have been re-designed and re-named in many places, especially since Reunification, and in particular the youth concentration camp for girls and young women at Uckermark, which was transformed into an extermination site later in the war. Because language and language use play a central role in the interpretation of history, intense debates have been held regarding these re-designing and naming processes. This article will focus on the two main opposing positions at the core of these debates: one demands an explicit naming of the atrocities—along with the corresponding assumption of responsibility for them—while the other supports the use of what are, in my opinion, unclear language and naming practices. As an introduction, I will discuss how these two opposing poles, clarity and ambiguity, were already central to the language policies of Nazi Germany and later to those of the Allied forces: while one characteristic of so-called "NS-Deutsch" is its use of deceptive obfuscation (which can be observed particularly in the Nazis' prolific employment of euphemisms), the Allies, by contrast, attempted during their denazification efforts to promote explicit speech practices.

Following that introduction, I will discuss how debates about the naming of the most well known memorial sites over the last decades have demonstrated that people are still struggling for clear wording. A central issue in these debates is a representation of history that has been criticized for using linguistic means to equate the National Socialist system with that of the German Democratic Republic. I would like to exemplify this by an analysis of the new *Gedenkstättenkonzeption* (Memorial Sites Concept) of the Federal Government and the Neue Wache memorial site in Berlin. Against that background, there is an ongoing struggle concerning the naming of the memorial site at Uckermark. This memorial site is not counted among the principal German memorial sites—it is one of the sites of National Socialist crimes whose existence has long been suppressed. By using this example, I will show that the opposition of clarity and ambiguity is also a central point of contention in the debate outside of the official arena. Finally, it must be stated that the interpretation of the National Socialist past is a contested domain in Germany, as is the language in which it is negotiated.

The Employment of
Euphemisms as Part of a Cover-Up

During the era of National Socialism, language policy decisions were certainly founded on an awareness of the power of language. There were investigations into language use in Germany during that time period: apart from Victor Klemperer's well-known diary, later published as *LTI: Notizbuch eines Philologen*,[1] there were also people living in exile, Allied "language experts," or other observers outside of Germany who spoke of a "Nazi-Sprache" long before the end of the war, and described the language changes they observed.[2] Their descriptions do provide good insight into National Socialist language use; the features they identify are present at all levels of linguistic expression. For this article, however, I would like to focus on one characteristic in particular: euphemisms. Or, more broadly speaking: language as a means of cover-up.

Euphemisms are used to sugarcoat something disagreeable, to make it less offensive or to disguise it. They therefore quickly became an important component of "NS-Deutsch," particularly in regards to terminology surrounding the policy of extermination. There are innumerable examples of this: "Arisierung," "Euthanasie," "Liquidation," "Sonderbehandlung," "Evakuierung," "in den Osten schicken," etc. An important characteristic of "NS-Deutsch" is thus its concealment of the real meanings of words; and it is primarily the disagreeable side of reality that disappears behind such vague terminology. These camouflage words are often commonly known words that are then combined to give a new meaning: "Rasse" and "Hygiene" become "Rassenhygiene," "Verfall" and "Kunst" become "Verfallskunst."[3] Their precise meaning can only be derived from the concrete context in which they are used; it is this ambiguity that provides the camouflage.

The Allies also understood the power of language: after the defeat of Nazi Germany, they included language as a focus in their attempts at "Entnazifizierung." There were a variety of language policies and language-regulating measures taken in all four of the occupied zones. Public, or official names (for example, street names) were changed, schoolbooks were revised, and newspapers' and magazines' use of language was monitored. That was, however, no simple task during the chaotic postwar years. For that reason, National Socialist terms or symbols in schoolbooks, or place names on maps that were reminiscent of "Großdeutschland" were often just blacked out.[4] However, regardless of the difficulties observed in the concrete implementation of such measures, they do clearly indicate the extent to which the occupying Allied powers considered language and language use to be a significant factor. Aware of the powerful effect of language, the Allied Control Council announced censorship ordinances that were explicitly directed against obfuscating language in April 1946: "Für die schriftliche Kommunikation galt die Auflage, dass die Texte einfach zu verstehen sein sollten . . . und Fachwortschatz auf ein Minimum begrenzt werden sollte."[5] Thus, National Socialism's extensive use of euphemisms was supposed to be countered by the explicit naming practices introduced within the framework of the Allied occupying forces' re-education program.

In Reunified Germany: Clear Wording for One's Own History?

What came of that desire for clarity? What words are used to speak about the National Socialist past in Germany today? Those kinds of questions became particularly important again in the course of the Reunification process. For, although the allied "Siegermächte" had in the meantime become friendly nations, some of the governmental heads remained skeptical about the German Reunification efforts, Margaret Thatcher and François Mitterand surely being the best-known examples. International reporting from that time period also demonstrates the linguistic dimension of the link between those concerns and Germany's National Socialist past: "Etikettierungen von Kohls Verhalten als Zeichen einer 'großdeutschen Arroganz' in den dänischen Medien, die Heraufbeschwörung eines 'Vierten Reiches' in der britischen *Times* sowie in der französischen Presse unübersetzt verwendete Begriffe wie 'Reich,' 'Anschluss' oder die im Zusammenhang mit Kohls Zehn-Punkte-Plan gewählte Formulierung 'Blitzangriff' zeigen dies deutlich."[6] However, Germany was dependent upon the support of Western governments. It was necessary to promote a positive image of Germany during a time of racist persecutions, arson attacks, and pogrom-like assaults on refugee residences, sometimes lasting days and resulting in a number of murders.[7]

In the efforts to promote a positive image of Germany, the principal memorial sites having to do with the National Socialist period played an important role, demonstrating to the world that Germany had dealt with its own past. There was a radical re-design accompanied by lengthy, broad, and heated debates. One major discussion point was, and is, the language used to speak about the past. I would therefore like to turn to a discussion of the memorial sites in order to investigate how the National Socialist past is talked about in Germany today. In the first example, I will concentrate on this re-orientation of official remembrance; in the second one, however, I will show that the struggle to express the inexpressible is also going on outside the institutional framework.

The Memorial Sites "of exceptional national and international significance" and the Federal Memorial Sites Concept

As was the case with many other places of remembrance, the official, federal National Socialism memorial sites in Germany were often hard fought for by survivors and their relatives, as well as by the family members of those murdered. Their demands for dignified treatment of their place of suffering and for the appropriate memorialization of those who were murdered were often met with refusal. Nevertheless, many survivors remained active in the memorial institutions in both German states and reported from their perspective about the terror that they had experienced, advocating tirelessly for "Nie wieder!"

In the course of the Reunification efforts, the principal National Socialism memorial sites were put into the spotlight: they were no longer just for the local school children to visit, but were now representative places of international importance, demonstrating the success of Germany's "Vergangenheitsbewältigung." In the process, the responsible parties also changed: as of the 1990s, the individual federal states were no longer solely responsible for their local memorial sites, as had been the case in West Germany. The conceptual framework of the main, larger memorial sites such as Dachau, Bergen-Belsen, Buchenwald, and Ravensbrück now took on national importance. Its basis was a new, nationally uniform concept for memorial sites, the so-called *Bundesgedenkstättenkonzept*, which included the regulation of funding allocation. Closely linked to that however, was the thematic orientation of the sites. A decades-long debate broke out about how to adequately represent the past, as well as how to use language appropriately: the Federal Memorial Sites Concept was only approved by the Federal Cabinet in June 2008, after a debate lasting over fifteen years, and it remains controversial to this day. During the process, survivor associations either left the negotiations in protest or were not even included in the discussions concerning the re-designing of the larger concentration camp memorial sites. Their critical voices and those of others went unheard during the re-organization, despite numerous formal objections. Their perspective had no place in this re-writing of history.[8]

So what are the main points of dispute? From what perspective, for what purpose, and in what language is the National Socialist past negotiated? The line of attack is made clear in the following citation. It is taken from a draft of the Federal Memorial Sites Concept initiated by the ex-GDR civil-rights activist Günther Nooke, and submitted by the CDU/CSU parliamentary group in 2004:

> **Förderung von Gedenkstätten zur Diktaturgeschichte in Deutschland—Gesamtkonzept für ein würdiges Gedenken aller Opfer der beiden deutschen Diktaturen.** Der Bundestag wolle beschließen: I. Der Deutsche Bundestag stellt fest: Zu den konstitutiven Elementen des wiedervereinten Deutschlands gehört das Gedenken an die Opfer der beiden totalitären Diktaturen des 20. Jahrhunderts: Nationalsozialismus und Kommunismus . . . Sowohl die nationalsozialistische Herrschaft von 1933 bis 1945 als auch die kommunistische Diktatur von 1945 bis 1989 sind Kapitel unserer Nationalgeschichte.[9]

This example clearly shows the direction planned for the official remembrance culture and policy in reunified Germany: a second "totalitäre Diktatur," namely, Communism, is set alongside National Socialism. For it is not only the future development of remembrance sites concerning National Socialism that are being negotiated in this concept draft; it also includes the conceptual framework of sites at locations of past repression in the Soviet Occupation Zone, or what later became the GDR. Under the combined label of "Diktatur," all of the historical-political differences between the two eras seem to disappear. The draft of the text cited above was rejected; however, even if a few paragraphs were changed following protests, on the whole, the text's orientation remained unaltered: in the final version, there are more than seven pages on the GDR, as opposed to less than two pages on "NS-Terrorherrschaft."[10] This emphasis alone demonstrates "dass die Aufarbeitung des Nationalsozialismus gegenüber der DDR-Aufarbeitung in gewisser Weise als *erledigt* angesehen wird."[11]

The Neue Wache war memorial in Berlin is one of the memorial sites promoted by the Federal Memorial Sites Concept. It is a visible example of the efforts to establish a unifying historical narrative under the label of totalitarianism: in the former GDR, beginning in 1960, the Neue Wache had been known as the "Mahnmal für die Opfer des Faschismus und Militarismus." As part of its redesign in 1993, it became the "Zentrale Gedenkstätte der Bundesrepublik Deutschland für die Opfer von Krieg und Gewaltherrschaft." This re-orientation, made obvious by the effacing character of the new nomenclature, was accompanied by a long series of debates and protests, primarily by associations of the victims of National Socialism. As in the case of the critical discussions around the Federal Memorial Sites Concept, criticism was directed at the relativization of National Socialism through its equation with other repressive regimes, as well as at the blurring and distortion of historical facts, instead of clearly naming those responsible, the causes, and the consequences. The journalist Claudia Krieg examines a further aspect: "Die kommunistische Diktatur hat begrifflich die nationalsozialistische Diktatur abgelöst und zu einer allgemeinen 'Schreckensherrschaft' werden lassen. Von dieser waren auch die Deutschen (vor allem) betroffen, das wird allgemein so verhandelt. Die NS-TäterInnenschaft bleibt seit über 60 Jahren hinter 'Terror' und 'Schreckensherrschaft' verborgen. [Kulturstaatsminister Bernd] Neumann deklariert damit erneut die NS-Deutschen zu einem Kollektiv von 'Beherrschten.'"[12] The Neue Wache memorial site is thus no longer dedicated to the victims of fascism; the inscription on the memorial plaque next to the entrance could not have been formulated more generally. Perpetrators are not named, and the commemoration is undifferentiated: first the fallen are mentioned, then the victims of war and displacement, and finally those who were murdered during the era of National Socialism. However, the latter period is not named; instead, the vague term "Gewaltherrschaft" is repeated here. Only once do you see the words "totalitäre Diktatur": "Wir gedenken aller Frauen und Männer, die verfolgt und ermordet wurden, weil sie sich totalitärer Diktatur *nach 1945* widersetzt haben."[13] What they are referring to here, however, is not National Socialism, but the GDR.

The above examples are intended to provide a brief insight into the current political-linguistic tendencies in Germany concerning this issue. Today, it appears as though Germany's twentieth-century history is omnipresent, not least in the form of numerous memorial sites. However, instead of emphasizing the uniqueness of the German extermination campaign as such, uncritical parallels between National Socialism and the "DDR-Regime" are drawn. Under the label of totalitarianism and dictatorship, this equalization makes fundamental differences disappear. The meanings are shifted, and the result is muddle and confusion. The overall picture is not characterized by clear nomenclature, but, to employ a metaphor, seems to be painted with watercolors that are no longer clearly distinguishable from one another: a similar blurring effect found with the employment of euphemisms.

This summary will provide the background for the current debate surrounding the naming of the Uckermark memorial site. The following section will provide a brief outline of those discussions.

The Naming of the Memorial at the Former Youth Concentration Camp and Later Extermination Site at Uckermark

The Uckermark site is one of the innumerable locations of National Socialist terror whose existence has been denied; they are often described as "vergessene Lager" (another euphemism). It is about eighty kilometers north of Berlin, alongside the Ravensbrück Memorial Site. While the remembrance and memorial site for Ravensbrück, a former women's concentration camp, was already inaugurated in 1959 and is funded through the Federal Memorial Sites Concept, for many years no attention was paid to the existence of the neighboring former youth concentration camp.[14]

The Youth Concentration Camp at Uckermark was created between 1942 and 1945; according to estimates, 1,000–1,200 girls and young women were imprisoned there, mainly stigmatized as "asozial" or "sexuell verwahrlost." Some survivors report upon how they continued to face discrimination even after 1945; for this reason, they did not tell their stories for a long time.[15] There were prisoners who were Slovenian partisans, young women from the socialist workers' movement, as well as supporters of the "Swing-Jugend," that is, groups that expressed their opposition to the regime through swing music. Some young Sinti and Roma women and girls as well as other people who were persecuted on the basis of racism were also imprisoned there.[16] While it existed, the camp was called "Jugendschutzlager," making it sound like something harmless.

In the winter of 1944-45, a part of the Uckermark camp was altered to function as an extermination site for the neighboring Ravensbrück camp. The resistance fighter, ethnologist, and Ravensbrück survivor Germaine Tillion provides reports of mass murder by means of starvation, poisoning, firing squad, and as a result of hours-long roll calls in the freezing cold, after the prisoners had been forced to give up their warm clothes.[17] Moreover, Tillion reported that fifty to sixty women were selected every evening to be murdered in the Ravensbrück gas chambers. The exact number of prisoners murdered between January and April 1945 is unknown, but it has been estimated that about five thousand women were killed.[18]

For a long time, there were no references to the former existence of the Uckermark camp. Since the mid-1990s, the survivors' association Lagergemeinschaft Ravensbrück/Freundeskreis e.V. (hereafter abbreviated LGR/F) and a self-organized feminist, anti-fascist network that eventually became the Initiative für einen Gedenkort ehemaliges KZ Uckermark e.V. (hereinafter referred to as the Initiative), committed themselves to the remembrance of the site of this camp. Their lengthy efforts appear to have been worth it: they have been successful in raising awareness about the history of the camp through diverse public-oriented campaigns and by working on the formerly completely unmarked camp site. The number of people engaged in the remembrance of those who suffered there has increased greatly in recent years, and there have been many controversial debates about the current and future design of the memorial site.[19] Since 2011, the Uckermark Working Group has been working on a concept for the future memorial site and its conversion. This group is not a hierarchically organized, institutionalized structure, but rather an open committee of interested individuals, groups, and institutions. Just looking at its composition, it is clear how diverse the positions are from which people are negotiating and speaking: there are independent political activists, representatives of survivor associations, relatives of survivors, representatives of the Ravensbrück Memorial Site, a major, federal memorial site, local interest groups, and the mayor of the neighboring town of Fürstenberg/Havel. In addition, representatives from the responsible county and federal offices regularly take part in the meetings.

One of the main topics of debate concerning this future memorial site is what its official name should be (a debate that is long overdue). As a part of that process, the employment of euphemisms has once again become a major focus. Although the literature on the Uckermark camp is not very extensive, its naming is inconsistent even within that modest amount of documentation. It changes depending on the perspective of the individual(s) speaking about the camp, or rather the camps, since, due to the camp being transformed into a site of targeted extermination in the winter of 1944/45, we must speak here of two types of camps, and also name them. In the first part of the article, "'Uckermark' benennen oder die Mühe des Begriffs," the Director of the Ravensbrück Memorial Education Department Matthias Heyl gives a good summary of the names used to refer to the Uckermark camps.[20] For the period in which it was a youth concentration camp, he provides and discusses the names from the era of National Socialism, which make it sound less harmful than it really was, namely "Jugendschutzlager" and "Jugenderziehungslager," claiming them to be "zeitgenössisch." Subsequently, he provides a detailed description of the different naming practices used by the authors who have published on the subject post war. The difference often lies solely in the placement of the quotation marks which are supposed to label National Socialist euphemisms: we find "'Jugendschutzlager Uckermark,'" with the complete name in quotes, or "'Jugendschutzlager' Uckermark," which puts the factually inaccurate, trivializing historical term used for the camp type in quotation marks but not the geographical name, or no quotation marks at all.[21] Heyl also mentions "Mädchenkonzentrationslager" or "Jugendkonzentrationslager," which are the commonly used names and which some argue reflect the true function of these camps, but criticizes them, claiming that they are not historical and that the term "Konzentrationslager" is in and of itself a euphemism.[22] In spite of that, after having summarized all of the different names used, Heyl himself later argues in favor of a euphemism, namely: the historical NS euphemism "Jugendschutzlager"—but I will come back to that later.

We know from survivors' reports that the youth concentration camp was generally called "Jugendlager" by the prisoners themselves, including also the "Ravensbrückerinnen," as it belonged to the larger Ravensbrück complex that comprised the women's camp, the men's camp, the Siemens camp, and the youth camp. In contrast, there is to my knowledge no known historical name for the extermination site established there between January and April 1945, at least not from the side of the perpetrators. However, former Ravensbrück or Uckermark prisoners not only speak of a "Jugendlager," but also of a "Vernichtungslager."[23] In the literature on the subject, one can find names such as "Sterbezone,"[24] "Sterbe- und Selektionslager,"[25] or "Todeszone,"[26] but also the term "Vernichtungslager."[27]

Thus, a variety of terms are used for both camps, often interchangeably within an individual text when referring to Uckermark. When this occurs within running text, it can easily be managed by explaining what is meant by the changing terminology; in such a context, nomenclature such as "Jugendlager" can be clearly classified, for example. However, as a stand-alone, detached name of a memorial site, that would no longer be the case. In general, a name is made up of one or a few words. A name provides an image of what something is; it creates a picture in the mind; it "sticks." To this effect, what Uckermark is called has a profound effect on the image that is conjured up about what this camp actually was.

Broadly speaking, there are two contrasting positions by the most visible actors in this debate: the Lagergemeinschaft Ravensbrück/Freundeskreis e.V. and the Initiative für einen Gedenkort ehemaliges KZ Uckermark e.V. are demanding that there be a clear and unambiguous naming of the events that took place there, while the Ravensbrück Memorial Site representatives are advocating the adoption of the National Socialist euphemism "Jugendschutzlager" as the historical nomenclature. As there is no such historical nomenclature for the camp's second phase, it is not mentioned at all in the memorial sites' chosen name. In the following section, I will outline the different positions.

The LGR/F and the Initiative currently use the name "Jugendkonzentrationslager und späteres Vernichtungslager Uckermark." They consistently point out the importance for the survivors of its official recognition as a concentration camp in the 1970s: that recognition was necessary in order to be able to even apply for "reparations," even though such applications were unsuccessful in most cases.[28] Taking up a clear position is important to the Initiative, especially considering that the situation is such that many of the survivors continued and continue to suffer under the "asozial" stigma, based on the widespread concept that they themselves bear the blame for their admittance into a kind of re-education institution. For that reason, it also wants to support those survivors who to this day are still struggling for the explicit naming and thus broader recognition of this site as a concentration camp. One of these individuals is Maria Potrzeba, who spoke to that point on a radio show on WDR5 on September 16, 2012: "Ich habe gehört, dass aus 'Uckermark' auch eine Gedenkstätte werden soll und dass man das als 'Jugendschutzlager' bezeichnen will. Das darf nicht sein! Das ist kein 'Jugendschutzlager' gewesen. Es war wirklich kein Schutz! Es war Hunger, es war Strafe, es war Verachtung."[29]

At the same time however, the naming of the camp is understood as a process. In a speech for the inauguration of a memorial stone in April 2009, the Initiative says the following about the inscription on it:

> Die Inschrift des Gedenksteins stellte uns vor einige Schwierigkeiten. Eine Inschrift kann nur sehr verkürzt darstellen, was wirklich hier geschah. Zudem war dieser Ort ja nicht nur Konzentrationslager sondern ab Anfang 1945 auch Vernichtungslager. Um dieses Lager jedoch gegenüber den Vernichtungslagern im Osten abzugrenzen haben wir ... uns entschieden "späteres Vernichtungslager" als Begriff zu benutzen. Bewusst entschieden haben wir uns gegen den Begriff "Sterbelager" ... Der Begriff "Sterbelager" erweckt bei uns den Anschein, als wären hier Menschen zum friedlichen Sterben hergeschickt worden statt systematisch ermordet zu werden.[30]

However, the debate surrounding the current name, and especially the search for an appropriate name for the camp's second phase, is not over, as the following reference on the Initiative's website demonstrates:

> Seit einiger Zeit diskutieren wir ... über die Bezeichnung Vernichtungslager für die Monate Januar bis April 1945 ... Häufig gibt es den Einwand, die Bezeichnung würde das KZ Uckermark Orten und Geschehen wie in Belzec, Sobibor, Auschwitz u. a. Vernichtungslagern gleichsetzen. Wir wollten den Unterschied durch den Zusatz *späteres* Vernichtungslager deutlich machen ... Wir möchten mit einer Bezeichnung nicht verharmlosen oder verschleiern, was in den letzten Monaten vor der Befreiung dort geschehen ist ... Das Lager [wurde] nicht zum Hospiz, sondern zum Ort gezielter Vernichtung. Wir suchen nach einer Bezeichnung, die den systematischen und willkürlichen Mord an tausenden Menschen deutlich macht und die trotzdem die oben genannten Einwände berücksichtigt. Wir sind im Diskussionsprozess, Beiträge zu diesem Thema sind uns sehr willkommen.[31]

The Initiative is thus leading an open and transparent debate about the naming of the memorial site, and invites participation in the discussion. Their process is not arbitrary: they explicitly state their goal of clarity and unambiguity, and the employment of euphemisms such as "Jugendschutzlager" is rejected due to their consistently trivializing effect.

In contrast, the Ravensbrück Memorial Site uses the euphemistic, historical nomenclature for the Uckermark Camp, namely "Jugendschutzlager Uckermark," enclosed in quotation marks for the most part. At the same time, Ravensbrück's representatives are well aware of the effect of euphemisms. That point is made especially clear in the above-cited text by Matthias Heyl, who, as Director of the Ravensbrück Memorial Education Department, has represented his institution in discussions with the Uckermark Working Group. By no means is anyone alleging that this use of euphemisms is in order to conceal something: so how do Heyl and the memorial site justify their naming practices?

I would like to answer this question with the help of the "Besucherleitsystem" that the Ravensbrück Memorial Site has developed in recent years and to which Heyl refers in his article.[32] The visitor wayfinding system is meant to make it easier for visitors to orient themselves at the site: historical places are marked and briefly described on information columns. Areas belonging to the historical camp complex, but not to the memorial site, are also included in this wayfinding system: column 35, for example, provides information about the neighboring Uckermark camp. This column also exclusively uses the name "Jugendschutzlager Uckermark" (in quotation marks); the title makes no reference to the camp's second phase. Only in the column's brief text can one read of its later use as a "Sterbe- und Selektionslager" (without quotation marks), for which the English translation of the text actually reads "camp for dying prisoners." Heyl formulates his concerns (and therefore also those of the memorial site institution?), which he purports to address with his naming practice, in the following way: "Dass in dem Text des Besucherleitsystems der Gedenkstätte zum 'Jugendschutzlager Uckermark' die historischen Termini 'Jugenderziehungslager' und 'Jugendschutzlager Uckermark'—in Parenthese . . . gesetzt—verwendet werden, versucht der Notwendigkeit Rechnung zu tragen, nationalsozialistische Begriffe in ihrer euphemistischen Position ebenso zu dekonstruieren wie in dem, was sie eben doch über ihre nationalsozialistische, ideologische Rahmung auszusagen wissen. Die Begriffe ganz zu bannen, indem man sie gar nicht verwendete, funktionierte nicht, nähme uns sogar Anlass und Gelegenheit, sie zu dekonstruieren."[33] A few paragraphs before, Heyl wrote that it was "notwendig und unabdingbar, die 'Mühe des Begriffs' auf sich zu nehmen—und das heißt, die Begriffe gerade dort, wo sie verharmlosend sind, als Deckbegriffe zu dekonstruieren und sichtbar zu machen. Hier hilft Konkretion, Darstellung dessen, was sich hinter dem Begriff tatsächlich verbirgt oder dahinter verborgen wurde."[34] Heyl and the memorial institution's editorial staff reject the name "Jugend-KZ" because, on the one hand, to them it seemed to be "als nachträgliche Bezeichnung problematisch," and on the other hand, as mentioned before, because the term "Konzentrationslager" was itself a euphemism. As far as their own retroactive naming of the camp's second phase as "Selektions- und Sterbelager," there was no detailed explanation of the choice.

Conclusion

If the positions in this discussion are compared, then one comes to an almost surprising conclusion: the goals appear to be the same! All participating actors are aware of the effect of euphemisms; all reject that effect; all appear to be more concerned with clarity, or "Konkretion." However, the directions they choose to take in their search for the appropriate nomenclature differ: the Lagergemeinschaft Ravensbrück/ Freundeskreis e.V. and the Initiative für einen Gedenkort ehemaliges KZ Uckermark e.V. are looking for a name that would provide the most clarity, as well as visibility, to both of the camp's phases. They are open to criticism, and call on others to take part in the search and engage in the discussions together. The Initiative does not "ban" National Socialist euphemisms, as Heyl suggests in the above citation; it names and discusses them, but in the body of the text rather than in the title. In contrast, the Ravensbrück Memorial Site institution already attempts "Dekonstruktion" in its naming of the Uckermark camp: the quotation marks are supposed to quasi "unmask" the National Socialist euphemism. However, even Heyl, as their representative, must point to the body of the text for a deeper discussion.[35]

At the beginning of this article, I discussed how powerful language and language use is for the construction of our perception of reality. Armed as they were with this same knowledge, the National socialists used many euphemisms as camouflage words during the era of National Socialism. Later, those expressions were supposed to be replaced with clarity during the Allied forces' efforts at denazification. Unfortunately, those efforts were not very successful: I have attempted to demonstrate with the use of a few examples how some dominant representations of history in Germany are not characterized by a clear description of facts, but rather by vagueness. The fundamental differences between National Socialism and the political system in the GDR disappear behind such fuzzy terms as "tyranny" and "totalitarianism."

Precisely in view of the above outlined functions of euphemisms, and the very real consequences of their use, one must in conclusion ask why they should be held to, especially in the context of memorial and remembrance politics. Why reproduce names that serve to cover up the truth, if we are committed to the critical spirit of the Enlightenment? Why does the Ravensbrück Memorial Site institution determinedly hold on to the National Socialist euphemism "Jugendschutzlager" in their naming of the Uckermark camp? As we have seen, it is not based on any desire to sugarcoat the truth. No, the memorial institution also wants to encourage a discussion about language and its effects. However, the arguments provided for the use of National Socialist terminology as a name for the Uckermark camp are not convincing. Even Heyl himself clearly demonstrates in his article that he is aware that what is actually meant by the employment of particular euphemisms can only be inferred from the concrete context. However, a name is more often than not heard or read in isolation, without any such clarifying context, and quotation marks used for the purpose of "deconstruction" and "Darstellung dessen, was sich hinter dem Begriff tatsächlich verbirgt oder dahinter verborgen wurde"[36] are certainly insufficient. The quotation marks are not heard in spoken language, and what remains is simply the National Socialist euphemism, and its effect: the image that it creates in our minds, the concept that it communicates to us about what it is supposed to be.

As mentioned above, Heyl and the Ravensbrück Memorial Site institution argue as part of their opposition to the proposal of the title "Jugendkonzentrationslager" that "Konzentrationslager" is itself a euphemism. That is true. That term has often been used in a diminishing way for prisoner camps worldwide, trivializing the harm suffered in them. However, in this case the term is used in a clear context so that its meaning is no longer arbitrary. *In and of itself*, "Konzentrationslager" does remain a euphemism, but in the context of National Socialism, it has lost its masking effect. It stands much more clearly for the terrible cruelty that it is meant to name. The image of a National Socialist concentration camp is surely clearer than that of a "youth *protection* camp" (protection for whom, by whom, from whom?). For that reason, the naming of the camp as a "Konzentrationslager" also plays a central role for survivors who are struggling for recognition of the suffering that they experienced there: on a legal, societal, and also quite personal level.

I find the critical discussion of "Jugendkonzentrationslager" as a "nachträgliche Bezeichnung" confusing: is it not about finding an accurate label, instead of reproducing "NS-Deutsch"? In his article "Kristallnacht: Murder by Euphemism," Rabbi Benjamin Blech criticizes the use of euphemisms as follows:

> *Kristallnacht* is German for "the night of crystal." And seventy years after the horrible events of 1938 should have given us by now sufficient perspective to expose the lie of a horrible WMD—Word of Mass Deception—that epitomizes the key to the most powerful

methodology for murder perfected by the Nazis. How, after all, were the Nazis able to commit their crimes under the veneer of civilized respectability? . . . They glorified the principle of murder by euphemism . . . We must pledge never again to allow evil to enter our lives disguised as the good and the noble.[37]

The debate surrounding the naming of the Uckermark memorial site is not over. As far as I am concerned, the use and reproduction of National Socialist euphemisms (within inaudible and non-self-explaining quotation marks) is wrong, regardless of any good intentions. The suggested euphemistic naming as "Jugendschutzlager" also leaves the camp's second phase invisible. The name "Jugendkonzentrationslager," however, clearly denotes what Uckermark was, already in the name. Finding appropriate words to convey the camp's second phase in its name is no easy feat, and the discussion participants are still in the midst of that process. My choice of the words "extermination site" (*Vernichtungsstätte*) reflects one of the suggestions currently discussed within the Initiative. This is an attempt to make the camp's second phase visible already in its title, without minimizing it, nor equating it with extermination camps in German-occupied Poland.

Let me end by saying that our choice of words is also a matter of an individual's position, and for what or for whom that individual feels a sense of responsibility. In Germany, many who investigate how people use language to speak about National Socialism are the descendants of perpetrators, and/or were socialized in a perpetrator context. That affects our perspective, the "glasses" through which we see the world. In that regard, Karin Doerr and Kurt Jonassohn make a thought-provoking observation in their article *The Persistence of Nazi German*:

> The use of inappropriate vocabulary is noticeable in many other German publications on the subject, as for example in German school books . . . Although clearly stating their rejection of the Nazi period, these German authors are unable to find a neutral language and a compassionate tone in their dealings with Nazi atrocities. Very few scholars have remarked on this phenomenon, such as Walter F. Renn and Elisabeth Maxwell. Both associate this use of the Nazi language with siding with the perpetrator instead of showing an understanding for the side of the victims and survivors of the Holocaust. They warn about continuing the use of Nazi terminology, particularly euphemisms, such as *Endlösung* instead of "destruction or mass murder of the European Jews."[38]

Although we are certainly incapable of simply taking off our "glasses," we could attempt to look over their rims. A good place to start would be to listen to and also empower the perspectives of survivors.

—Translated by Jessica Ring, Subtext Network Berlin/Seattle

Notes

[1] Victor Klemperer, *LTI: Notizbuch eines Philologen* (Leipzig: Reclam, 1980).

[2] Dirk Deissler, *Die entnazifizierte Sprache: Sprachpolitik und Sprachregelung in der Besatzungszeit* (Frankfurt am Main: Peter Lang, 2004), 31.

[3] Cornelia Schmitz-Berning, *Vokabular des Nationalsozialismus* (Berlin: de Gruyter, 1998).

[4] Schmitz-Berning, *Vokabular des Nationalsozialismus*, 98.

[5] Schmitz-Berning, *Vokabular des Nationalsozialismus*, 92.

[6] Torben Fischer and Matthias N Lorenz, eds., *Lexikon der "Vergangen-heitsbewältigung" in Deutschland: Debatten- und Diskursgeschichte des Nationalso-zialismus nach 1945* (Bielefeld: Transcript, 2007), 273.

[7] AutorInnenkollektiv Autofocus Videowerkstatt, *The Truth Lies in Rostock ¾ Die Wahrheit liegt (lügt) in Rostock* (Germany, UK, 1993), accessed September 10, 2013, http://www.youtube.com/watch?v=4gboC2bsv8w&feature=youtube_data _player.

[8] Sylvia Degen and Claudia Krieg, "Offenes Gedenken auf dem Uckermark-Gelände: Erinnerungsarbeit, politische Auseinandersetzung und Kritik der Nutzbarmachung von Geschichte zur nationalen Identitätsbildung im vereinten Deutschland," in *Unwegsames Gelände: Das Jugendkonzentrationslager Ucker-mark: Kontroversen um einen Gedenkort* (Gütersloh: Fördergemeinschaft wissen-schaftlicher Publikationen von Frauen, 2013).

[9] BT-Drs. 15/3048, "Drucksache des Deutschen Bundestages 15/3048: Förde-rung von Gedenkstätten zur Diktaturgeschichte in Deutschland—Gesamtkonz-ept für ein würdiges Gedenken aller Opfer der beiden deutschen Diktaturen" (Deutscher Bundestag, April 5, 2004), 1, accessed January 10, 2014, http:// dip21.bundestag.de/dip21/btd/15/030/1503048.pdf. (Bold in original.)

[10] BT-Drs. 16/9875.

[11] Werner Nickolai, *Gedenkstättenpädagogik und Soziale Arbeit* (Münster: LIT Verlag, 2013), 261. (Emphasis in original.)

[12] Claudia Krieg, "Neuauflage der Totalitarismustheorie: Zum Erinnerungsdis-kurs und dem neuen Bundesgedenkstättenkonzept," *Standpunkte* 19 (Novem-ber 2008), p. 6, accessed January 10, 2014 http://www.rosalux.de/fileadmin/ rls_uploads/pdfs/Standpunkte/Standpunkte_0819.pdf.

[13] Luisenstädtischer Bildungsverein e.V., "Neue Wache," *Berlin von A Bis Z*, accessed January 10, 2014, http://www.luise-berlin.de/berlinaz/indexabz.htm. (Emphasis SD.)

[14] Katja Limbächer, Maike Merten, and Bettina Pfefferle, *Das Mädchenkonzen-trationslager Uckermark* (Münster: Unrast, 2005). Just as in the title of the book referenced in this note, the term "Mädchenkonzentrationslager" is also used for the Uckermark camp. That is because this camp was specifically designed for girls and young women. However, more recent research suggests that there were also some boys imprisoned there. By using the term "youth concentration camp," I would like to include them on a linguistical level. Furthermore, the term seeks to point out the connection between the Uckermark camp and the other

two *Jugendkonzentrationslager* in Moringen and Łódź ("Jugendverwahrlager Litzmannstadt").

[15] Cf. Chris Rotmund, "Fürsorge als Ausgrenzung: Das Konzentrationslager für Mädchen und junge Frauen Uckermark" (Thesis, Hochschule für Angewandte Wissenschaften, Hamburg, 2006), 39, accessed January 10, 2014, http://www.gedenkort-kz-uckermark.de/assets/downloads/2006_rotmund-diplomarbeit.pdf.

[16] Cf. Martin Guse, "Das Jugend-KZ Uckermark—1942 bis 1945," Bundeszentrale für politische Bildung, accessed November 3, 2013, http://www.bpb.de/geschichte/nationalsozialismus/ravensbrueck/60709/jugend-kz-uckermark?p=1.

[17] Cf. Germaine Tillion and Anise Postel-Vinay, *Frauenkonzentrationslager Ravensbrück* (Lüneburg: zu Klampen, 1998), 274, 297, 299.

[18] Initiative für einen Gedenkort ehemaliges KZ Uckermark e.V., "Reader for the International Antifascist Feminist Working Camp at the Site of the former Youth Concentration Camp Uckermark 2009," accessed January 10, 2014, http://www.gedenkort-kz-uckermark.de/assets/downloads/baucamps/2009_Reader_baucamp.pdf.

[19] Cf. Forschungswerkstatt Uckermark, ed., *Unwegsames Gelände: Das Jugendkonzentrationslager Uckermark: Kontroversen um einen Gedenkort* (Gütersloh: Fördergemeinschaft wissenschaftlicher Publikationen von Frauen, 2013).

[20] Matthias Heyl, "Uckermark benennen oder die Mühe des Begriffs," in *Unwegsames Gelände: Das Jugendkonzentrationslager Uckermark; Kontroversen um Einen Gedenkort*, ed. Forschungsgruppe Uckermark (Gütersloh: Fördergemeinschaft wissenschaftlicher Publikationen von Frauen, 2013), 61–72.

[21] Heyl, "Uckermark benennen," 64.

[22] Heyl, "Uckermark benennen," 64.

[23] Bernhard Strebel, *Das KZ Ravensbrück: Geschichte eines Lagerkomplexes* (Paderborn: F. Schöningh, 2003), 460. And my personal conversations with the survivors Irma Trksak (January 2014) and Esther Bejarano (November 2013).

[24] Christa Schikorra, *Kontinuitäten der Ausgrenzung: 'Asoziale' Häftlinge im Frauen-Konzentrationslager Ravensbrück* (Berlin: Metropol, 2001), 193.

[25] Strebel, *Das KZ Ravensbrück*, 459.

[26] Simone Erpel, *Zwischen Vernichtung und Befreiung: Das Frauen-Konzentrationslager Ravensbrück in der letzten Kriegsphase* (Berlin: Metropol, 2005), 80.

[27] Simone Erpel, "Das 'Jugenschutzlager' Uckermark als Vernichtungslager," in *Das Mädchenkonzentrationslager Uckermark*, 2nd ed. (Münster: Unrast, 2005), 215–33.

[28] Initiative für einen Gedenkort ehemaliges KZ Uckermark e.V., "Rede Befreiungsfeier April 2009," accessed January 10, 2014, http://www.gedenkort-kz-uckermark.de/assets/downloads/berichte/2009_RedeBefreiungsfeier.pdf.

[29] Potrzeba quoted in Monika Mengel, "Maria Potrzeba, Überlebende: Im Mädchen-KZ Uckermark," *Erlebte Geschichten* (WDR 5, September 16, 2012), accessed January 10, 2014, http://www.wdr5.de/sendungen/erlebtegeschichten/potrzebamaria102.html.

[30] Initiative für einen Gedenkort ehemaliges KZ Uckermark e.V., "Rede Befreiungsfeier April 2009."

[31] Initiative für einen Gedenkort ehemaliges KZ Uckermark e.V., "Gedenkort ehemaliges KZ Uckermark." (Emphasis SD.)

[32] Heyl, "Uckermark benennen," 70.

[33] Heyl, "Uckermark benennen," 70.

[34] Heyl, "Uckermark benennen," 63.

[35] Heyl, "Uckermark benennen," 63.

[36] Heyl, "Uckermark benennen," 63.

[37] Benjamin Blech, "Kristallnacht: Murder by Euphemism," *Aish.com*, August 11, 2008, accessed January 10, 2014, http://www.aish.com/ho/i/Kristallnacht-Murder-by-Euphemism.html.

[38] Karin Doerr and Kurt Jonassohn, "The Persistence of Nazi German," *Montreal Institute for Genocide and Human Rights Studies: MIGS Occasional Paper*, April 1999, accessed January 10, 2014, http://migs.concordia.ca/occpapers/n_german.html.

Language and the Perpetrators

"Lieber, guter Onkel Hitler": A Linguistic Analysis of the Letter as a National Socialist Text-Type and a Re-evaluation of the "Sprache im/des Nationalsozialismus" Debate

Geraldine Horan, University College London

GIVEN THE LARGE NUMBER OF TEXTS produced by National Socialists during the period 1933–45 and before, why begin this analysis with the opening greeting from a letter sent to Hitler by a young teenager: "Lieber, guter Onkel Hitler"? The intention here is to shift the focus from the *language of* and *in* National Socialism to *discourse* in National Socialism, with a particular emphasis on language use in context as a shared, communicative phenomenon. In this article I will argue that in analyzing National Socialist discourse as part of communicative practice, the letter should be considered as constituting a significant text-type, as revelatory in its use of language as speeches and propaganda texts. The significance of letters lies in their combination of fixed, recognizable, yet also malleable features. Letters are "defined partly by the functions of communication," yet "letters may include poetry and narrative; they remain as letters and as a distinct genre in terms of the purposes they serve."[1] Thus, letters provide the analyst with certain ritualized linguistic features, such as the opening and closing greetings, while also varying in style and content. Moreover, letters can reveal a great deal about the relationship of the writer and the addressee, including potential imbalances in power and a shared language (or lack thereof). Unlike the speeches and printed propaganda texts produced by National Socialists, letters provide insights into the instrumentalization of National Socialist language by the writer and the negotiation of status, power, information, ideas, and wishes that constitute the letter as a text-type.

My analysis will draw in particular on the historical sociolinguistic concept of language history "from below," which stresses the importance of including long-ignored texts in linguistic studies, texts produced by "ordinary" people, those who did not hold positions of power and are not the authors of official, authoritative texts.[2] The corpus for my analysis consists of four letters written to Hitler and other NSDAP leaders between 1924 and 1945, published in an edited volume by Henrik Eberle entitled *Briefe an Hitler* in 2007. As the analysis will show, the letters show evidence of a participatory discourse between individuals, who may not have been members of the NSDAP, and leaders of the party. From this, I will argue that the "Sprache im/des Nationalsozialismus" debate that has dominated investigations of NS language over the past seventy years should be abandoned in favor of a more nuanced, differentiated analysis that focuses on the participatory nature of discourse in National Socialism and acknowledges the linguistic involvement of marginalized voices, including those of women and children.

The "Sprache im/des Nationalsozialismus" Debate

Linguists have for almost seven decades pursued the question of whether there was (and is) an identifiable "Nazi language," and the role it may have played in promoting, justifying, and even concealing the atrocities committed during the NS regime. Starting with Victor Klemperer's *LTI* (1947) and Eugen Seidel and Ingeborg Seidel-Slotty's *Sprachwandel im Dritten Reich* (1961), followed by Cornelia (Schmitz-)Berning's *Vokabular des Nationalsozialismus* (1964, revised in 2000), Karl-Heinz Brackmann and Renate Birkenhauer's dictionary *NS-Deutsch* (1988) and Robert Michael and Karin Doerr's *Nazi-Deutsch / Nazi German: An English Lexicon of the Language of the Third Reich* (2002), a recognizable vocabulary has been defined, codified, and attested. Therefore, despite the intervention of some German linguists, outlined below, the notion of a "Nazi language" persists. Where attention should now be focused, I would argue, is on placing this vocabulary within its social and communicative context, on the language as part of the individual's communicative repertoire.

The debate over whether the appropriate label should be "Sprache *im* Nationalsozialismus" or "Sprache *des* Nationalsozialismus," although appearing to focus on the significance of the preposition, extended far beyond this, and came to define linguistic approaches to the subject. Since the 1960s, no analysis of language use or discourse in National Socialism has been able to take place without acknowledging the methodological issues raised. As part of the "structural turn" in German linguistics in the 1960s, Peter von Polenz's articles in 1963 and 1967 criticized the *Einzelwortmethode* ("single-word method") that contributed to the notion of a National Socialist language, as it did not sufficiently distinguish between diachronic and synchronic methods, and confused linguistic critique (*Sprachkritik*) with linguistic analysis.[3] Victor Klemperer's *LTI* was criticized for its methods and findings: as a non-linguist, his focus on single words, and his moral and aesthetic judgement of the language as toxic was regarded as flawed and misleading.[4] Linguists writing on language use in National Socialism in the 1970s were careful to maintain the view that there was no identifiable language *of* National Socialism. As Gerhard Voigt states, "Von einer Sprache des Nationalsozialismus wird nicht mehr gesprochen," thereby confirming the divide between the "science" of linguistics, which avoided dabbling in personalized theories of fascism, and subjective critique of language.[5] Similarly, Wolfgang Werner Sauer's description of NS language as an "occupation" refuted the fear of language commentators that the German language had been irreparably damaged, and contextualized the language within the political, discursive context of the time.[6]

More recent contributions have attempted to bridge the metholodogical divide in a re-examination of the terminology "Sprache im Nationalsozialismus" and "Sprache des Nationalsozialismus." With the benefit of thirty years' hindsight, in 1999 von Polenz re-entered the debate to point to the heterogeneity of language use "des/im/ zum Nationalsozialismus," distinguishing in particular between the "Sprache des Nationalsozialismus," the language of the NSDAP from 1920 onwards, and "Sprache im Nationalsozialismus," which encompassed the language of National Socialism and other manifestations of political language.[7] In a more decisive stroke, having examined the development of scholarship on language and National Socialism, Waltraud Sennebogen concluded that one should only refer to "Sprache im Nationalsozialismus," and that this topic "bietet ausgezeichnete Möglichkeiten für die Sprachkritik, vor allem in Verbindung mit sprachhistorischen Ansätzen."[8] It is this link between linguistic critique and language history that I would now like to explore further: the emergence of linguistic approaches such as critical metaphor analysis, discourse analysis, and historical sociolinguistics facilitates a more nuanced and differentiated understanding of language use in National Socialism.

NS Discourse in Language History: Continuities and Ruptures

Linguists and many *Sprachkritiker* agree that National Socialist language did not appear out of the blue in 1933. Klemperer regarded many of its features as emanating from a misdirected form of Romanticism; Berning refers to Paul de Lagarde, Houston Stewart Chamberlain, and Friedrich Nietzsche as possible sources.[9] Von Polenz points to National Socialist discourse as having emerged from an increasingly radical political language of violence, originating from the second half of the nineteenth century.[10] In parliamentary and political discourses of the Weimar Republic, NSDAP rhetoric did not stand out as unique or aberrant, and the language of the National Socialists in 1933 was largely the same as it had been in preceding years.[11]

Recent studies have identified particular linguistic features of key NS texts, such as Hitler's *Mein Kampf,* including Felicity Rash's investigation of the influence of existing racist and anti-Semitic language on Hitler's metaphors, and Paul Chilton's exploration of the relationship between metaphors, memes, and cognitive models.[12] These are important areas of inquiry, as Rash's identification of patterns and frameworks of metaphor and their borrowing from previous texts goes a considerable way in explaining why NS racial and anti-Semitic language was accepted by the population, as many of these terms and expressions would have been familiar to readers, supported and espoused by some with right-wing, anti-Semitic sympathies. Drawing on the notion of "memes" and "ideational epidemiology," Chilton analyzes the possible reasons why *Mein Kampf* was received so positively by contemporary readers, and why its offensive, inflammatory messages were propagated by millions. Chilton comes to the compelling, if chilling, conclusion that the use of metaphor and the processes of cognitive blending, which involve transferring an idea or word from one domain to another, constitute the means for the successful propagation of these "memes" (i.e., anti-Semitic, ultra-nationalistic ideas).[13] Von Polenz argues that the effectiveness of NS language lay in its broad appeal to different sections of the population, including "traditional" vocabulary for the conservative voter, such as *Arbeit,* or *Ehre,* and reactionary vocabulary for the right-wing, radical voter, promising *Ausmerze, Ausradierung.*[14] NS language had to be both familiar and striking in order to enjoy broad appeal, but carefully targeted so as not to alienate larger sections of the population. This combination provides some suggestion of why it was used so readily by certain members of the population, not just those occupying positions of authority in the National Socialist state, and why the influence of NS language on post-1945 German is so contested.

Language History "from Below": Participation in National Socialist Discourse

In his introduction to *Germanic Language Histories "from Below,"* Stephan Elspaß states that the avoidance or even active removal of non-standard variants "has led to a language historiography in which a major part of the language community (i.e., those writers with no access to printing) and the written language produced by these members of the community is simply not represented."[15] This comment seems to be particularly pertinent to the question of language use in National Socialism, since, with few exceptions, linguistic studies have focused on official, overtly political, propaganda texts, with little insight into the production of NS language by members of the population and the linguistic interaction between individuals and the state. Gerhard Bauer touches on it in his analysis of language use in the regime, in which he describes individuals' attempts to negotiate their way through official and ideological language, by complying, remaining silent, or creating small opportunities for linguistic rebellion.[16] Wells's analysis of the denunciation letter as a sociolinguistic text-type similarly provides some clues to the individual's strategic use of NS language, often for very personal reasons.[17] Taking this a step further, using the "the community of practice" model from sociolinguistics, I have explored the possibility that members of the population "performed" their National Socialist identity through language, and engaged in different levels and types of performance, depending on their personal beliefs and individual needs.[18] Further examination of private or semi-private ego-documents, such as letters and diaries, would enable a greater understanding of how the ideological and administrative language of the National Socialist state became integrated into everyday idiolectical and group discourses.

For further investigations, linguists could take their lead from historical scholarship: the question of participation in the National Socialist regime has preoccupied historians for several decades, not least since the fall of the Berlin Wall and the collapse of the Soviet Union, which provided fresh impetus to study life in a dictatorship and the role of state terror in ensuring compliance. The focus shifted from a hierarchical imposition of power from the top to a view from below, with an analysis of political practices and discourses on a local level.[19] Although many democratic forms of political participation were eliminated or robbed of any significance under the National Socialists, the population "were not just victims who were silenced or driven in retreat to their private spheres . . . certain avenues remained open through which citizens could express their opinions, articulate their interests, and seek to satisfy them. One of the ways citizens participated in the Nazi system was to mail countless letters of supplication, complaint, or accusation to the officials at all levels. These letters were usually efforts to get some 'action' from the state, but some of them were simply expressions of loyalty and even love for Hitler and Nazism."[20] The popularity of letter-writing to the regime should not be underestimated: in his analysis of denunciation letters, Robert Gellately, for example, estimates that "Hitler's Chancellery . . . received at least one thousand letters and petitions every working day, and according to the postwar testimony of one official there might have been twice that many."[21] The letters provided the regime with some insights into the mood of the people; denunciation letters in partiuclar represented a form of localized and individual terror, enabling the regime to extend its reach into neighborhoods and homes. In his analysis of letters written to the *Kreisleiter* in Eisenach, a medium-sized town in Thuringia, John Connelly argues that the question of whether the population internalized NS ideology and believed in it fervently is less important than the evident external-ization of NS ideology. Letter-writers to the *Kreisleiter* were at pains to demonstrate their support for National Socialism by using appropriate key words and catchphrases associated with NS ideology, thereby par-ticipating in "anticipatory compliance" (vorauseilender Gehorsam).[22]

Analysis of a Selection of National Socialist Letters

A collection of letters written to Hitler in the years 1924 to 1945, edited by Henrik Eberle, provides significant insights into the partici-patory nature of NS discourse, demonstrating that it was a part of the communicative process between the individual and the party (and state). Eberle compiled the volume from previously unpublished documents in the Moscow archives, and divides the letters into four chronological sec-tions: "Hitlers Charisma wächst: Briefe der Jahre 1924 bis 1932"; "Auf dem Weg zum Gipfel: Kult, Protest und Zustimmung 1933 bis 1938"; "Führergeburtstage 1933 bis 1945: Huldigung mit Untertönen"; "Krisen und Krieg 1938 bis 1945: Verfall der Popularität." The titles encapsulate the main themes and tone of the letters written during each period and are intended to show the changes that occurred, from the NSDAP's rise to power through to defeat in 1945. Some letters are reproduced in full, others are abridged and accompanied by Eberle's commentary, combining explanation and interpretation. While one must be cautious of the selective nature of the collection and the editing process, the letters nonetheless provide a very useful source for linguistic analysis, as they demonstrate the desire of many individuals to commu-nicate with the National Socialist leadership. In most cases, the writ-ers initiated the communication themselves, and for many, it remained a one-sided communication. In his introduction, Eberle characterizes the letters as "Glückwünsche und Bittgesuche, gut gemeinte Vorschläge und wütende Protestbriefe."[23] Those who wrote them demonstrated an ability to use NS rhetoric, also to imitate and, to some small degree, to innovate. The letter-writers employ a range of registers, from the formal to the informal and personal, but all communicate a personal desire to contact Hitler personally and establish a connection with him:

> Doch schon allein die Tatsache, dass Tausende von diesen Briefen geschrieben wurden, zeigt ein Vertrauen zur Regierung, das es so vorher und danach nie wieder gegeben hat. In ihren Briefen an Hitler, den sie als Führer akzeptierten, öffneten die Menschen ihr Herz. Sie berichteten von dem, was sie bewegte . . . Verehrung und Wut finden sich in diesen Briefen, nicht selten aber auch demütiges Flehen.[24]

Particularly striking are the highly personalized letters expressing admiration and adoration for Hitler. To refer back to the title of the article, Annelene K., from Heydekrug in the Memel Territory, wrote to Hitler on May 7, 1933, addressing him as "Lieber, guter Onkel Hitler" and signing off as his niece, aged 13¾.[25] She was not his niece, and the contents of the letter are very far removed from usual family correspondence. The letter praises Hitler, expresses loyalty to him, also on behalf of her fellow inhabitants of the Memel Territory, particularly its youth, and expressing the wish that the region become part of Germany once again. The loyal fellow inhabitants referred to in the collective "wir" do not include "Juden," "Szameiten," and "Litauer": "Vom kleinsten Kinde an bis zum größten Menschen, Juden und Szameiten ausgeschlossen, ruft hier alles voller Begeisterung nur 'Heil Hitler!' . . . Die Juden und Litauer müssen dann noch alle raus, nicht wahr?"[26] Annelene K. then describes the persecution suffered by the German minority, "Heil Hitler dürfen wir auch nicht rufen . . . Ja, lieber Onkel Hitler, wir sind hier wie in der Gefangenschaft."[27] Her own personal risk in writing the letter is also described, in particular her plan to send it via her uncle, who would appear to be a biological uncle, in Tilsit, and her request that the reply be sent to him, because if she is found out, the "Kommandant" will shoot her. For the same reason, she also implores Hitler not to mention the letter in his radio speeches, as this will bring further trouble. The letter displays a clear ability to use NS expressions, including "Heil Hitler," "Schandurteil gegen das Memelgebiet," "Hakenkreuz"; she compares herself to "Horst Wessel, dessen Lied nicht nur ich, sondern die ganze Jugend hier täglich singt."[28] Sensationalist anti-Semitic sentiments also feature prominently in the letter: "Die Juden nehmen uns nicht nur das Brot weg, sondern sie schlachten sogar zu Ostern Christen ab. Jedes Kind fürchtet sich vor Ostern, nach einem jüdischen Geschäft zu gehen." She implores Hitler "Komm doch möglichst bald, und erlöse uns von den Juden und Litauern."[29] Intertwined with this political, ideological, religious language is also a rather informal register: "Die [Juden und Litauer] machen sich hier schon fürchtbar mausig" and "Wenn ich zu ihnen sage 'Heil Hitler!', dann wollen sie mich verhauen."[30] In Eberle's collection, this hybrid style is employed frequently by letter-writers, and demonstrates how individuals were able to "externalize" NS ideology, to use Connelly's expression, and combine it with a personalized, intimate style.

The use of anti-Semitic rhetoric in a letter that contains personal, private matters is a striking but not unusual feature of Eberle's collection. A letter sent by Frau Barth on March 4, 1934, for example, begins with a typical face-saving strategy of apologizing for bothering Hitler, but stating that her problem is so great that in desperation she finds herself compelled to write.[31] This is followed by an outline of her situation; namely, that "Ein Judenweib hatte meine 20 Jahre bestehende Ehe zerstört"; what follows is a detailed description of how she has been reduced to poverty at the hands of "das Judenweib" and the "Marxistengesetz," which deny her the pension she deserves. Her personal pain at her husband marrying another women and having lost her pension entitlement is transformed into a political and ideological matter through her references not only to pension rights and sums of money, but also to the comparison she makes between her husband's Jewish wife and herself, as a German woman:

> Das dürfte wohl nicht dem Sinne des Nationalsozialismus entspre-chen, dass im heiligen Dritten Reich ein Judenweib einer ehrbaren deutschen Frau gegenüber so bevorzugt wird . . . Wenn man mich als deutsche Frau und Mutter heute noch nicht einmal einem Judenweib gleichstellt, sondern diese finanziell 2- bis 4-fach bevor-zugt, so ist das nicht nur eine unbillige Härte, sondern es entspricht nicht der Gerechtigkeit des nationalsozialistischen Staates.
>
> Daher kann ich nicht glauben, nach dem, was der Herr hoch-verehrter Reichskanzler in seinem Buch *Mein Kampf* über Juden schreibt, [dass er] diese Bevorzugung eines Judenweibes billigt.[32]

The references to "Judenweib," "ehrbare deutsche Frau," "Gerechtigkeit des nationalsozialistischen Staates," and *Mein Kampf* demonstrate the writer's willingness to engage in National Socialist discourse, includ-ing anti-Semitic rhetoric, and to combine it with her own personal situation. As such, her participatory discourse is both personal and political-ideological.

Participation in National Socialist discourse, according to Eberle's collection of letters, also took the form of composing poems and song strophes dedicated to Hitler and the NSDAP. A Frau Klose's homage to Hitler, sent in the early summer of 1933, is a typical example of an attempt to express loyalty and devotion to him in poetic form:

> Adolf Hitler 1933.
> A lle Menschen jubeln Dir zu,
> D u gibst Hoffnung, Freud und Ruh!
> O Du unser Heil!
> L ast und Mühe hast Du viel!
> F est im Auge doch das Ziel!
>   Adolf Hilter Heil!
>
>
> H och Hitler! Ruft die ganze Welt,
> I n allen Herzen bist Du Held!
> T reu zu Dir, halten wir!
> L asst sein Lob erklingen hier!
> E s wird mehr gelingen,
> R uft "Hitler hoch" im Ringen.[33]

The poem represents an attempt by an individual to replicate the kind of personalized, sentimental tributes to Hitler produced by official propagandists, and as such illustrates the participatory nature of the discourse: this woman felt empowered to write the poem and to send it to Hitler, requesting that she be given permission to publish it in newspapers in Berlin, Munich, and Wiesbaden. Her desire to publish it also indicates that she had sufficient confidence that it was worthy of sharing with members of the public. The reply, from Brückner, Hitler's aide, however, highlights the rupture in participation between the individual and the NSDAP. Brückner conveys his thanks from Hitler, but denies permission to publish the poem, "da der Führer eine Verherrlichung seiner Person grundsätzlich ablehnt." Commenting on the reply, Eberle at first expresses surprise at its negative tone, given the prominence of the *Führerkult* during the National Socialist regime, but then remarks that poems like these were outside of official control and therefore not considered desirable.[34] The fact that many poems like these were sent to Hitler, particularly after the NSDAP took power, so many that the chancelleries were unable to reply to each individually, would suggest that individuals felt that they were permitted and perhaps even encouraged to echo official propaganda and innovate, within certain limitations, and were therefore an integral part of the co-creation of NS language in a variety of guises and styles.

The letters show the writers' willingness to combine private and political discourse in a seemingly effortless way: for instance a letter sent by a family from Berlin-Siemensstadt on April 12, 1935, entitled "Kinderlogik. Oh, dieser Kinder!" containing an amusing story of a conversation between the family's two young children.[35] The seven-year-old girl declares that she wants to marry the best man in all of Germany, and it is soon revealed that this is Hitler. Horrified by this declaration, her younger brother calls the father to intervene. There then follows a discussion about who of the NSDAP leaders is married, with mention of Goebbels, his wife and children, and of Göring's recent marriage. The daughter expresses her worry that Hitler is alone: "Warum soll er denn allein bleiben? Wenn er der allerbeste Mann in Deutschland ist, dann kriegt er auch die allerbesten Kinder." Her father reassures her that he is not lonely: "Er hat uns alle, Männer, Frauen und Kinder in Deutschland und weit darüber hinaus. Wir lieben ihn alle. Das ist mehr wert als die Liebe nur eines Menschen."[36] The tone is light-hearted and sentimental, with considerable space devoted to the conversation, recounted in direct speech, using informal, childish formulations: "'Pfui, du bist ein olles Ekel,' schuchzt unser Schwälbchen."[37] Potentially face-threatening content, including references to Hitler's marital status and childlessness, is countered by statements of his special status as leader, above "normal" relationships.[38] The letter promotes the image of a happy, loyal German family, for whom conversations about Hitler are a part of their intimate circle of communication, and conversely, provide ample material to demonstrate in a semi-official context that Hitler is a central part of their lives. The family received a personalized reply on June 5, 1935, affirming that their little anecdote had been well-received: "mit der netten, so lebendigen kleinen Episode haben Sie dem Führer eine wahre Freude bereitet."[39]

Oppositional Discourse

Not all letters from members of the public in Eberle's collection were supportive and full of praise. A number of them expressed dissatisfaction with NSDAP actions and policies, and in the process employed a more oppositional, even combative discourse. A letter from Edita Badke from March 25, 1934, inquiring about her husband, who had been arrested five months previously, is an example of a more critical engagement with National Socialism. After the usual opening greeting "Sehr geehrter Herr Reichskanzler!" she begins with the reprimand: "Zum dritten Male wende ich mich an Sie. Es kann nicht wahr sein, dass Sie meine Schreiben nicht erhören wollen."[40] She retreats from further face-threatening statements by stating that she can only assume that Hitler had not received her letters personally, otherwise he would have answered. The rest of the letter is dedicated to providing a description of her husband's good character, and assurances that despite their hardship, both she and her husband are satisfied with life in the NS regime. In contrast to other letters, she does not express her loyalty and admiration, but rather expresses resignation and capitulation: "Ich versichere Ihnen immer wieder, dass wir mit dem zufrieden sein wollen, was Sie uns geben" and "Aber ich habe das Vertrauen wiedergefunden auf eine bessere Zukunft, drum will ich alles hinnehmen, nur bitte ich Sie, seien Sie doch nachsichtig, und geben Sie meinem Mann die Freiheit wieder."[41] Although the only obvious displays of National Socialist language are in the opening and closing greetings, the latter being "Mit großer Zuversicht und Dank verbleibe ich mit deutschem Gruß," the letter nonetheless belongs to the participatory discourse of National Socialism: Editha signals her compliance with, if not loyalty to, the regime, and her recognition that Hitler is responsible for her and her husband's destiny.

Moving Beyond "Nazi Language": Conclusions

Over the past seventy years much effort has been expended in the field of linguistics in arguing over the labeling of language use in National Socialism, and debating what the choice of label says about the analyst's atttitude to the language. In this article, I have argued for a critical reassessment of the *Sprache im/des Nationalsozialismus* debate. Rather than debating which preposition is most appropriate, we should not only consider "im" vs. "des," but also "während," "vor" and "nach," and "zu." Because this runs the risk of descending into further lexical, semantic, and morphological navel-gazing, and because it sounds rather like a grammar lesson on German prepositions, let me add that rather than focus on language, the emphasis should shift to "discourse." Any understanding of "Nazi language" as a collection of recognizable ideologically-charged and organizational vocabulary can only result from an analysis of its use in context.

As this brief analysis of a highly selective number of letters illustrates, "ordinary" people, including those usually considered to be peripheral to political discourse from a historical perspective, namely women and children, should be considered as participants in National Socialist discourse as much as those in positions of power and authority. The number of letters written by the population and the instrumentalization of National Socialist language to express loyalty and/or to ask for help, or even complain, would seem to suggest that many individuals felt that they were entitled to participate, imitate, or be innovative within the discursive context. What the letters demonstrate is a shift in the role and function of National Socialist language from a group discourse, in competition with other interlinking and opposing discourses, to one that had general, prescriptive currency.[42] In order to explore this transition from group to national discourse, a more detailed, systematic linguistic analysis of a range of text-types is required, including ego-documents. Eberle's edited volume points to the existence of tens of thousands of letters housed in archives, libraries, and private collections in Germany and elsewhere that have not yet been the subject of linguistic study.

This analysis has drawn on Elspaß's concept of language history "from below," because this is relevant to a broader understanding of language use in National Socialism. In his study of letters written by German immigrants to the United States in the nineteenth century, Elspaß states that he not only wishes to present a linguistic history of simple, everyday folk, but also to chart the historiography of the language, from its sociocommunicative varieties to its role as a standardized form.[43] This, I would argue, is where scholarship on language use in National Socialism should focus. As outlined at the start of the article, there is a considerable body of literature identifying and defining key NS words and phrases; yet the discourse that made use of these words and phrases was a fundamentally social phenomenon. In his 2013 study *Sprache unterm Hakenkreuz* (Language under the Swastika), Horst Dieter Schlosser stresses the importance of pragmatic, communicative features of the language, arguing that individuals used language in a network of situations dominated by National Socialist ideology. Therefore, not only the use of key ideological language should be scrutinized; even apparently "harmless" language should be examined for its ideological content.[44] For those who wrote letters to NS leaders, it is true that the communication was often largely a one-way process, as many of the letter-writers never received a reply, or if they did, it was brief, formulaic, and did not often match the length and intensity of the sender's letter. Nonetheless, this did not deter many, including women and children (if the stated authorship of letters is indeed authentic), from putting pen to paper, and to harnessing NS language for a variety of personal as well as political motives. Focusing on the letter as an interactive text-type, in that it is intended in most cases to elicit a response of some kind from the addressee, I argue that NS discourse should be regarded as a participatory discourse; that its use and effectiveness is best measured not only in terms of persuasiveness and manipulation, but rather in the population's willingness and ability to use it. It is not just the language we must analyze, in terms of words and phrases, but also the communicative space that the language inhabits.

Notes

[1] David Barton and Nigel Hall, "Introduction," in *Letter Writing as a Social Practice*, ed. David Barton and Nigel Hall (Amsterdam: John Benjamins, 2000), 1–14, here 6.

[2] Stephan Elspaß, *Sprachgeschichte von unten: Untersuchungen zum geschriebenen Alltagsdeutsch im 19. Jahrhundert* (Tübingen: Niemeyer, 2005), and Stephan Elspaß, "A Twofold View 'from Below': New Perspectives on Language Histories and Language Historiographies," in *Germanic Language Histories "from Below" (1700–2000)*, ed. Stephan Elspaß, Nils Langer, Joachim Scharloth, and Wim Vandenbussche (Berlin: Walter de Gruyter, 2007), 3–9.

[3] Peter von Polenz, "Sprachkritik und Sprachwissenschaft," *Neue Rundschau* 74 (1963): 391–403, here 401–2; Peter von Polenz, "Sprachpurismus und Nationalsozialismus. Die 'Fremdwort'-Frage gestern und heute," in *Nationalismus in Germanistik und Dichtung: Dokumentation des Germanistentages in München vom 17. bis 22. Oktober 1966*, ed. Benno von Wiese and Rudolf Henß (Berlin: Schmidt, 1967), 79–112, here 105.

[4] Victor Klemperer, *LTI* (Stuttgart: Reclam, 1975), 83; Gerhard Voigt, "Bericht vom Ende der 'Sprache des Nationalsozialismus,'" *Diskussion Deutsch* 5 (1974): 445–64; Wolfgang Werner Sauer, "Die Okkupation der Sprache durch die Nationalsozialisten oder: Ist die deutsche (Sprach-)Geschichte manchmal noch aktuell?," *Osnabrücker Beiträge zur Sprachtheorie* 7 (1978): 38–56; Wolfgang Werner Sauer, "Schlag nach bei Berning? Anmerkungen zur Renaissance der Vokabularien zur ns Sprache," *Diskussion Deutsch* 15 (1984): 319–24. More recently, Siegfried and Margaret Jäger have rehabilitated Klemperer's status as a commentator on National Socialist language and praised the validity of his findings, claiming that his approach is very similar to that adopted by modern-day critical

discourse analysts; Margaret Jäger and Siegfried Jäger, *Gefährliche Erbschaften: Die schleichende Restauration rechten Denkens* (Berlin: Aufbau, 1999), 41.

[5] Voigt, "Bericht vom Ende der 'Sprache im Nationalsozialismus,'" 445.

[6] Sauer, "Okkupation," 38–56.

[7] Peter von Polenz, *Deutsche Sprachgeschichte vom Spätmittelalter bis zur Gegenwart*, vol. 3 (Berlin: de Gruyter, 1999), 547.

[8] Waltraud Sennebogen, "Tarnung—Leistung—Werbung," in *Tarnung—Leistung—Werbung: Untersuchungen zur Sprache im Nationalsozialismus*, ed. Albrecht Greule und Waltraud Sennebogen (Frankfurt am Main: Peter Lang, 2004), 11–29, here 19–20.

[9] Klemperer, *LTI*, 194; Cornelia Berning, *Vom "Abstammungsnachweis" zum "Zuchtwart": Vokabular des Nationalsozialismus* (Berlin: de Gruyter, 1964), 102–103. See also Cornelia Schmitz-Berning, *Vokabular des Nationalsozialismus* (Berlin: de Gruyter, 1998).

[10] Von Polenz, *Deutsche Sprachgeschichte*, 552.

[11] Sauer, *Der Sprachgebrauch von Nationalsozialisten*, 45; Voigt, "Bericht vom Ende der 'Sprache des Nationalsozialismus,'" 464.

[12] Felicity Rash, *The Language of Violence* (New York: Peter Lang, 2006); Paul Chilton, "Manipulation, Memes and Metaphors. The Case of *Mein Kampf*," in *Manipulation and Ideologies in the Twentieth Century: Discourse, Language, Mind*, ed. Louis de Saussure and Peter Schulz (Amsterdam: John Benjamins, 2005), 15–43.

[13] Chilton, "Manipulation, Memes and Metaphors," 16, 24–41. In devising his theoretical framework, Chilton draws on Richard Dawkins, *The Selfish Gene* (Oxford: Oxford University Press, 1976) and Dan Sperber, *Explaining Culture: A Naturalistic Approach* (Oxford: Blackwell, 1996).

[14] Von Polenz, *Deutsche Sprachgeschichte*, 550.

[15] Elspaß, "A Twofold View 'from Below,'" 4.

[16] Gerhard Bauer, *Sprache und Sprachlosigkeit im "Dritten Reich"* (Cologne: Bund, 1988).

[17] Christopher J. Wells, "Sprachhistorische und soziolinguistische Überlegungen zu einer dubiosen Textsorte: Der Denunziantenbrief," *Soziolinguistica: Internationales Jahrbuch für europäische Soziolinguistik* 13 (1999): 209–34.

[18] Geraldine Horan, "Er zog sich die 'neue Sprache' des 'Dritten Reiches' über wie ein Kleidungsstück," *Linguistik online* 30, no. 1 (2007): 57–80, here 61–64. http://www.linguistik-online.de/30_07/horan_a.html (accessed February 12, 2014).

[19] Sheila Fitzpatrick and Robert Gellately, "Introduction to Practices of Denunciation in Modern European History," in *Accusatory Practices: Denunciation in Modern European History, 1789–1989*, ed. Sheila Fitzpatrick and Robert Gellately (Chicago: University of Chicago Press, 1997), 1–21, here 4.

[20] Fitzpatrick and Gellately, "Introduction," 6.

[21] Robert Gellately, "Denunciations in Twentieth-Century Germany: Aspects of Self-Policing in the Third Reich and the German Democratic Republic," *Accusatory Practices*, 185–222, here 204.

[22] John Connelly, "The Uses of the *Volksgemeinschaft*," *Accusatory Practices*, 153–84, here 182–83.

[23] Henrik Eberle, ed., *Briefe an Hitler: Ein Volk schreibt seinem Führer; Unbekannte Dokumente aus Moskauer Archiven—zum ersten Mal veröffentlicht* (Bergisch Gladbach: Bastei Lübbe, 2007), 9.

[24] Eberle, *Briefe an Hitler*, 12–13.

[25] Eberle, *Briefe an Hitler*, 133–34.

[26] Eberle, *Briefe an Hitler*, 133.

[27] Eberle, *Briefe an Hitler*, 134.

[28] Eberle, *Briefe an Hitler*, 134.

[29] Eberle, *Briefe an Hitler*, 134.

[30] Eberle, *Briefe an Hitler*, 133.

[31] Eberle, *Briefe an Hitler*, 179.

[32] Eberle, *Briefe an Hitler*, 181–82.

[33] Eberle, *Briefe an Hitler*, 135.

[34] Eberle, *Briefe an Hitler*, 135.

[35] Eberle, *Briefe an Hitler*, 218–21.

[36] Eberle, *Briefe an Hitler*, 220.

[37] Eberle, *Briefe an Hitler*, 220.

[38] The expression "face-threatening" is taken from the linguistic discipline of Pragmatics, and is used to refer to any utterance that is considered impolite by the addressee and threatens his or her self-image (Penelope Brown and Stephen C. Levinson, *Politeness: Some Universals in Language Use* [Cambridge: Cambridge University Press, 1987], 68–71).

[39] Eberle, *Briefe an Hitler*, 221.

[40] Eberle, *Briefe an Hitler*, 195.

[41] Eberle, *Briefe an Hitler*, 195–96.

[42] Sennebogen, "Tarnung—Leistung—Werbung," 20.

[43] Elspaß, *Sprachgeschichte*, 20.

[44] Horst Dieter Schlosser, *Sprache unterm Hakenkreuz: Eine andere Geschichte des Nationalsozialismus* (Cologne, Weimar, and Vienna: Böhlau, 2013), 11.

"German was heard so often in our Dutch home": German Nazi Refugees in the Netherlands and Their Ambivalent Relationship with Their Mother Tongue

Simone Schroth

IN HIS AUTOBIOGRAPHICAL REPORT *Untergetaucht unter Freunden*, German-born refugee Claus Victor Bock describes how he survived the German occupation by hiding in Amsterdam as a member of the Dutch-German community of artists Castrum Peregrini. In order to capture the atmosphere in the group, he states that nobody belonging to this circle gave it a second thought when two Dutchmen presented a third with a volume of German poetry, thereby demonstrating a positive relationship with the language of those endangering their existence, focusing on its aesthetic values.[1] While the situation in the Castrum was certainly a special, if not unique one, Bock's remark strikingly illustrates a two-fold phenomenon that will be central to this article. Whether German or Dutch, those having to fear persecution by Hitler's henchmen in the occupied Netherlands found themselves confronted with a dilemma: for the Germans, the language of their home country had become the language of those forcing them into exile and threatening their lives beyond the German borders. For their host country, whose intelligentsia had traditionally shown a lively interest in German literature and philosophy, German became the language of the occupiers. This article will focus on autobiographical texts written by the first group and examine to what extent their authors' fate influenced their relationship with their native language: how and to what degree did they distinguish between "German" and "Nazi"? In the cases of those who avoided using their mother tongue, was this a decision motivated by their contempt for the system they fled, or by a desire to accelerate their integration into their new surroundings? Did they react to the fact that their persecutors had caught up with them and brought their language to all occupied countries? The second group, Dutch with an affinity to German language and culture, will be considered whenever this seems useful with regard to crucial points. The majority of the primary sources used in this article will come from migrants who were not famous at the time they went into exile and whose memories of the years between 1933 and 1945 are often their only publications. These range from Anne Frank's *Diaries* and texts from an anthology published by German-Dutch couple Volker Jakob and Annet van der Voort that contains twenty-seven accounts based on transcribed interviews (1988) to Eva Schloss's *After Auschwitz*, published in 2013. Edith Velmans, the daughter of a Dutchman and a German, has a special status: it was her mother who came to the Netherlands in 1918 to get married and her grandmother who joined her family twenty years later as a refugee. *Edith's Book* (2001; first published in 1998 as *Edith's Story*) contains excerpts from the author's teenage diaries.

As a first step, it is necessary to briefly examine the connection between language and identity, as it is important to establish the significance of being forced to change one's language environment. In his essay on German-Dutch writer Elisabeth Augustin, Heiko Stern explains that an individual's identity is developed through three interplaying factors: personal development and the fact that every individual depends on society with regard to both social as well as historical influences. He points out that language plays a crucial role in connection with all three factors and concludes that an individual's relationship with language corresponds to his or her personal development.[2] To illustrate his point, Stern refers to a passage from Tove Skutnabb-Kangas's *Bilingualism or Not: The Education of Minorities*, which is quoted here at greater length than in Stern's text:

> The mother tongue can also be defined as *the language one identifies with*, a social psychological definition, the language through which in the process of socialization one has acquired the norms and value systems of one's own group. The language passes on the cultural tradition of the group and thereby gives the individual an identity which ties her to the in-group, and at the same time sets her apart from other possible groups of reference (the language acting as a preserver of boundaries). Since this socialization process to a large extent occurs with the aid of language, language itself comes to constitute a symbolic representation of the group. Identification with a language, i.e. *internal identification*, as a consequence becomes a symbolic act.[3]

Skutnabb-Kangas's analysis is doubly useful for our purposes: firstly, it stresses the importance of language and language acquisition for one's personal development and thereby makes obvious what a drastic change any voluntary or involuntary move from one language to another must represent in the life of any individual. Secondly, it refers to the mechanisms of group-formation through language that we will find described in some of our sources.

While certain experiences mentioned in the autobiographical texts to be examined in this article could be called universal in the sense that they form part of accounts given by migrants of any period or origin, it is also necessary to put Skutnabb-Kangas's characterization of the power of language into a concrete historical context. In his reflections on what he named "Lingua Tertii Imperii" (LTI, the language of the Third Reich), Victor Klemperer does just this:

> [T]he most powerful influence was exerted neither by individual speeches nor by articles or flyers, posters or flags; it was not achieved by things which one had to absorb by conscious thought or conscious emotions. Instead Nazism permeated the flesh and blood of the people through single words, idioms and sentence structures which were imposed on them in a million repetitions and taken on board mechanically and unconsciously . . . But language does not simply write and think for me, it also increasingly dictates my feelings and governs my whole spiritual being the more unquestioningly and unconsciously I abandon myself to it. And what happens if the cultivated language is made up of poisonous elements or has been made the bearer of poisons? Words can be like tiny doses of arsenic: they are swallowed unnoticed, appear to have no effect, and then after a little time the toxic reaction sets in after all.[4]

Having experienced the rise of National Socialism in their home country, refugees would be well aware of the corruption their mother tongue was subjected to. As described above, possible reactions to this would be to either dissociate oneself completely from the German language as a whole or to distinguish between the varieties of German used pre- and post-1933.

When German troops invaded the Netherlands in May 1940 and defeated its army in five days of fighting, this marked the end of the country's hope to maintain its neutral status as it had during the First World War. It also marked the beginning of five years of occupation which remain difficult to characterize: while there was resistance against the occupiers, there were also those who welcomed the new rulers, for example the members of Anton Mussert's Nazi party, the NSB (Nationaal-Socialistische Beweging), which counted 27,000 members in June 1940 and whose membership numbers reached their peak with over 75,000 members in 1941.[5] With more than 100,000 of the about 140,000 so-called "Volljuden" (a term used by the persecutors) murdered in the concentration camps,[6] the Netherlands are the Western European country with the lowest survival rate of Jewish citizens.

Since 1933, about 35,000 German-Jewish refugees had come to the Netherlands.[7] At the same time, Germans without a Jewish background fled to the Netherlands, too. Klaus Mann is an example of this. From his professional activities between 1933 and 1936, it becomes obvious that he profited from the affinity with German literature and philosophy embodied by mediator figures such as Nico Rost (1896–1967) and Menno ter Braak (1902–1940). Both had been actively engaged in introducing German key texts to Dutch readers for decades and even intensified their efforts to remain doing so when it became obvious that many authors and thinkers would have to fear for their lives under Hitler's regime, and both used their contacts to support Klaus Mann in his activities devoted to the promotion of German literature during his time in Amsterdam.[8] Publishing houses such as Querido (who accepted Mann's novels *Mephisto* and *Der Vulkan* in their original German versions and also took on his journal *Die Sammlung*) and Allert de Lange provided a platform for the texts written by those in exile.[9] In his essay "Die Rezeption der deutschen Exilliteratur in den Niederlanden in den Jahren 1933–1940," Hans Würzner states that in the period between Hitler coming to power and the occupation of the Netherlands an important part of German literature emigrated to the Netherlands.[10]

Würzner's comment is useful with regard to understanding the "cultural setting," and it will help us put information into context. The reflections of the aforementioned Nico Rost, a Dutch writer, journalist and translator with a special interest in German literature, will be referred to in connection with the distinction between German and Nazi literature. However, we must not forget that the situation of writers in exile is, in many ways, a specific one: living in a different country forced them to reconsider their use of their mother tongue, which was at the same time their medium of expressing their creativity and their means of striving for financial security.[11] At the same time, they perceived their status and influence as representatives of German art as a responsibility to preserve and promote their language and culture outside Nazi Germany, which would not allow the artists to completely dissociate themselves from that language and culture.

A few characteristic quotes will give us an idea of the surroundings the refugees found themselves in. Miep Gies, who would retrieve Anne Frank's writings after the arrest of the group of German Jews that Frank belonged to and that Gies had supported during their twenty-five months in hiding, remembers the situation in Amsterdam in the thirties as follows:

> Each day, more and more refugees from Germany were moving into our neighbourhood [Amsterdam Zuid], mostly Jews, and the joke became that on the number 8 streetcar "the ticket taker also speaks Dutch." Many of these refugees were more affluent than the Dutch workers in the neighbourhood, and they created a stir when seen in furs or with other fancy possessions.[12]

Other accounts provide corresponding information. In her autobiographical text "Westerbork—Theresienstadt—Auschwitz," German-born Renate van H. describes the situation as follows: "Amsterdam-Zuid. Das war eine Welt für sich. Da wohnten damals fast ausschließlich deutsch-jüdische Emigranten. Überall wurde Deutsch gesprochen. Da gab es Schlachter mit deutscher Wurst und Bäcker mit deutschem Brot."[13] In the same publication, the anthology published by Jakob and van der Voort mentioned above, Carlotta M (born in 1918) chooses the title "Wir lebten auf einer deutschen Insel" for her contribution.[14]

The fact that it was possible to export German language and customs into Dutch exile illustrates the point made by Tove Skutnabb-Kangas about language and group-formation: the circumstances would to a certain extent prevent German refugees from integrating into the society of their host country as they remained in that "world of its own." A closer look at our sample texts, however, shows that the question of what position the authors should adopt towards the authors' mother tongue plays a role in most of their accounts and that the co-existence of both languages and cultures in their individual lives had its problems.

In the present essay the sample texts written by German (and, in one case, Austrian) refugees are compared with regard to three questions: 1) How explicitly are negative feelings towards the Germans and their language voiced, and is there a clear distinction between "Germans" and "Nazis"? 2) To what extent do these emotions influence the authors' attitude towards the native language? 3) What conflicts arise from these circumstances, for example between family members belonging to different generations? The books of Nico Rost and Miep Gies—who at the age of eleven had left her native Vienna for the Netherlands as part of a campaign to nurse children back to health after the First World War and became naturalized by marrying a Dutchman in 1941—provide a complementary "Dutch perspective."

Of the publications analyzed for this article, it is the most famous one that provides material for all of the questions listed above: Anne Frank's writings from her time in hiding, produced between the summers of 1942 and 1944. Referring to these texts requires a brief comment on the edition used here: since the 1980s, Anne Frank's original diary entries (the so-called version a) and an incomplete, rewritten manuscript intended for publication after the war (version b) are available in a critical edition that offers a synoptic view of the two versions, complemented by the text known as *The Diary of a Young Girl*, edited by Anne Frank's father, Otto Frank.[15] Also, it is important to mention a feature that distinguishes Anne Frank's writings from the other primary sources used in this article: while all the sample texts belong to the autobiographical genre, Anne Frank's are the only ones that were composed during the occupation (and, due to her not returning from the camps, not revised by the author after 1944). The others were produced decades after the war.

Due to the fact that the Frank family belonged to a group of eight Jews hiding in the center of Amsterdam, it would be inappropriate to describe their situation as "typical" once they left Amsterdam Zuid in order to escape deportation.[16] There is, however, an aspect of their existence in hiding that can be regarded as characteristic of migrant communities: the different levels of linguistic proficiency depending on the generation an individual belongs to and his or her working situation. In her autobiography, Miep Gies makes several references to this phenomenon and clearly contrasts the language skills of the younger and older Frank family members:

> The new language had come hardest for Mrs. Frank, probably because she was at home so much. It had been much easier for Mr. Frank, out in the world of Amsterdam all the time, and the children had taken to it like ducks to water.[17]

In Anne Frank's *Diaries*, we find this confirmed: her sister Margot is described as the Dutch teacher of the hiding place, and we learn that there is an agreement with regard to the mutual correcting of mistakes: the members of the group are encouraged to correct each other as it is assumed they will all benefit from this approach (March 19, 1943 and November 17, 1942, both version b).

In this context, the publications of Eva Schloss, *Eva's Story* (1997) and *After Auschwitz* (2013), illuminate the process.[18] Schloss, whose Vienna-based family emigrated to the Netherlands via Belgium, keeps referring to her own struggle with the Dutch language (see Schloss a, 32 and 44). The most interesting observation, however, can be found in *After Auschwitz*:

> At first, of course, I hardly spoke any Dutch—another frustration. I had just mastered French! Soon I was enrolled in yet another new school, facing what were becoming familiar hurdles: new language, new teachers to impress—and new gangs of girls to somehow become a part of. At home my parents still spoke to each other mostly in German, while Heinz and I took to speaking a strange hybrid of French and Dutch. We were rapidly becoming a mixed-up family, with our experience as refugees leaving traces in all areas of our lives.[19]

Like Gies, Schloss contrasts the experiences of members of different generations. What is striking is that she highlights the negative impact living in exile has on her family, stressing the fact that it affected "all areas." This ties in with Stern's and Skutnabb-Kangas's reflections on language and identity: it is impossible to separate one from the other.

In the case of Anne Frank, it seems safe to state that being in hiding, which meant spending the better part of her days with adults while being separated from friends and schoolmates, prevented a similar development that could have caused a rift between generations: although the command of Dutch and German differed among the individual family members, the Franks did not become a mixed-up family as they lived very closely together in their hiding place. At the same time, her relationship with her mother tongue is rather difficult to evaluate. On the one hand, many of her comments make it obvious that it is Dutch she regards as "her" language: she shows disdain for the mistakes made by the adults in the hiding place and develops her own method to transcribe their accents (see for example the entries of September 2 and November 17, 1942, both version b). The spelling and grammar mistakes she herself makes when recording some of her own rare utterances in German clearly show that she did not often use it in writing, although she lists "learning German" among her tasks (see May 16 and May 20, 1944, both version a). On the other hand, her father wanted to provide both his daughters with what has been described as "a classic German cultural education"[20] and regularly studied German texts with them, for example Goethe and Schiller's plays (see October 29, 1942, version b). However, the "Favorite Quotes Notebook" Anne Frank kept while in hiding only contains very few excerpts from German sources: apart from "Sprüche von Goethe," and Käthchen's "Himmelhoch jauchzend, zum Tode betrübt" monologue from *Egmont*, and Shakespeare in the Schlegel-Tieck translation we only find—ironically—a few lines from Richard Wagner's *Siegfried*, although the latter, as is duly noted, was selected "only because of the alliteration."[21] This gives the impression that the continuous contact with German literature Anne Frank experienced while in hiding was motivated more by Otto Frank's wishes than by his daughter's interests.

It also seems justified to assume that the Frankfurt-born diarist's preference for Dutch is an indication of her dissociation from her native nationality and maybe even an attempt to prepare for a change on that level. On April 11 and May 22, 1944 (both version b), she expresses the strong desire to become Dutch after the war. In the final paragraph of the diary entry dated October 9, 1942 (version b, thus revised in spring/summer 1944), Anne Frank states that she is not German anymore and that there are no greater enemies in the world than Germans and Jews: "Er bestaat geen groter vijandschap op de wereld dan tussen Duitsers en Joden." In this context, it is also important to mention that the term "Nazis" does not feature in her texts: whenever she refers to the occupiers, they are "Germans" (although it should be noted that she is not alone in this; see for example the use of "Germans" in Velmans and Gies).

The only other author in our sample voicing her anti-German feelings as vehemently—and with an even more explicit link between language and nationality—is Edith Velmans. When her mother's mother emigrates to the Netherlands in the late thirties, this is described as follows:

> Mother spent a great deal of time tending to her; consequently, I grew resentful that I always had to share my mother with Omi. It also bothered me that since Omi's arrival, German was heard so often in our Dutch home. I hated that language, and like most people I knew, I disliked Germans. Even though I excluded Mother's relatives from my prejudice, I absolutely refused to identify with them in any way. I was Dutch and so was Mother. I wanted her to speak Dutch all the time—she spoke it flawlessly, without an accent.[22]

Velmans, at the time a teenager like Anne Frank, clearly links her contempt for the language with that she feels for the people—it is obvious she resents the Germans as the occupiers of her country. For the sake of objectivity, it should also be added that her aversion might at least partly have had its origin in a young person's wish not to stand out or be different from those surrounding her—a phenomenon also described by German refugee Gerhard L. Durlacher (born in 1928), who felt embarrassed by his mother's mistakes in the new language.[23] In her contribution to Jakob and Van der Voort's anthology, Eva N (born in 1923) expresses similar feelings when reflecting on her wish to be "wie die Nachbarskinder auch" and explains how her mother and stepfather were forced to start learning Dutch due to the fact that their children refused to use their mother tongue (see Jacob and Van der Voort, 196). Ursula P (born in 1922), who came to the Netherlands at the age of eleven, goes one step further by establishing a clear link between the feelings of discomfort about her parents' imperfect command of Dutch and their general situation as refugees, which she perceived as humiliating:

> Was mich aber eigentlich am meisten irritierte, war, dass die Eltern plötzlich so unbedeutend geworden waren, so anonym. Das empfand ich damals sehr stark. In Frankfurt hatte es immer geheißen "Guten Tag, Herr Doktor, guten Tag, Frau Professor" (typisch deutsch, übrigens), und jeder zog den Hut vor ihnen. Hier waren sie einfach irgendwelche deutschen Emigranten, die sich anzupassen hatten, was wir [P and her siblings] eigentlich nicht verstanden. Zum Beispiel erinnere ich mich noch gut an Vaters verzweifelte Bemühungen, Niederländisch zu lernen. Jeden Morgen las er laut die Zeitung vor. Seine Antrittsvorlesung in Leiden im Jahr 1935, die zuvor von einer befreundeten Sozialistin ins Niederländische übersetzt worden war, war fast nicht zu verstehen. Es war entsetzlich. Später hat er seine Seminare einfach auf deutsch gehalten. Mutter kam sehr viel besser mit dem Holländischen zurecht, sprach es aber auch nicht fehlerfrei.[24]

Consulting other sources also clearly shows the dangers of overinterpretation: in her transcribed interview, Helga B, who was born in Dülmen, North Rhine Westphalia, as the child of a bi-national marriage, reports how, after emigrating in 1939, her mother would have liked to have transformed the family tradition of speaking Dutch for an hour on Sundays into a weekly hour of German, but finally had to accept her daughters' refusal.[25]

With regard to Velmans, it also has to be pointed out that in her case, the contrast between being very critical of the German language in some contexts while enjoying its aesthetic value in others is much stronger than in the case of Anne Frank. In her diary entry of July 4, 1940, Velmans describes her birthday party: "Mother sang Schubert, . . . my friend Dolf played Schumann's Papillons on the piano . . . Then Father gave us his own hysterical version of a poem by Schiller, mixing up all the lines; I laughed so hard tears ran down my cheeks."[26] Moreover, it is worth noting that in the same paragraph, she comments: "I never expected to have such an incredible birthday in these difficult times. What a shame Mother's birthday had to fall on the day of Holland's capitulation." This remark can be seen as proof that Velmans, while enjoying performances in German, always saw these in connection with the political events. This indicates that, with regard to German language and culture, it was not possible for her to see them in isolation from the knowledge of living in a country occupied by Germans.

An example of German being readily accepted as a literary language can be found in Helga B's account: when confined indoors during the occupation, she managed to avoid boredom by reading her mother's editions of Goethe, Schiller, Lessing, Uhland, and others.[27] Here the classics become a kind of lifeline. At the same time, it creates an intriguing contradiction with Helga B's previously mentioned refusal to use German in conversation with her mother and sister.

The stark contrast between being exposed to persecution by Germans (which includes the camp language that inevitably belongs to the situation) and using one's love for German literature as a mental, almost spiritual support, is most clearly seen in a text by Nico Rost, who supported Klaus Mann's literary activities in pre-war Amsterdam. Although the Dutchman was not a refugee and therefore, strictly speaking, does not match the criteria used for the selection of texts employed in this article, there are certain features that justify taking a closer look at his book *Goethe in Dachau* (1946).[28] It is possible to relate this publication to several of the sample texts. The publication, a diary the author kept during his imprisonment in the concentration camp between June 1944 and April 1945, starts with the Goethe quote "Die alte Erde steht noch, und der Himmel wölbt sich noch über mir" and is, like the whole diary, used by the writer to stimulate his will to persevere.[29] This strategy of

consciously integrating his love for literature in his daily strive to cope
with camp life quickly turns into a leitmotif: Rost discusses the significance of Bettina von Arnim with a fellow inmate and wonders if a friend
in another camp will be able to read his copy of *Wilhelm Meister*.[30] This
can, to an extent, be compared to the "reading while in hiding" described
by Helga B. In Rost's case, though, dealing with literature becomes a way
of instigating a political debate, too: when a Dutch doctor refuses to get
a volume of Goethe or Lessing from the hospital library for Rost, Rost
engages him in a discussion about this.[31] Like Velmans's account of her
birthday party, many of the entries in *Goethe in Dachau* contain passages
that link the experience of atrocities to declarations of interest in German
literature. On June 29, 1944, Rost expresses his wish to read as many
German classics as possible while in the camp, especially Goethe. In the
following paragraph, he wonders about the fate of those he left behind
at home.[32] Later, he marvels about the availability of books in the camp
library, and wonders whether the previous owner of a book, who had
a Jewish name, might still be alive. When the situation culminates in a
typhoid epidemic in the spring of 1944, he declares that it is possible to
derive pleasure from literature even when facing death; after quoting Kurt
Tucholsky, he continues: "An interest in literature while facing death?
Well, why ever not?"[33] The most useful entry for our purposes is that of
July 13, 1944. Reflecting on his previous involvement in the promotion
of German literature in his home country and the fact that he increased
his efforts when his German friends started to encounter increasing difficulties, Rost points out:

> Indeed, there is a German literature that will last, and a Nazi lit-
> erature that will disappear sooner or later. Here is what I think:
> why should we stop reading Lessing or Hölderlin, Goethe or
> Lichtenberg, even during occupation? People are avid readers, and
> there are so many texts waiting to be translated . . . Nazi literature,
> whether Dutch or German, is absolutely unacceptable![34]

Although Anne Frank's statement with regard to the "greatest enemies in
the world" does not contain a reflection on the consequences of political
events on one's attitude towards language and culture, what is notewor-
thy here is that Rost bases his whole credo on a distinction we do not find
in Anne Frank's texts: that between Germans and Nazis.

This observation can also be linked to an aspect we have already
discussed in a different context: the majority of the autobiographical texts consulted here come from authors who were in their teens
when they left Germany for the Netherlands. As previously discussed,
this might, in some ways, have facilitated their learning Dutch, for
example via their exposure to the school system of their host country.
At the same time, belonging to what might be called the "younger

generation" had an effect that can be described as negative: depending on their age when emigrating, they might only remember very little, if anything, of pre-Nazi Germany—unlike their parents, who, like Nico Rost, were able to relate their feelings for their home country to experiences untarnished by discrimination and to relate their love for its literature to a tradition preceding linguistic contamination as described by Klemperer.

The testimony of members of the "older generation" demonstrates that reactions to their status as migrants from Germany range from almost apologetic to outright defiant: one of the contributors to Jakob and Van der Voort's collection, Ilse M, who came to the Netherlands as a young woman, begins her autobiographical account with the confession that she answers her daughter's Dutch letters in German because her written Dutch is not quite flawless; she then continues by saying that "Ich denke und träume eigenartigerweise deutsch."[35] In contrast, Hans B, who is approximately ten years her senior, says:

> Deutsch spreche ich auch heute noch besser als alle anderen Sprachen, und ich mache im Gegensatz zu vielen anderen keinen Hehl daraus, dass ich in Deutschland geboren und aufgewachsen bin. Ich hab's mir nicht ausgesucht und brauche mich dafür nicht zu schämen.[36]

The fact that most of the testimonies in Jakob and Van der Voort's anthology reveal the contributors' need to comment on their attitude towards their mother tongue can be seen as another confirmation of the crucial role language plays in any individual's life as well as of the impossibility of completely disconnecting one's language from one's experiences during the Third Reich.

It has been possible to identify recurrent elements such as the use of literature as a lifeline. But it has also become obvious that we have to beware of conclusions that cannot be supported sufficiently by quotes from the source texts: while it is tempting to diagnose politically motivated reservations on the basis of comments on language and culture and vice versa, this can lead to an overinterpretation.

Some of the phenomena that were identified in several texts—for example the link between language and group identities or the attitudes of members belonging to different generations—can be described as "typical of texts dealing with emigration and the fate of refugees." At the same time, it has become obvious that the publications have to be put in context, since autobiographical details such as the age of the authors in the thirties and forties and how much time elapsed between their experiencing Nazi persecution and writing their autobiographical texts must not be ignored. In all of the testimonies considered in this article, the enormous difficulty of establishing, and sometimes even defending, one's personal identity in a host country being occupied by one's own native country has become evident—an issue that occupies their reflections until much later in their lives.

Notes

[1] See Claus Victor Bock, *Untergetaucht unter Freunden: Ein Bericht, Amsterdam 1942–1945, Castrum Peregrini* 166–67 (Amsterdam: Castrum Peregrini Presse, 1985), 65. See also Michael Philpp, "*Castrum Peregrini*—Eine deutschsprachige Zeitschrift in den Niederlanden," in *Ungenaue Grenze: Deutsch-niederländische Beziehungen in Vergangenheit und Gegenwart*, edited by Jattie Enklaar and Hans Ester (Amsterdam: Rodopi, 1994), 195–213; here, 196.

[2] See Heiko Stern, "Sprache zwischen Exil und Identität: Die Konstitution von Heimat durch Sprache bei Elisabeth Augustin," in *Jews in German Literature Since 1945: German-Jewish Literature?*, edited by Pól Ó Dochartaigh (Amsterdam: Rodopi, 2000), 77–94; here, 87.

[3] Tove Skutnabb-Kangas, *Bilingualism Or Not: The Education of Minorities*, translated by Lars Malmberg and David Crane (Clevedon: Multilingual Matters, 1981), 15. Original emphasis.

[4] Victor Klemperer, *The Language of the Third Reich: LTI: Lingua Tertii Imperii*, translated by Martin Brady (London: Continuum, 2011), 14.

[5] See http://www.niod.nl/nl/vraag-en-antwoord/nationaal-socialistische-beweging-nsb (accessed January 14, 2014). See also Loe de Jong, *Het Koninkrijk der Nederlanden in de Tweede Wereldoorlog*, vol. 10a (The Hague: Martinus Nijhoff, 1980), 203.

[6] See J. C. H. Blom, "Die Niederlande im Zweiten Weltkrieg," in *Die Niederlande und Deutschland: Nachbarn in Europa*, edited by Joachim F. E. Bläsing, Jac Bosmans, Horst Lademacher, Wichard Woyke et al. (Hannover: Niedersächsische Landeszentrale für Politische Bildung, 1992), 93–111; here, 101. See also Loe de Jong, *Het Koninkrijk der Nederlanden in de Tweede Wereldoorlog*, vols. 8a and b (The Hague: Martinus Nijhoff, 1978), 70 and 887.

[7] See http://www.niod.nl/nl/projecten/duits-joodse-vluchtelingen-nederland-1933–1945 (accessed January 14, 2014).

[8] See Presse- und Kulturabteilung der Königlich Niederländischen Botschaft Bonn, "Menno ter Braak, Nietzsche, der Nationalsozialismus und die deutsche Exilliteratur," *nachbarn* (42: 1999) 102–26.

[9] See *nachbarn 42*, 115–16.

[10] See Hans Würzner, "Die Rezeption der deutschen Exilliteratur in den Niederlanden in den Jahren 1933–1940," in *Ungenaue Grenze: Deutsch-niederländische Beziehungen in Vergangenheit und Gegenwart*, edited by Jattie Enklaar and Hans Ester (Amsterdam: Rodopi, 1994), 223–36; here, 225.

[11] For a detailed discussion of this phenomenon, see for example Susanne Utsch, *Sprachwechsel im Exil: Die "linguistische Metamorphose" von Klaus Mann* (Vienna: Böhlau, 2007).

[12] Miep Gies, *Anne Frank Remembered: The Story of the Woman Who Helped to Hide the Frank Family* (London: Bantam, 1987), 25.

[13] Renate van H., "Westerbork—Theresienstadt—Auschwitz," in *Anne Frank war nicht allein: Lebensgeschichten westfälischer Juden in den Niederlanden*, ed. Volker Jakob and Annet van der Voort (Berlin: Dietz, 1988), 221–29; here, 224.

[14] Carlotta M, "Wir lebten auf einer deutschen Insel," in *Anne Frank war nicht allein*, ed. Jakob and Van der Voort, 144–51; here, 145.

[15] *The Diary of Anne Frank: The Revised Critical Edition*, edited by David Barnouw and Gerrold van der Stroom, translated by Arnold J. Pomerans, Barbara M. Mooyaart-Doubleday, and Susan Massotty (New York: Doubleday, 2003). In this article, references to Frank's diary entries will be by date, so that readers can refer to any available edition. For the sake of accuracy, it is crucial to state which version a quote originates from.

[16] See Loe de Jong, *Het Koninkrijk der Nederlanden in de Tweede Wereldoorlog*, vol. 6a (The Hague: Martinus Nijhoff, 1975), 51–52.

[17] Gies, 52; see also Gies 32.

[18] See Eva Schloss with Evelyn Julia Kent: *Eva's Story: A Survivor's Tale by the Stepsister of Anne Frank*, New Edition (Edgeware, Middlesex: Castle-Kent 1999) and Eva Schloss with Karen Bartlett, *After Auschwitz: A Story of Heartbreak and Survival by the Stepsister of Anne Frank* (London: Hodder & Stoughton 2013). These will be referred to, respectively, as Schloss a and Schloss b. The author's mother would become Otto Frank's second wife in the early fifties.

[19] Eva Schloss, *After Auschwitz*, 57–58.

[20] See Ton Broos, "De boekenplank van Anne Frank," in *Neerlandistiek de grenzen voorbij: Handelingen Vijftiende Colloquium Neerlandicum* (Woubrugge: Internationale Vereniging voor Neerlandistiek, 2004), 71–82; here, 78. Available on http://www.dbnl.org/tekst/_han001200301_01/_han001200301_01_0006.php (accessed 13 January 2014).

[21] Anne Frank, *Het Mooie-zinnenboek*, edited by Gerrold van der Stroom (Amsterdam: B. Bakker, 2004).

[22] Edith Velmans, *Edith's Book* (London: Penguin Books 1999), 9–10.

[23] See Gerhard L. Durlacher, "Niet verstaan," in Durlacher, *Verzameld Werk*, 8th ed. (Amsterdam: Meulenhoff, 1999), 474–503; here, 486.

[24] Jakob and Van der Voort, 213.

[25] Jakob and Van der Voort, 240.

[26] Velmans, 32.

[27] See Jakob and Van der Voort, 242–43.

[28] Nico Rost, *Goethe in Dachau: Literatuur en werkelijkheid* (Amsterdam: Veen, 1946). Available from http://www.dbnl.org/tekst/rost001goet01_01/. See also http://www.stiftung-sozialgeschichte.de/ZeitschriftOnline/pdfs/Goethe_in_Dachau.pdf, especially footnote 31, for more information on prison and camp libraries (both accessed January 14, 2014).

[29] Rost, 9.

[30] Rost, 40 and 31.

[31] Rost, 10.

[32] Rost, 19.

[33] Rost, 35, 31 and 214. The quotation, which was translated by Simone Schroth, is from the last page given here.

[34] Rost, 27; translation by Simone Schroth.

[35] Jakob and Van der Voort, 205.

[36] Jakob and Van der Voort, 127.

"Whose text is it anyway?" Influences on a Refugee Memoir

Andrea Hammel, Aberystwyth University

ROM THE 1930s ONWARDS German-speaking refugee writers who fled from National Socialist Central Europe to the UK had to make a stark choice regarding the language of their literary production: some continued to write in German, and if they were well-known or lucky, their works were translated into English (Anna Gmeyner, Stefan Zweig) as publication opportunities in German were very limited. Others tried to switch to English as soon as possible (Robert Neumann, Hilde Spiel). A small group of writers continued to write in German and ceased to publish until after the war (Max Herrmann-Neiße, Martina Wied).[1] But all of these writers were adults when they came to the UK, mostly educated in Germany and Austria. What about the young refugees who came to the UK as children, who were not able to finish or, in some cases, even start their education in their country of origin?

A Kindertransport Memoir

There have been a growing number of autobiographical works written by refugees from National Socialism over the last twenty years. In the UK many of the authors were former child refugees who arrived on a *Kindertransport*. The term Kindertransport is usually applied to the rescue of nearly 10,000 unaccompanied minors mainly from Jewish family backgrounds from Germany and Austria to Britain between December 1938 and the outbreak of the Second World War in September 1939. With the increasing interest since the end of the twentieth century in the Kindertransport as a British refugee movement, more and more autobiographical narratives have been written and published in English. However, this public interest in the UK is a relatively recent phenomenon. Ruth David is an example of a Jewish girl from Germany who fled to the UK on a Kindertransport aged ten. She was born Ruth Oppenheimer in Fränkisch-Crumbach in the Odenwald region of Hesse in Germany in 1929. Her mother Margarethe was the second wife of Moritz Oppenheimer, the owner of a cigar manufacturing business; both parents came from prominent Jewish families; Ruth had five siblings. In "Child of Our Time" she describes how her formerly well-respected family was affected by National Socialist persecution and became ostracised in the village community. Attempts were made for all members of the family to emigrate. Ruth escaped in 1939 and lived in a girls' hostel in the Lake District until she was 17. All the Oppenheimer children survived the Shoah; however, their parents were murdered in Auschwitz in 1942. As an adult she lived in the UK and the US.

In the late 1980s and early 1990s she decided to write a memoir in English. Her memoir is dedicated to her children, Margaret and Simon Finchley, and the text states that their questions about her life were her motivation for writing her life story (MS 3).[2] However, after finishing the memoir in the early 1990s, David decided to make it available to a larger audience and tried to find a publisher for the English-language manuscript, which was entitled "Child of Our Time." Initially she was unsuccessful in the UK. In contrast, there was more interest in Germany, as she had established contacts with individuals who were active in commemorating the former Jewish citizens of the region David had fled from in 1939. Two local historians from her former hometown of Fränkisch-Crumbach, Hilde Katzenmeier and Ottilie Born-Hauenstein managed to interest the Landeszentrale für politische Bildung Hessen in the text.[3] This institution commissioned a translation into German and facilitated the publication of the translated text in 1996. Thus Ruth David's English-language manuscript was first published in a German translation by Gerd Hofmann and Petra Marzinzig entitled *Ein Kind unserer Zeit*. Some years later David managed to place the manuscript with I. B. Tauris in the UK and an English version was published in 2003. As with many texts of this kind, the translation and publication history is complex and there are significant differences between the three versions: the English-language manuscript, the publication in German, and the publication in English. In this article I will discuss the three different versions of Ruth David's text to outline issues of English and German in relation to life writing by former child refugees, and translation and the various influences on the translation and editing process.

Social Memory

These are, however, not the only influences. Although an autobiographical text represents an individual experience and the readership is looking for authenticity in the text, it has to be acknowledged that such texts are not written in a social vacuum. The memory researcher Aleida Assmann writes about the concept of social memory, which is defined as the memory of a whole group, which they recall through constant re-imagining and re-telling.[4] The former Kindertransportees are a group with such a social memory. The development of this social memory was significantly aided by the Kindertransport reunion movement. Although almost 10,000 children entered the UK between December 1938 and September 1939, after the war many former Kindertransportees did not see themselves as part of a group. 1988 saw the first major reunion of former Kindertransportees in London. A period of intense activity followed and there were a number of large-scale meetings and conferences in the UK and abroad. Although now smaller in scale, they continue to this day under the auspices of the Association of Jewish Refugees.[5] There is evidence that a large number of the surviving Kindertransportees continue to support this group identity and the formation of social memory. When the AJR sent out 1,500 questionnaires to former Kindertransport refugees in 2008, over 1,000 were returned, an almost unprecedented response rate and an indication of a strong and continuing group identification process. Most Kindertransport memoirs were written and published after 1988, which is an indicator of the group's newly acquired group identity and its developing social memory.

A factor contributing to the increasing number of Kindertransport memoirs is perhaps the passage of time and the fact that the generation of older refugees were passing away. For a long time former Kindertransport children had been seen as a group of refugees to whom "nothing happened at all," as explained in Dorit Bader Whiteman's book *The Uprooted*.[6] They were seen to have survived in the comparative safety of Britain and considered too young to remember their hardship and emotional plight. Nowadays, of course, we know that early childhood experiences can have a profound effect on the development of a person. It has thus become the norm in Kindertransport memoirs to write about the difficulties of the children adjusting to separation and new circumstances. In the case of Ruth David's memoir, the chapters dealing with the actual journey from Germany to England are entitled "Departure from Germany" in the manuscript, the corresponding translation is "Ausreise aus Deutschland" in the German translation, but "The Kindertransport" in the English publication. This change can already been seen as due to the re-imagining and re-telling of the communal memory: the term Kindertransport became more and more popular and entered the general public's imagination in Britain from the late 1990s onwards.

Comparing the three chapters we realize that the one most recently published, the English-language text, contains added material detailing the adjustment difficulties of Ruth and her fellow Kindertransportees in their hostel, something that is not discussed in detail in the other two versions. There is a cyclical relationship between individual and social memory: memories that are selected strengthen the identity of a group and the identity of the group consolidates the memory. This is clearly the case regarding memoirs by former Kindertransportees. One major question in current research on the topic is the change in perception of the Kindertransport from a success story to a flawed policy. Whereas earlier memory texts emphasised the gratitude the Kindertransportees felt towards their carers, those who organised the rescue and the British government who granted admission to the child refugees, more nuanced views have come to the fore over the last ten years. The publication of Louise London's *Whitehall and the Jews 1933–1948: British Immigration Policy and the Holocaust,* which is highly critical of British immigration policy, can be seen as a watershed in this respect.[7] The German-language publication of David's text and the later English-language publication fall on either side of this divide and thus clearly reflect this change. In *Child of Our Time* we find a passage which cites the name of a girl that received regular beating for wetting her bed: "Lore was not the only child who was beaten, but in her case it was a regular event, as her intense unhappiness at leaving home at the age of five had provoked her enuresis" (*Child* 109). Here David shows the lack of understanding among the adults for the traumatic experiences of the children. The beatings are downplayed in the earlier German-language version and no real details are given. In the later English language version, David even quotes from a published memoir of a fellow Kindertransportee who lived with her in the hostel, which shows how individual story interacts with social memory.

Language Choice and Translingualism

All these are influences on an autobiographical text which point to a tension between the individual, authentic autobiographer and the social context. Translation is a further influence. The cultural critic and translation studies researcher Lawrence Venuti argues in his book *The Scandals of Translation* that translations work against our desire in Western culture to be able to trace a text back to a single author. We value self-expression and originality. In contrast, translation is seen as "derivative, neither self-expression nor unique" creating the "fear of inauthenticity, distortion, contamination."[8] The issue of authenticity will always have a special place in discussions on writing about the Shoah. First, there is the fact that the National Socialist ideology denied Jews and other oppressed groups their voice and ultimately their right to exist. Thus survivors of this ideology rightly feel their need to assert their voice. Second, this becomes more acute due to the fact that Holocaust denial continues to this day. Thus, fear of the loss of authenticity is a very real problem when it comes to autobiographies dealing with the Shoah, for their authors, their readers, and potentially their translators too.

However, translation is a necessity if texts about the experiences of the Shoah are to be made available to a larger audience. However, as Alan

Rosen has investigated in *Sounds of Defiance*, translations into English are not value-neutral, as the English language plays a very specific role regarding Holocaust narratives, both due to its marginality in relation to the events of the Holocaust, it being "neither the primary language of the perpetrators nor the victims,"[9] and due to its dominant status in Western culture since the second half of the twentieth century.

But is the English language as marginal in relation to Holocaust writing as he makes it out to be? The perspective changes if one pays attention to the refugee experience, which Rosen does not: this relates to an area of discussion within Holocaust Studies as to the exact definition of a Holocaust survivor. In the *AJR Journal*, the publication of the Association of Jewish Refugees, a longstanding debate was held in 2010 on whether refugees were Holocaust survivors.[10] The majority of the former refugees who contributed felt that they were not Holocaust survivors. However, as a researcher I would argue that the experience of someone like Ruth David, who lived through the November Pogroms in 1938 fearful for her life aged ten and suffered the loss of her parents murdered in Auschwitz in 1942, is the experience of a survivor. Her writing should thus be counted as Holocaust writing.

David experienced the November Pogrom in 1938 through the medium of German but a lot of her later experiences were through the medium of English. Although she chose to become a teacher of French and German in the British secondary education system, and was thus capable of writing in German, when she decided to write her life story, she did so in English. This might be partially due to the fact that she wanted to write her story for her English-speaking children; however, she also admitted that she felt more at ease writing in English.[11] We could speculate whether the English language allowed David to distance herself from the trauma of her earlier life as well and in what way other English language literature on the Holocaust influenced her decision.

In fact, David should be considered a translingual writer, someone who writes in a language that is not her mother tongue, as defined by Stephen Kellman, in *The Translingual Imagination*.[12] Stephen Kellman focusses on mainly well-known writers and texts; however, he acknowledges that many writers do not become translingual out of choice:

> Much translingual writing . . . is the literature of immigration. . . . Immigration is often reluctant, the product of vast historical forces over which the individual has little control. . . . Eva Hoffman recounts how, at the age of thirteen, she was uprooted from her beloved Cracow by her apprehensive Jewish parents and resettled in Vancouver where English inevitably supplanted her native Polish. Though certain feelings persist—like *tęsknota*, a blend of nostalgia, sadness, and longing—that she can articulate only in Polish.[13]

David migrates as a child as well and, as we have discussed above, it can be argued that English replaced German as her primary language. However, she clearly remembers the fact that German was her first language and she points this out in her memoir. She uses some German terms in her English-language memoir, to express an intense emotional memory. She begins the narrative with the German word for emigration:

> Auswanderung: emigration: In German the word is vivid, less abstract than in English. Aus; "out"; wandern: "to wander." When I was a young child this word was part of our daily vocabulary for as long as I can remember. The word frightened me. Where would we go? How would we wander? Like pilgrims? Like beggars? What would we take with us? What would we leave behind? I soon discovered that wherever we went, it would not be a place where German was spoken. This I found particularly frightening. How could I ever learn to speak another language? (*Child* 1)

With this opening paragraph David makes linguistic differences central to her memoir. This is interesting and unusual. Many memoirs of former child refugees remember the language acquisition process, for example those of Martha Blend or Ellen Davis,[14] but very few discuss linguistic differences, and even fewer make it as central as David does. On the other hand, it is also important to note that her text, though written in English, was first published in a German translation: while the names of the translators are prominently displayed on the title page of the published book, the fact that the text is a translation from an English-language manuscript is not mentioned or discussed in the narrative.

The visibility or invisibility of translation in general has been an issue for debate for Translation Studies researchers for many years. Only more recently has there been research on the visibility of translation in Holocaust texts specifically. Piotr Kuhiwczak has shown the complex history of even well-known Holocaust texts. Kuhiwczak points out that we as readers do not always know "whether we are dealing with a translation or not."[15] A publication by another Kindertransportee, Ingrid Jacoby, is a case in point. Although based on Jacoby's diary, written when she was a child and adolescent, and although Jacoby stresses the immediacy of the diary genre, in the published book the reader is never told whether it is a self-translation or a translation by somebody else. It has to be one or the other, because we learn from the content of the diary that the diarist switched from writing in German to writing it in English, but we never learn when or why. The publication is in English and the content of the diary shows that the young Jacoby must have been writing in German at first, since she clearly did not have the ability to write in English at the time. Despite reading entries such as "Today Mr R said that he'd send me away if I don't learn to speak English"[16] or "Mr Robins has written to Mummy saying I should try and learn English soon,"[17] the issue of translation and the identity of the translator are never mentioned in the publication. In my correspondence with Jacoby she has stated that she translated her German entries herself, but that there was not much to translate, since most of the three volumes of the diaries she published were written in English. However, this information is not given in any of the publications; this is a significant omission as the diary entries cited above demonstrate the significance for the child refugee Jacoby of the fact that she had to learn the English language.

As discussed, translingualism is defined by Steven Kellman as writing in one's second or third language. In his study he discusses how this might affect text production and content. First, however, as in the case of Ruth David, how do we define which is our first, second, or third language? If we follow Kellman's literal definition of mother tongue, that is the language David spoke with her mother from the earliest age, this was clearly German. Even after emigration, David managed to continue speaking German more than most refugees, as she lived in a hostel in the Lake District together with other German-speaking refugee girls. Two German-speaking refugee women had been put in charge of the girls as matron and cook, and the hostel was thus a German-speaking environment. However, English clearly became more and more important for David, since she lived in England and received an English education from age ten. By the time she wrote her memoir in the 1990s she had lived in an English-speaking environment for over half a century. So choosing to write her memoir in English seems a logical choice. However, Kellman points out that a number of writers use a second language to express what they cannot express in their first language.[18] It might indeed have been easier to express traumatic events such as the fear of the ten-year-old during the November Pogrom in 1938, the separation from her parents, or the difficult time in the hostel in a second language, a language David clearly mastered as an educated adult who has learned to live with her traumatic past. Kellman suggests that translingualism can be seen "as a form of self-begetting, as the willed renovation of an individual's own identity."[19] For child refugees like David, building an identity more often than not involves more than one language.

The mother tongue can only become the first language if it continues to be used and developed after the first few years of a person's life. For example, there are a number of former child refugees who lost the ability to speak their mother tongue altogether after fleeing to the UK.[20] As Kellman points out, language is closely linked to identity building, and the mother tongue is an important building block in this process. However, it is clearly not the only one. For former Kindertransportees, maintaining the language of their birth parents or, on the other hand, losing this ability is often important for their identity formation. It is bound

up with the trauma of separation from the birth parents, be it tempo-
rary or permanent. This is still a neglected area for linguistic research as
is the subject of translingualism regarding memory literature by former
Kindertransportees.

Although all six siblings in David's family spoke German as children,
English became important to her, as did French and Spanish for her five
brothers and sisters at some stage in the 1930s and early 1940s. Her
two oldest half-brothers had emigrated to South America in the 1930s;
Hannah, only four years older than Ruth, had also emigrated to England,
but had been considered too old to go to school and had had to work
in agricultural jobs before emigrating to the US in 1947. David's two
youngest siblings had stayed with their parents the longest and were
deported with them to a number of camps in France. Eventually, the children had been helped to escape and survived the war in France in hiding,
living with French families. These different experiences during emigration
and the war led to different languages becoming important to the different siblings. David writes in the original manuscript: "We had to acquire
three new languages: English, French, and Spanish, but we no longer
have a common language: German is not spoken by all of us and we do
not communicate as easily as siblings should" (MS 206). "German is not
spoken by all of us" is a slightly ambiguous statement but it probably
refers to David's youngest siblings' inability to speak German. Michael
and Feodora were eight and four years old in 1938. Having lived for years
in hiding with French families, it is likely that they would not have been
able to speak German any more after the war.

Editorial and Translation Choices

Here we have one of the differences between the three different versions
of the text: the manuscript, the published German translation, and the
published English version. The fact that German cannot be used as a language for communication becomes a more deliberate act in the German
translation: "Wir mußten drei neue Sprachen lernen: Englisch, Französisch
und Spanisch, aber wir haben keine gemeinsame Sprache mehr. Deutsch
wird nicht mehr gesprochen, und so können wir nicht mehr auf so einfache Weise kommunizieren, wie es im Falle von Geschwistern sein sollte"
(*Kind* 152), "Deutsch wird nicht mehr gesprochen" signifies a decision
against speaking German and an implied reaction against the German language rather than a statement of necessity due to the fact that some of the
siblings simply do not speak it any more. The published English-language
version puts yet another spin on the statement: "German has been put
behind us" (*Child* 154). This is only one of the significant differences
between the three versions of David's text. Although the German translation is generally a close rendering of the English-language manuscript,

here it seems to imply an emphasis on the rejection of the German language by former refugees, a feeling that the author of the original memoir does not share. The later English-language published version tries to create distance between David's early and present-day life.

David clearly wrote her original manuscript for a British readership. For example, in the text of the original manuscript David explains the geography of Germany for her intended audience: "I had never seen the sea myself. Germany was a large country with only a short northern coastline" (MS 47). The German translation stays close to the English original: "Bis dahin hatte ich selbst das Meer noch nie gesehen. Deutschland ist ein großes Land, hat aber nur einen kleinen Küstenstreifen im Norden" (*Kind* 37). However, such a statement is presumably superfluous for a German readership, which would be aware of the geography of Germany. As it was commissioned by an institution that seeks to educate German citizens about political systems and historical processes, we can assume that the translation was deliberately respectful of the original text as a testimony, and left statements like the above unchanged.

Although it is clear from the unfolding narrative that Ruth David had to emigrate and does not live in Germany anymore, this does not necessarily mean that the reader of the German translation will assume that David originally wrote for an English-speaking audience. However, this is clearly the case. For example, David explains in the memoir that she was worried about not being able to read in a language other than German, but links this statement to her lack of knowledge about the original versions of *David Copperfield* and *The Adventures of Tom Sawyer*. She explains the German term "Heimat" in the English-language original manuscript: "I realized that we had to leave our 'Heimat,' a very evocative word to Germans, a combination of home, hearth, and country" (MS, 46). This again is translated into German, although we must assume that German readers have their own associations with the term. However, there is an additional explanation for readers of the late twentieth century, outlining what the term meant for Germans in the 1930s: "'Heimat' läßt im Deutschen Assoziationen zu Heim, häuslichem Herd und Land aufkommen. Das Wort beinhaltet sehr viel für mich und für alle Deutschen aus jener Zeit" (*Kind* 36). This personal intervention ("Das Wort beinhaltet sehr viel für mich") is an extraordinary addition to the English language manuscript, added by the translators with permission from David. For the German publication it was obviously felt that a translation from English to German was not enough, and a personalised explanation was needed. The English-language published version does not differ from the original manuscript.

It is important to note, however, that overall the published English-language version shows more radical changes from the manuscript than does the translation into German. Piotr Kuhiwczak points out that there are "other forms of text production like transcription, . . . co-authorship, or editing which often disguise a radical re-writing and translation."[21] Besides translation into German, the German version of David's text has undergone editing and rewriting. The translation studies scholar Theo Hermans argues that "translation involves a network of active social agents, who may be individuals or groups, each with certain pre-conceptions and interests."[22] Although it is difficult to disentangle all influences, the comparison of the different versions is an interesting task.

Among the most striking differences between the three different versions of David's text are the editorial changes undertaken for the English publication, especially concerning historical background information that she provided in the English-language original manuscript and was then translated into German for the German-language publication. For the English published version the links David made in the original English-language manuscript between past and present anti-Semitism, for example, have been cut almost completely. For instance, while the German version contains references to pogroms in York in the year 1189 and Strasburg in 1394, and to the banishment of all Jews from England by Edward I in 1289, these have been removed without providing any replacement in the published English-language version. A further example is the portrayal of the history of provincial Jewry in Germany. The original manuscript reads:

> How did the Jews earn a living? This was not easy . . . They were allowed to trade, particularly cattle, and many country Jews had to become cattle dealers. The other profession open to them was money lending . . . However, when wily King Edward I decreed the Jews' expulsion from England, he ordered that all debts to Jews were still to be paid—into the king's own coffers! Thus grasping of goods and property continued to happen in all places wherever Jews were driven out or murdered, not least in the Germany of the Third Reich . . . Having found comparative safety in the country, the Jewish community of Fränkisch-Crumbach continued and multiplied during the 19th century in the same measure as their Christian compatriots. (MS 12)

In the German translation, published as *Ein Kind unserer Zeit*, we read:

> Was taten die Juden um ihren Lebensunterhalt zu verdienen? Es war nicht einfach. . . . Der Handel war ihnen erlaubt, besonders mit Vieh, so dass viele der Landjuden Viehhändler wurden. Der andere ihnen erlaubte Beruf war der des Geldverleihers. . . . Als der listige Edward I die Ausweisung der Juden aus England verfügte, befahl er, dass alle noch offenen Schulden an die Juden noch bezahlt werden müssten, in die Schatullen des Königs! Derartige Zugriffe

auf das Vermögen und den Besitz fanden immer wieder dort statt,
wo Juden vertrieben oder ermordet wurden, einschließlich der Zeit
des Dritten Reiches . . . Die jüdische Gemeinde von Fränkisch-
Crumbach bestand, dank der vergleichsweisen Sicherheit, die sie auf
dem Land gefunden hatte, und verdoppelte sich im Verlauf des 19.
Jahrhunderts, wie auch der christliche Anteil der Dorfgemeinschaft.
(*Kind* 13–14)

The English-language publication has undergone significant editing
and is much shorter: "How did the Jews earn a living? This was not
easy . . . They were allowed to trade, particularly cattle, and many country Jews had to become cattle dealers. Having found comparative safety
in the country, the Jewish community of Fränkisch-Crumbach continued
and multiplied during the nineteenth century in the same measure as their
Christian compatriots. (*Child* 5).

These changes are significant, because by cutting the reference to the
expulsion of Jews under Edward I from England, the text shows anti-
Semitism as a historical phenomenon specific to Germany, rather than a
more widespread prejudice.[23] To cut out references to expulsions of Jews
in a text for a British audience might allow the British reader to believe
that such incidents never happened in Britain, a belief that David was
clearly writing against in the English-language original manuscript. David
reports that the editors at the British publishing house I. B. Tauris had
asked for most historical references to be cut because David was not a
historian by profession.[24] It could be argued that a subtle genre shift from
memoir to autobiography took place with the preparation of the English-
language publication: memoirs are concerned with the historical context
of the memoirist's world, whereas in an autobiography the individual's
life is at the center.[25]

There are other small but significant differences: in all three versions
David focuses on her hometown's mayor, an ardent National Socialist,
who created difficulties for her family, especially for her father, who had
owned a cigar factory that he was eventually forced to sell for a very low
price. The mayor's wife is portrayed as more sympathetic to Ruth's family's plight. In the manuscript we read: "I heard only recently, that Mrs T.,
the Bürgermeister's wife, was willing to sell her milk secretly. Why would
she do this? And did her husband know?" (MS 67) From the context of
the passage it is open to the reader's interpretation whether the milk was
sold directly to David's family or to their non-Jewish maid Mina. The
German version is much more detailed and it seems to express that the
milk was sold to the family:

An dieser Stelle möchte ich der Frau des Bürgermeisters meine
Achtung aussprechen. Ich erfuhr erst kürzlich davon, dass sie meiner
Familie heimlich Milch verkaufte, denn es war uns verboten, die

Geschäfte des Orts zu betreten. Uns Kindern erschien es selbstverständlich genug zu essen zu haben. Woher die Lebensmittel kamen,
wussten wir nicht, es wurde uns nicht gesagt. Es muss also jemand
geholfen haben, und ich bin Frau T. für ihre Hilfe sehr dankbar. Ob
ihr Ehemann darüber Bescheid wusste? Es gibt so vieles, was wir
nicht verstehen können. (*Kind* 49)

Here we find a commentary by David about the situation of the children and her inability to understand what was going on at the time, even
retrospectively. The German translators added information they managed
to obtain from speaking to Ruth David while they were translating the
text. Both times the additions ("denn es war uns verboten, die Geschäfte
des Orts zu betreten. Uns Kindern erschien es selbstverständlich genug
zu essen zu haben. Woher die Lebensmittel kamen, wussten wir nicht,
es wurde uns nicht gesagt" and "Es gibt so vieles, was wir nicht verstehen können.") are in a very personal style and more akin to verbal comments than written style, which supports the idea that they stem from
verbal communications between the translators and David.[26] The English
publication is again much shorter and reads: "I heard recently that Mrs
Trinkaus, the Bürgermeister's wife, was willing to sell milk secretly to
Mina. Why would she do this? And did her husband know?" (*Child* 38)
Is it important that in one version the Mayor's wife sells the milk to the
family and in the other to the non-Jewish maid, Mina? Peter Newmark
argues that "translation is concerned with moral and factual truth."[27] If
we go along with this view, the difference is highly significant. Selling
milk to the Jewish family directly would be considered a more serious
transgression of National Socialist policy than selling it to the non-Jewish
maid. Lawrence Venuti argues that: "A translation always communicates
an interpretation."[28] If this is the case, it can be argued that editorial
changes are part of the same complex web of interpretation.

We can find many examples of this process in David's text; for example, in the manuscript we read: "The devil we had to face was Hitler, with
his massive array of supporters and accomplices" (MS 6). This is translated into German quite literally: "Das Böse, mit dem wir konfrontiert
wurden, war Hitler mitsamt seiner großen Komplizenschar" (*Kind* 9).
But it is truncated in the English publication: "The devil we had to face
was Hitler" (*Child* 2). Again we can speculate that the British publisher
did not only want to portray anti-Semitism as a German phenomenon
but as a phenomenon that focusses on Hitler as the evil individual. Ruth
David reports that she did not always feel in control of her autobiographical narrative during the translation and editorial process.[29] We are in the
fortunate position to be able to have access to the original manuscript as
well as the two published versions of the text and to have had the chance
to ask the author about the translation, editing, and publishing process

regarding the different versions of the text. For future research it seems desirable to be able to investigate and question the various social agents that are involved in these processes affecting the text.

Conclusion

Investigating the many influences on an autobiographical text might go against "the prevailing sense of authorship"[30] in Western culture but we seem to have no choice. The process lays bare some of the changes over time regarding texts by former refugees. David's text was written in English with a British readership in mind, but was initially deemed only to be of interest to a German-speaking public. The Landeszentrale für politische Bildung and the publishers who commissioned the translation treated the text as testimony, and the translators were reluctant to change the text even when it made sense for a German readership. Interest in English-language texts increased as public interest in the Shoah became more and more global, and Holocaust education is now on the school curriculum in many English-speaking countries. Those former refugees like David who wrote their memoirs in English occupy a very specific position in the discussion of the position of the English language in this field. English is the language in which they think and write about the Shoah. In the UK, with the surviving former Kindertransportees, we have a group who have built and developed a social memory, a process that is conducted in the English language. For these groups at least, English has become more central to Holocaust memory than some critics acknowledge.

As researchers it is our task to disentangle choice of language, social memory, and editing and translation processes as inevitable influences on a text and make more readers aware of them.

Notes

[1] See Richard Dove, *Journey of No Return: Five German-Speaking Literary Exiles in Britain, 1933–1945* (London: Libris, 2000); see also Andrea Hammel, *Everyday Life as Alternative Space in Exile Writing: The Novels of Anna Gmeyner, Selma Kahn, Hilde Spiel, Hermynia Zur Mühlen and Martina Wied* (Bern and Oxford: Peter Lang, 2008).

[2] I am working with three different versions of the text: Ruth L. David, "A Child of our Time," manuscript (no place, no date, in possession of the author) henceforth cited as MS; Ruth L. David, *Ein Kind unserer Zeit: Autobiographische Skizzen eines jüdischen Mädchens; Kindheit in Fränkisch-Crumbach, Kindertransport nach England, Leben im Exil*, translated from English by Gerd Hofmann and Petra Marzinzig (Frankfurt am Main: dipa-Verlag, 1996) henceforth cited as *Kind*; Ruth David, *Child of our Time: A Young Girl's Flight from the Holocaust* (London: I. B. Tauris, 2003), henceforth cited as *Child*.

3 See Hilde Katzenmeier, Rudhart Knodt, Stefan Kunz, and Ottilie Born Hauenstein, eds., *Geschichte der Juden in Fränkisch-Crumbach* (Fränkisch-Crumbach: no publisher, 2007).

4 Aleida Assmann, *Der lange Schatten der Vergangenheit: Erinnerungskultur und Geschichtspolitik* (Frankfurt am Main: C. H. Beck, 2011).

5 See http://www.ajr.org.uk/kindertransport, accessed December 15, 2013.

6 Dorit Bader Whiteman, *The Uprooted: A Hitler Legacy* (New York: Plenum Books, 1993), 1.

7 Louise London, *Whitehall and the Jews 1933–1948: British Immigration Policy and the Holocaust* (Cambridge University Press, 2000).

8 Lawrence Venuti, *Scandals of Translation: Towards an Ethics of Difference* (London: Routledge, 1998), 31.

9 Alan Rosen, *Sounds of Defiance: The Holocaust, Multilingualism & the Problem of English* (Lincoln and London: University of Nebraska Press, 2005), x.

10 See for example, *AJR Journal*, September to December 2010.

11 Ruth David in conversation with the author, London, February 2011.

12 Steven G. Kellman, *The Translingual Imagination* (Lincoln and London: University of Nebraska Press, 2000), 1–16.

13 Kellman, 17.

14 Martha Blend, *A Child Alone* (London: Vallentine Mitchell, 2001); Ellen Davis, *Kerry's Children: A Jewish Childhood in Nazi Germany and Growing Up in South Wales* (Bridgend: Seren, 2004).

15 Piotr Kuhiwczak, "The Grammar of Survival. How do we read Holocaust testimonies?," in *Translating and Interpreting Conflict*, ed. Myriam Salama-Carr (Amsterdam: Rodopi, 2007), 61–73; here 70.

16 Ingrid Jacoby, *My Darling Diary: A Wartime Journal—Vienna 1937–39, Falmouth 1939–44* (Penzance: United Writers Publication, 1998), 30.

17 Jacoby, *My Darling Diary*, 30.

18 Kellman, *Translingual Imagination*, 26.

19 Kellman, *Translingual Imagination*, 21.

20 See Andrea Hammel, "'Why is your Czech so bad?' Czech Child Refugees, Language and Identity," in *Exile to and from Czechoslovakia in the 1930s and 1940s*, ed. Charmian Brinson and Richard Dove (Rodopi: Amsterdam, 2009), 215–28.

21 Kuhiwczak, "The Grammar of Survival," 71.

22 Theo Hermans, "Norms and the Determination of Translation: A Theoretical Framework" in *Translation, Power and Subversion*, ed. Roman Alvarez (Clevedon: Multilingual Matters, 1998), 25–51; here, 26.

23 For a further discussion of this point, see Andrea Hammel, "The Destabilisation of Personal Histories: Rewriting and Translating of Autobiographical Texts by German-Jewish Survivors," *Comparative Critical Studies* 1, no. 3 (2004): 295–308; here 297. The article just referenced was written, however, before I had any knowledge of the original manuscript of the text.

[24] Ruth David in a conversation with the author, London, February 2011.

[25] Helen M. Buss, "Memoirs," in *Encyclopedia of Life*, vol. 2, ed. Margaretta Jolly et al. (London, Fitzroy and Dearborn, 2001), 595–96.

[26] Ruth David remembers speaking to the translators on several occasions, but does not remember the exact remarks she made. Ruth David in a conversation with the author, London, February 2011.

[27] Peter Newmark, *About Translation* (Clevedon: Multilingual Matters, 1991), 1.

[28] Venuti, *Scandals of Translation*, 5.

[29] Ruth David in a conversation with the author, London, February 2011.

[30] Venuti, *Scandals of Translation*, 31.

Stigma and Performance: Victor Klemperer's Language-Critical Reflections on Anti-Semitic Hate Speech

Arvi Sepp, University of Antwerp / Free University of Brussels

A s OF 1942, THE GERMAN-JEWISH professor of Romance languages Victor Klemperer undertook a thoroughgoing analysis of Nazi language in his diaries. In his journal, he provides concrete and painstakingly precise notes of his reflections on fascist institutions, his gradual exclusion from society as a Jew, the circumstances of ordinary people under National Socialism, including laws, working conditions, and the media. The following essay will offer a new way of approaching Klemperer's critique of language by drawing on Erving Goffman's examination of the consequences of exclusion and discrimination from the perspective of his theory of stigma, as formulated in his study *Stigma: Notes on the Management of Spoiled Identity* (1963), and on Judith Butler's analysis of the role injurious speech plays in constituting the subject in her book *Excitable Speech: A Politics of the Performative* (1997). This essay sets out to illustrate how the language Klemperer investigates in his diary can be understood as hate speech, arguing that the Nazis' racial classification "Jew" creates a Jewish identity among those who, like Klemperer, had both converted and assimilated into German society. By studying both direct and indirect statements and the vocabulary used in them, the diarist continuously strives to discover his interlocutors' attitudes towards the National Socialist typology of identity and therefore, by extension, towards him.

It is in this context that Klemperer stresses the dangers of the ways in which National Socialist ideology politicizes all aspects of language: "Words can be like tiny doses of arsenic: they are swallowed unnoticed, appear to have no effect, and then after a little time the toxin sets in after all."[1] In defiance of this tendency, the author attempts to remove himself from the power of racial classification in Nazi discourse by shielding his national identity from National Socialism's anti-Semitic eugenics and Social Darwinism: "Belonging to a nation depends less on blood than on language."[2]

Stigma

"The Jew" as a biological embodiment of the purpose-oriented spirit of modernity became the focal point of National Socialist ideology: through the "purifying" effect of exterminating "the Jew," technology would be placed in the service of nature as a now liberated and reinvigorated force. The reactionary modernism represented by National Socialism fashioned a destructive synthesis of counter-Enlightenment and science, persecution and racial biology, and pogrom and bureaucratically organized mass murder.[3] In this respect, Poliakov, Delacampagne, and Girard emphasize that, for the racist, the Other is invariably anyone who embodies a *difference* that the racist wants to eliminate at all costs.[4] Without a doubt, the difference that the racist therefore fears the most is the difference that cannot be immediately recognized, and so ostensibly represents an *internal* danger to one's integrity. Racism becomes all the more fervent the nearer the alien is to the racist, the closer it lives to the racist, and the harder it is to distinguish it from the racist. In this case, when even science heads towards completely ruling out intrinsic differences between the two, racism calls on a form of science that has gone utterly astray, in order to underline the biological foundations of difference nonetheless. Of all "Others," it is precisely "the Jew" who is the least "Other," who is the least different. As a result of its combination of the alien and the familiar, the Jewish community has often been treated as a scapegoat, particularly by "Individuen und Völkern, die vom Problem ihrer Integrität besessen waren, das heißt der Angst, daß sich das zerbrechliche Bild der Allmacht, mit dem sie sich identifizieren, auflösen kann."[5]

In National Socialist propaganda, as can be seen from the textbook *Geschichte als nationalpolitische Erziehung* (1939), for example, this fear of the invisible dangers of Jewish "Verräter und Zerstörer" was systematically stoked. This book claims that "Juden, die sich als Deutsche getarnt haben" made a significant contribution "zu Niedergang und Zerfall" in Europe.[6] In this vein, the diarist identifies an "übermäßig gesteigerte[n] Gebrauch von *tarnen*"[7] in National Socialist discourse when it attempts to warn of the "schädlichen" influence of the Jewish population. Klemperer experiences his typological classification into the racial category "Jew" by the National Socialists as a degrading stigma, and his increasing experience of discrimination can be read in this sense, in the words of Hilarion Petzold "wie ein Kapitel 'angewandter Stigmatheorie.'"[8] In turning now to the consequences of this stigmatization, isolation, and designation as a Jew for Klemperer's self-understanding, Erving Goffmann's stigma theory, as set out in his 1963 study *Stigma: Notes on the Management of Spoiled Identity*, will provide a potentially rich point of departure.

By stigma, Goffman understands a substantial threat to identity, brought about socially in the tension between the discursively constructed notions of "normality" and "abnormality":

> The term stigma . . . will be used to refer to an attribute that is deeply discrediting. . . . An attribute that stigmatizes one type of possessor can confirm the usualness of another, and therefore is neither creditable nor discreditable as a thing in itself.[9]

The tension between the decreed racist conception of normality and the prescribed and readily accepted negative image of the "Jew" greatly affected Klemperer's self-understanding in the Third Reich. All aspects of society were subject to the racial code "Aryan/Jewish" and social groupings were for the most part determined by the racial norm, and, as Klemperer puts it on the eve of the boycott, because of this dichotomy, one's immediate environment gradually became irreconcilably and violently torn apart:

> Even more hopeless. The boycott begins tomorrow. Yellow placards, men on guard. Pressure to pay Christian employees two months' salary, to dismiss Jewish ones. No reply to the impressive letter of the Jews to the President of the Reich and to the government. [. . .] No one dares make a move. The Dresden student body makes a declaration today: United behind . . . and the honor of German students forbids them to come into contact with Jews.[10]

Hannah Arendt stresses that in periods of persecution and discrimination, the aforementioned social stigma can or must be transformed into an important defensive measure through which Jewish identity can be defined: "Wenn man als Jude angegriffen ist, muß man sich auch als Jude wehren."[11] An *affirmative* recognition—of the sort that Arendt speaks of—of having been attributed an identity externally cannot, however, be found in Klemperer's diaries at all, and so he barely develops any form of internal solidarity with the Jewish collective. Then again, when considering racist exclusion, Klemperer continually resorts to the collective "wir" form to refer to the persecuted Jews as a group of which he is a part. The diarist described himself as a Jew because, in practice, he belonged to the grouping of those who were persecuted and not, for instance, because he had performed an internal volte-face or transformation: "I judge as a Jew, because as such I am particularly affected by the Jewish business in Hitlerism."[12]

The diarist continually employs the collective "we" form in order to categorize the fate of a section of the population that the Nazis had designated as "Jews." In this respect, and here I agree with Heidrun Kämper, this is a case of "unfreiwillige Gruppenidentität."[13] Examples of this include: "We—threatened Jewry";[14] "we Jews";[15] "we J-people";[16] "We star-bearers."[17] Speaking in the "we" form can be explained to a great degree by the external circumstances surrounding a form of institutional persecution and marginalization that collapses together an utterly heterogeneous group, which Klemperer places at the center of his *LTI*:[18] "But now we were simply the group of Dresden people who had to wear the star, the group of factory workers and street-cleaners and the occupants of the Jews' houses and the prisoner of the Gestapo; and, as in prison or the army there was an immediate sense of mutuality which obliterated earlier common ground and individualities."[19]

Jewish Identity and Anti-Semitism

Klemperer's Jewish identity is therefore primarily determined negatively and externally: it was never ethnicity, historical consciousness, culture, or religion that defined his self-identity, rather it was formerly education, job, and social status; these had, however, been rendered meaningless as parameters used for measuring individuals under National Socialism's racist codification. Klemperer's highly prized means for evaluating his position along the lines of professional achievement, intelligence, and reliability were discredited and marginalized in one fell swoop. Soon after Hitler came to power, for example, Klemperer experienced a loss of respect, marginalization, and finally outright isolation both socially and professionally.

In Nazi society, the close relationship between ethnic propaganda, pseudo-scientific racial biology, and social status generated a hegemonic category of the "normal." Anti-Semitism and anti-intellectualism were two aspects of National Socialist ideology that directly affected Klemperer from the beginning of the regime; indeed, as a German-Jewish professor, whose identity was built squarely on the foundations of "Deutschtum" and "Akademikerstatus" that were now denied him by the Nazis, the diarist felt completely uprooted. Filled with terror and horror, the diarist notes the propaganda directed at Jewish professors:

> Notice on the Student House (likewise at all the universities): "When the Jew writes in German, he lies," henceforth he is to be allowed to write only in Hebrew. Jewish books must be characterized as "translations."—I only note the most ghastly things, only fragments of the madness in which we are unceasingly immersed.[20]

In the early days of Nazi rule, these symbolic acts of violence led Klemperer to develop a most acute sensitivity towards gestures, actions, choices of words, and political opinions in his social circles. Klemperer and his wife Eva had always maintained close contact with both Jewish and non-Jewish acquaintances, whom they tended to meet often at dinner parties and functions. Klemperer's perception of the communication conducted in these conversations became profoundly sensitized as of 1933, due to his experiences of stigma. The pain that the diarist felt in Nazi society can be traced back to this sudden racist de-subjectification.

The subject, when confronted with stigmatization at the same time as he or she is exposed to a corresponding process of social isolation, attempts to redefine itself through self-reflection and social relationality.[21] With regard to being forced to take emeritus status, Klemperer recorded the reactions of friends and colleagues: "On Saturday evening the Kühns were here, Wengler, Annemarie and Dressel. They took my elimination very lightly."[22] Their attitude led to his later willingness to communicate with these people. Even Klemperer's protégé Johannes Thieme, who enthusiastically proclaimed his support of National Socialism during a visit to Klemperer, became a *persona non grata*: "That was dreadful and the end of that. Thieme—of all people—declared himself for the new regime with such fervent conviction and praise. He devoutly repeated all the phrases about unity, upwards, etc. . . . I shall not forgive him *that*."[23]

The stigma attached to being a Jew was legally consolidated through the Nuremberg Race Laws and, as a result, Klemperer's isolation from communication was even more intense. His social networks sustained considerable damage in the first years of the Third Reich.[24] In the light of his exclusion, in the early period of the anti-Semitic policies Klemperer began to adopt private strategies for offsetting his treatment. He organized meetings at home with people of similar opinion and circumstances, while turning his back on acquaintances who had been disloyal to him. Ever since his dismissal in 1935, his contact with former academic colleagues was limited to correspondence with his friends Professors Dember and Blumenfeld, who had by that time emigrated. His personal contacts became ever scarcer throughout the course of the year, and he immediately cut ties with many one-time friends and acquaintances who were not categorically opposed to political movements that he rejected, such as Zionism and communism, as well as to the NSDAP. Klemperer groups his friends and acquaintances into three categories according to their responses to the discrimination he is experiencing: "*The loyal and the brave; In the stocks; The tepid.*"[25] People who had once been his friends broke off contact with him, while he himself ceased contact with particular people who had been unfaithful to him:

> We become ever more lonely, I become ever more mistrustful. Especially since Martha Wiechmann swung over to the Hitler front. Why has there been not a word from Annemarie Köhler for months? Why has Johannes Köhler not phoned, as agreed, to arrange an excursion by car together?—The Isakowitzes are getting ready to emigrate to London, after that we shall be quite alone.[26]

In his professional life, the bulk of his colleagues gave him a wide berth, "like a plague corpse,"[27] and, faced with the rapid nullification of his personal and social integrity by the regime, he saw himself and his fellow Jews "condemned to be Negro slaves, to be literally pariahs until our end."[28]

In September 1941, the intensifying social ostracization and political disenfranchisement of the Jews since 1933 resulted in the decree that
Jews should be labeled with the so-called *Judenstern*, which, in hindsight,
Klemperer saw as representing the harshest blow of the twelve years of
Nazi dictatorship.[29] Through this, the Jewish population was marked
with a clearly recognizable stigma. Every infringement of this decree was
met with severe consequences, whether in the form of fines or prison sentences. For Klemperer, this *Erinnerungszeichen* or memento was a humiliation that indicated only worse to come in the future:

> This Jewish armband, come true as Star of David, comes into force
> on the nineteenth. At the same time a prohibition on leaving the
> environs of the city. Frau Kreidl Sr. was in tears, Frau Voss had pal-
> pitation. Friedheim said this was the first blow so far, worse that
> the property assessment. I myself feel shattered, cannot compose
> myself. . . . The newspaper justification: After the army had got to
> know, through Bolshevism, the cruelty, etc., of *the Jew*, all possibil-
> ity of camouflage must be removed from the Jews here, to spare the
> comrades of the people all contact with them.[30]

A few days later, Klemperer refers to this in his diary, writing: "Yesterday,
as Eva was sewing on the Jew's star, I had a raving fit of despair."[31]
For the professor of Romance languages, the introduction of the
Judenstern signified ultimate and explicit expulsion from the German
Volksgemeinschaft. Klemperer pursued private methods for coping with
this stigmatization in order to defy anti-Semitic discrimination and marginalization. Although he resisted his degradation and stigmatization by
keeping hold of his intellectual universality and integrity, the very physical feeling of humiliation can barely go unnoticed.[32] The injuring of
his identity caused by being stigmatized with the *Judenstern*, through
which he was exposed moreover to real physical danger, is triggered
in particular by his *negative singularization* in "Aryan" society: "This
waiting in front of shops, which is often my lot, is particularly horri-
ble. . . . [T]he whole world eyes my star. Torture—I can resolve a hundred times to pay no attention, it remains torture. Also I never know
whether someone walking or driving past is not in the Gestapo, whether
he will not insult me, spit on me, arrest me."[33]

For Klemperer, the writing of a diary and the reflections within it on
what he called the LTI or *Lingua Tertii Imperii* (The Language of the
Third Reich) constituted a critical stance toward and a critical assessment
of National Socialism. Connected with this critical stance and assessment,
the diarist complained about the way in which the Jewish community
appeared to have uncritically surrendered itself, and, for this very reason,
he distanced himself from the Jewish population.[34] While he felt required
to adopt a stance on Jewishness when faced with being forced to adopt

the name "Israel" in 1939, being moved into the *Judenhaus* in 1940, and being forced to wear the Star of David in 1941, by and large his comments rarely expressed loyalty to the Jewish community: "The Jews are certainly visited by misfortune and are in the right; but altogether likeable? I think not."[35] The diarist shows himself to be increasingly indignant about the Jews' apparent internalization of anti-Semitic ways of thinking, which, according to him, illustrated the catastrophic potential of anti-Semitic hate speech.

Performance of Hate Speech

The radical disruption of Klemperer's life and the injuries to his identity caused by the anti-Semitic policies of extermination created an existential vacuum for him, and by writing his diary he sought to resist being alienated from his own existence. Protecting one's sense of identity was one of the main functions of Jewish diary-writing in the Third Reich, and served as a form of defense mechanism in the face of stigmatization, vilification, and fear of death, a defense mechanism that, in the case of Klemperer, enabled him to some extent to assert himself as an individual and a human being.

In *Excitable Speech*, Judith Butler provides a plausible account of ways in which injurious speech works to constitute the subject. Drawing on J. L. Austin's concept of performativity[36] and Louis Althusser's theory of interpellation,[37] Butler understands identity as the result of a discursive process of designation, which produces material effects through regulated repetition. Performative speech acts bring into being that which they designate, and are therefore able to produce reality by their very nature: performativity is therefore "that discursive practice that enacts or produces that which it names."[38] Like Althusser, Butler speaks of a subaltern subject that is assigned an identity on the basis of its external characteristics being named. Butler's description of this process, which she undertakes specifically in relation to gendered identity, also applies to racial or racist categorizations: the Nazi's racial classification "Jew" simultaneously created a Jewish identity even for converted and assimilated Jews like Klemperer. Because this racial-biological categorization functions as an illocutionary form of speech that, in the moment it is uttered, injures the subject and, through this very injuring of the subject, constitutes the subject, it performs the function of an address.[39] In this respect, for Klemperer, the act of being recognized as a Jew becomes an act of constitution:[40] Klemperer is called into being as a Jewish subject. Nevertheless, he despairs of having a Jewish perspective imposed on him: "Once again I have come back to the Jewish theme. Is it my fault? No, it is the fault of Nazism and Nazism alone."[41]

Although this *negative* understanding of Jewish identity is hugely controversial and rejected by many and on many accounts, Klemperer ascribes, *nolens volens*, to this logic, and therefore analyzes National Socialist everyday life "through Jewish spectacles."[42] As mentioned above, Klemperer sets out from a negative definition of Jewish identity in which National Socialist violence is clearly inherent, and he is compelled as a matter of fact to deploy the ethnic binary German/Jewish as an analytical tool for his observations. This racial dichotomy reduces people to a dominant characteristic, so that a collective subject is created against which people can be measured and therefore be either accepted or rejected. The disorientation experienced through the force of classification combined with one's uncertainty about the future leads to the subject becoming generally unsettled and feeling a total loss of control. Butler puts it this way:

> To be injured by speech is to suffer a loss of context, that is, not to know where you are. Indeed, it may be that what is *unanticipated* about the injurious speech act is what constitutes its injury, the sense of putting its addressee out of control.[43]

As Klemperer records in perfect detail, in a circular from the Interior Minister on August 18, 1939, Jews were requested to make their Jewishness obvious on the basis of their names alone by adding the names "Israel" or "Sara" to their legal names:

> [S]ince the idea is only to protect the German national comrades from Jewish names, but also, more importantly, to safeguard them from any contact with the Jews themselves, the latter are most carefully segregated. And one of the principal means of this kind of segregation is to point to their names. Anyone who does not have an unmistakably Hebraic name, one which has not established itself in German, such as Baruch or Recha, has to add "Israel" or "Sara" to his forename.[44]

Underneath the imposition of the names Israel or Sara one can already see a direct indication of the Nazis' planned course of action; these names no longer signified that the people named were born into a chosen people, but quite the opposite: they signified their death sentences.[45] The discursive production of Otherness that somewhat painfully turns Victor Klemperer into "I, Victor-Israel Klemperer"[46] functions by means of a semantic displacement that transforms the designation of belonging to the Jewish religious community into a racial category; what once was "a Jew" is therefore simplified into "the Jew."

In the chapter "Elements of Anti-Semitism: Limits of Enlightenment" from *Dialectic of Enlightenment*, Adorno and Horkheimer highlight the de-specification and stereotypification of the image of the Jew in modernity: "They who were never allowed untroubled ownership of the civic right which should have granted them human dignity are *again* called '*the Jews*' *without* distinction."[47] Klemperer's diaries give a pertinent example of the ways in which National Socialism reduced the individual to a species. In National Socialist propaganda, the names of Jewish people were always supplemented with the generic name "der Jude" (the Jew), such as, for example, in the case of Karl Marx or Heinrich Heine: as Klemperer notes, "The Jew Marx, the Jew Heine, not simply Marx or Heine, is a special technique for hammering something home stylistically which had already occurred in the ancient *epitheton ornans*."[48] The generalizing usage of an allegorizing singular aims to degrade or malign the Jewish population and is the prevalent means of using speech and text in National Socialism as a means to agitation: "The concentration of hate has this time turned into utter madness. Not England or the USA or Russia—*only*, in everything nothing but *the Jew*."[49]

The Holocaust evidently did not only aim to destroy the body, but was also present in language. As Butler points out with recourse to Althusser, linguistic injury comes about from forms of address that interpellate the subject and constitute it as such. Interpellation or categorization as "the Jew" represents the social exclusion of the subject and serves as the linchpin in its destruction. The injurious address—such as "You have to stand, Jew!"[50] or "Go on in, Jew!"[51]—is essential to the use of stereotypes for reducing the individual to its definitive ethnic and racial identity, as Klemperer notes with reference to the way in which he was officially designated by the Gestapo: "When I am referred to officially it is always 'the Jew Klemperer'; when I have to report to the Gestapo there are blows if I don't announce sufficiently 'smartish' [*zackig*]: 'The Jew Klemperer is here.'"[52] Through the name one receives, Butler suggests, one is not merely addressed, but, depending on the degree to which this address is injurious, one is also proportionately degraded and humiliated.[53] The axiological result of *hate speech* is extremely effective; injurious speech functions as a "slap in the face" so to say: anti-Semitic hate speech therefore not only represents violence, it *is* violence. One's "administrative" designation as a Jew and one's eradication as a Jew merge into one another almost inseparably. In this light, Klemperer observes in his diary: "[Y]esterday afternoon in the Jews' House in Strehlener Strasse. A notice on every door: 'Here resided the Jew Weiler . . .'—'Here resided the Jewess . . .' These are the people who have been evacuated, whose household goods have been sealed up and are gradually being removed."[54]

The widespread yet absurd stereotype of demonic *Weltjudentum* inevitably collided with the appearance and behavior of actual Jewish individuals. In personal contact with the Gestapo, the philologist was requested to recall his imperceptible phylogenetic stigma, and thus in the local Gestapo office in Bismarckstraße he was forced to register explicitly with the words: "I am the Jew Victor Israel Klemperer": "A Gestapo fellow by the counter: 'Get back there, you swine!' Upstairs in the 'more lenient' Room 68 . . . a small fellow at the door sneering and coarse: '. . . You have to say loudly and clearly: 'I am the Jew Victor Israel Klemperer.' 'Now you go outside and say it . . .' I do so."[55]

Klemperer's degrading and distancing de-humanization by means of the repetition of the invective "Schwein" or "Judenschwein"[56] and his de-subjectification by means of being compelled to refer to himself as "the Jew" were accompanied by a feeling of powerlessness and having been deprived of his rights as well as by a loss of self-worth. The dualistic logic of the collective symbol "Tier" in hate speech serves to create a categorical distance from its victims. The all-too-frequent and Manichaean pairing of the collective singulars "der Deutsche" and "der Jude" served as an official attack on the universality of the individual and had severe and ominous repercussions for "arische" (Aryan) public opinion. When Frau Belka, a worker in the company in which Klemperer had been forced to work, made use of the Nazi-sanctioned ethnic or administrative dichotomy German/Jewish, the diarist was given proof of his painful exclusion from the community: "The effect of propaganda: Frau Belka has repeatedly asked me: 'Do you have a *German* wife?'—'Does Jacobi have a *German* wife?' Etc. That shakes me more than the foreign word 'Aryan'. It demonstrates how very successful the Jews have been 'totally cut off' in popular consciousness."[57]

The question quoted above, which may well not demonstrate an intentionally and unashamedly anti-Semitic bent on the part of Frau Belka, shows just how firmly the discourse of racial segregation had nested itself in the everyday language of the "Aryan" population. Statements of this kind are particularly injurious to Klemperer, because they undermine any notion of a German-Jewish symbiosis, which he had cherished until then, and whose failure he did not always want to believe, even in the Third Reich.

But it was not only the "Aryan" population that was infiltrated by the "poisonous nature of the LTI";[58] even Jewish self-understanding was affected by the linguistic violence of the Nazis, in that, through re-articulating the dichotomy German/Jewish, people actually classified *themselves* into the ethnic matrix. It proved exceptionally difficult for people to remove themselves from the hegemonic discourse and to keep a distance in their own speech from the prevalent babble of propaganda that had been drummed into them. In view of this, Klemperer angrily criticizes his fellow Jews but includes himself with the offenders as well: "Ich ärgere mich über das Nachplappern der LTI-Wörter durch die Juden und sündige doch selbst."[59]

Klemperer offers numerous examples of Jews "parroting" the LTI, and among them are Elsa Glauber and Carl Jacoby. Elsa Glauber, a fellow Jew forced to live in the *Judenhaus* in the Zeughausstraße in Dresden, showed herself to be very receptive to contamination by National Socialist vocabulary. She emphasized that both of her sons needed to be "fanatical Germans," as "[o]nly fanatical Germanness can cleanse our Fatherland of this current un-Germanness [*Undeutschheit*],"[60] and especially because the adjective "fanatical" served as a key term in National Socialist jargon.[61] Klemperer reacted with indignation: "Don't you realize that you are speaking the language of our mortal enemies and thus admitting defeat and thus putting yourself at their mercy and thus betraying that very Germanness of yours?"[62]

Thus the anti-Jewish logic was involuntarily adopted by the Jews themselves, and the perception of others projected onto their own self-perception. The anti-Semitic form of address as "Jew x,"[63] which linguistically injures, discriminates against, and excludes Jews, was adapted in an exemplary fashion by the Jewish Dr. P., who before 1943 "had felt himself to be a German and a doctor, nothing more and nothing less":

> He [Dr. P.] appropriated all of the Nazis' anti-Jewish expressions, and especially those of Hitler, and uttered them so incessantly that he himself could probably no longer judge to what extent he was ridiculing either the Führer or himself, or whether this self-deprecating way of speaking had simply become second nature. He was in the habit of never speaking to any member of his Jewish group without prefixing his name with the term "Jew." "Jew Löwenstein, you are to use the small cutting machine today."—"Jew Mahn, here is your medical certificate for the tooth Jew [*Zähnejuden*] (by which he meant our dentist).[64]

The influence of National Socialist dogma and its vocabulary led to a peculiar confusion of the roles of victim and perpetrator. The passage cited tellingly underlines how the language of the enlightened and culturally integrated *Bildungsbürger* Dr. P., who had previously "wasted no time thinking about the problems of religion and race,"[65] had reversed into its discursive opposite. It is unclear whether his imitation of anti-Semitic discourse is concerned with hatred or self-hatred, is playful or serious, or even whether all of these possibilities come into play simultaneously. In any case, it expresses the conflicting position of the assimilated German Jew, who wanted to prove his unmistakable Germanness, yet was all the time condemned to failure because the Nazi regime deemed him definitively and exclusively a Jew. His adoption of the LTI indicates an awareness of his own Otherness with which he can barely cope.[66]

For Klemperer, the fact that Nazi language and its apposite racial ideology have crept into the psyche of the victim is, quite literally, extremely painful: "Every day it was a slap in the face once again, worse than the *Du* and the Gestapo's swear-words, I never prevailed against it with protest or explanation, I never became inured to it."[67] In stark opposition to the racist separation of Jews and Germans allegedly on the basis of blood, which he saw as utterly artificial, Klemperer insists that language and culture are of the greatest importance in the individual's sense of belonging:

> [A]ll the elements of culture, which one absorbs consciously or unconsciously, are carried along by the river of language. Music, painting, architecture provide individual aspects—language contains the totality of the intellectual. And the totality of the intellectual cannot be separated from language. . . . If I have grown up in a language, then I am under its spell forever; I can in no way, through no act of my will, withdraw from the nation whose spirit lives in it, and no stranger's command can detach me from it.[68]

The acceptance of racial doctrine, which according to Klemperer is exemplified by the stereotyping that comes about as a result of using the definite article in "*the* Jew," condemns people to an animalistic existence and completely disregards both Western civilization and its intellectual history. Faced with the sudden meaninglessness of his lifelong efforts to assimilate himself and be educated, which he had hoped would bring him social recognition, the diarist feels that his humanness has been both debased and degraded. It is in the pseudoscientific faith in the notion of race that Klemperer sees the embodiment of the fundamental characteristics of National Socialist ideology: anti-individualism, antihumanism, anti-intellectualism, oversimplification, and emotional excess. What clearly emerges from Victor Klemperer's diary entries is how his marginality encouraged his pursuit of self-awareness: writing is a process that serves to reflect the origins of and the potential tensions in one's own identity.

—Translated by Michael Wood, University of Edinburgh

Notes

[1] Victor Klemperer, *The Language of the Third Reich: LTI—Lingua Tertii Imperii; A Philologist's Notebook* (London: Continuum, 2002), 15–16.

[2] Victor Klemperer, *I Will Bear Witness: A Diary of the Nazi Years 1942–1945* (New York: The Modern Library, 2001), entry of January 28, 1943, 195.

[3] Enzo Traverso, *Moderne und Gewalt: Eine europäische Genealogie des Nazi-Terrors* (Cologne: ISP, 2003), 149.

[4] Léon Poliakov, Christian Delacampagne, and Patrick Girard, *Über den Rassismus: Sechzehn Kapitel zur Anatomie, Geschichte und Deutung des Rassenwahns* (Frankfurt am Main: Klett-Cotta im Ullstein-Taschenbuch, 1984), 189–90.

[5] Poliakov, Delacampagne, and Girard, *Über den Rassismus*, 190.

[6] Dietrich Klagge, *Geschichte als nationalpolitische Erziehung* (Frankfurt am Main: Volk und Führer. Deutsche Geschichte für Schulen, 1939), 37.

[7] Victor Klemperer, *Ich will Zeugnis ablegen bis zum letzten: Tagebücher 1942–1945* (Berlin: Aufbau-Verlag, 1995), entry of June 12, 1942, 125. This passage is not printed in the English translation of Klemperer's diaries: cf. Klemperer, *I Will Bear Witness, 1942–1945*.

[8] Hilarion Petzold, "Identitätsvernichtung, Identitätsarbeit, 'Kulturarbeit'—Werkstattbericht mit persönlichen und prinzipiellen Überlegungne aus Anlaß der Tagebücher von Victor Klemperer, dem hundertsten Geburtstag von Wilhelm Reich und anderer Anstöße," *Integrative Therapie* 22, no. 4 (1996): 371–451; here, 396.

[9] Erving Goffman, *Stigma: Notes on the Management of Spoiled Identity* (Harmondsworth: Penguin, 1963), 13.

[10] Victor Klemperer, *I Will Bear Witness: A Diary of the Nazi Years 1933–1941* (New York: The Modern Library 1999), entry of March 31, 1933, 10.

[11] Hannah Arendt, *Ich will verstehen: Selbstauskünfte zu Leben und Werk* (Munich: Piper, 1996), 107.

[12] Klemperer, *I Will Bear Witness, 1933–1941*, entry of April 16, 1941, 382.

[13] Heidrun Kämper, "Zeitgeschichte—Sprachgeschichte. Gedanken bei der Lektüre des Tagebuchs eines Philologen. Über die Ausgaben von Victor Klemperers Tagebuch 1933–1945," *Zeitschrift für Germanistische Linguistik* 24, no. 3 (1996): 328–41; here, 332.

[14] Klemperer, *I Will Bear Witness, 1933–1941*, entry of March 30, 1933, 9.

[15] Klemperer, *I Will Bear Witness, 1933–1941*, entry of April 3, 1933, 11.

[16] Klemperer, *I Will Bear Witness, 1933–1941*, entry of July 18, 1941, 421.

[17] Klemperer, *I Will Bear Witness, 1942–1945*, entry of March 19, 1944, 303.

[18] Irene Heidelberger-Leonard maintains in this respect that Klemperer ultimately reconciled with his Jewishness, but in my opinion, this is not a case of Klemperer changing his attitude or of Jewish solidarity. See Irene Heidelberger-Leonard, "'Über Zwang, Jude, über Unmöglichkeit, Deutscher zu sein'. Überlegungen zu Victor Klemperers Tagebüchern 1933–1945," in *Identités—existences—resistances: Réflexions autour des Journaux 1933–1945 de Victor Klemperer*, ed. André Combes and Didier Harlem, special issue, *Germanica* 27 (2000): 59–70; here, 65.

[19] Klemperer, *The Language of the Third Reich*, 183.

[20] Klemperer, *I Will Bear Witness, 1933–1941*, entry of April 25, 1933, 15.

[21] Cf. Goffman, *Stigma*, 149–50.

[22] Klemperer, *I Will Bear Witness, 1933–1941*, entry of May 7, 1935, 122.

[23] Klemperer, *I Will Bear Witness, 1933–1941*, entry of March 17, 1933, 6. Emphasis in original.

[24] Cf. Klemperer, *I Will Bear Witness, 1933–1941*, entry of December 31, 1933, 45.

[25] Klemperer, *I Will Bear Witness, 1933–1941*, entry of October 5, 1935, 135. Emphasis in original.

[26] Klemperer, *I Will Bear Witness, 1933–1941*, entry of April 24, 1936, 161.

[27] Klemperer, *I Will Bear Witness, 1933–1941*, entry of October 19, 1938, 136.

[28] Klemperer, *I Will Bear Witness, 1933–1941*, entry of October 2, 1938, 269.

[29] Cf. Klemperer, *The Language of the Third Reich*, 213.

[30] Klemperer, *I Will Bear Witness, 1933–1941*, entry of September 15, 1941, 429.

[31] Klemperer, *I Will Bear Witness, 1933–1941*, entry of September 20, 1941, 434.

[32] Cf. Victor Klemperer, *Ich will Zeugnis ablegen bis zum letzten: Tagebücher 1933–1941* (Berlin: Aufbau-Verlag, 1995), entries of June 23–July 1, 1941, 632–33. This passage is not printed in the English translation of Klemperer's diaries: cf. Klemperer, *I Will Bear Witness, 1933–1941*.

[33] Klemperer, *I Will Bear Witness, 1942–1945*, entry of June 9, 1942, 71.

[34] Cf. Klemperer, *I Will Bear Witness, 1933–1941*, entry of January 16, 1935, 109.

[35] Klemperer, *I Will Bear Witness, 1942–1945*, entry of May 20, 1944, 316.

[36] Drawing on Austin's *How To Do Things With Words*, Butler sets out from the premise established in the philosophy of language that words perform actions by virtue of being uttered. In contrast to constative utterances, the essential characteristics of performative speech acts are, on one hand, that they prompt an *action*, and, on the other hand, that they either *succeed* or do *not succeed*, rather than being true or false (Cf. John L. Austin, *How To Do Things With Words* [London: Oxford University Press, 1962], 132–46).

[37] In "Ideology and Ideological State Apparatuses," Louis Althusser formulates the most important thesis of his theory of ideology in a nutshell as follows: "*All ideology hails or interpellates concrete individuals as concrete subjects*" (Althusser, "Ideology and Ideological State Apparatuses," in *Lenin and Philosophy, and Other Essays*, trans. Ben Brewster [London: New Left Books, 1971], 127–88; here, 173; emphasis in original). According to the French philosopher, we can compare the process of becoming a subject with what happens when a policeman addresses someone on the street: "'Hey, you there.'. . . [T]he hailed individual will turn around. By this mere one-hundred-and-eighty-degree physical conversion, he becomes a *subject*. Why? Because he has recognised that the hail was 'really' addressed to him" (ibid.,174).

[38] Judith Butler, *Bodies That Matter: On the Discursive Limits of "Sex"* (London: Routledge, 1993), 13.

[39] Judith Butler, *Excitable Speech: A Politics of the Performative* (London: Routledge, 1997), 24.

[40] Cf. Butler, *Bodies That Matter*, 27–28.

[41] Klemperer, *The Language of the Third Reich*, 82.

[42] Klemperer, *I Will Bear Witness, 1933–1941*, entry of February 20, 1941, 375. Emphasis removed from original.

[43] Butler, *Excitable Speech*, 4.

[44] Klemperer, *The Language of the Third Reich*, 82.

[45] Manuela Günter, "Writing Ghosts. Von den (Un-)Möglichkeiten autobiographischen Erzählens nach dem Überleben," in *Überleben schreiben: Zur*

Autobiographie der Shoah, ed. Günter (Würzburg: Königshausen & Neumann, 2002), 21–50; here, 35.

[46] Klemperer, *I Will Bear Witness, 1933–1941*, p. 266, entry of August 24, 1938.

[47] Theodor W. Adorno and Max Horkheimer, *Dialectic of Enlightenment: Philosophical Fragments* (Stanford, CA: Stanford University Press, 2002), 144.

[48] Klemperer, *The Language of the Third Reich*, 266.

[49] Klemperer, *I Will Bear Witness, 1942–1945*, entry of April 28, 1942, 45.

[50] Klemperer, *I Will Bear Witness, 1942–1945*, entry of March 16, 1942, 27.

[51] Klemperer, *I Will Bear Witness, 1942–1945*, entry of December 11, 1942, 174.

[52] Klemperer, *The Language of the Third Reich*, 78.

[53] Cf. Butler, *Excitable Speech*, 2.

[54] Klemperer, *I Will Bear Witness, 1942–1945*, entry of March 16, 1942, 29.

[55] Klemperer, *I Will Bear Witness, 1942–1945*, entry of August 2, 1943, 251.

[56] As the diarist shows by relating his own personal experience, the use of the offensive term "Schwein" was standard procedure during the Holocaust. Cf. for example: *I Will Bear Witness, 1942–1945*, entries of May 20, 1942, 60; June 11, 1942, 72; June 13, 1942, 75, and August 23, 1942, 130.

[57] Klemperer, *I Will Bear Witness, 1942–1945*, entry of May 3, 1944, 312.

[58] Klemperer, *The Language of the Third Reich*, 16.

[59] Klemperer, *Ich will Zeugnis ablegen bis zum letzten, 1942–1945*, entry of February 6, 1944, 483. This passage is not printed in the English translation of Klemperer's diaries: cf. Klemperer, *I Will Bear Witness, 1942–1945*.

[60] Klemperer, *The Language of the Third Reich*, 191.

[61] Cf. Klemperer, *The Language of the Third Reich*, 57–61.

[62] Klemperer, *The Language of the Third Reich*, 191.

[63] Cf. Klemperer, *The Language of the Third Reich*, 78.

[64] Klemperer, *The Language of the Third Reich*, 194.

[65] Klemperer, *The Language of the Third Reich*, 194.

[66] Cf. Irving Wohlfarth, "In lingua veritas. LTI mit und gegen Klemperer gelesen," in *Identités—existences—resistances*, ed. Combes and Harlem 103–46; here, 131.

[67] Klemperer, *The Language of the Third Reich*, 190.

[68] Klemperer, *I Will Bear Witness, 1942–1945*, entry of January 28, 1943, 196.

Literary Language

Reinventing Invented Tradition: *Vergangenheitsbewältigung* and the Literature of Melancholy

Mary Cosgrove, University of Edinburgh

Melancholy Traditions in Postwar German Literature

SINCE THE PUBLICATION IN 1964 of Raymond Klibansky, Erwin Panofsky, and Fritz Saxl's landmark iconological study of melancholy from antiquity to the early modern period, *Saturn and Melancholy*, interdisciplinary scholarship on literary melancholy in the field of German Studies has thrived.[1] Despite the many studies on literary melancholy since the 1960s, however, melancholy, understood as a set of traditions in Western writing and culture from antiquity to the present, has yet to be identified as a feature of German literature that deals with the legacy of National Socialism and the Holocaust. This oversight arises, to some degree, from the scholarly association of German melancholy traditions predominantly with the early modern period, the baroque period, Romanticism, and also the *fin-de-siècle* crisis of modernity; indeed, most postwar publications on melancholy in German literature stop their analysis before the twentieth century.[2] Consistent with the view of the Holocaust as a radical caesura in the history of Western civilization, this lapse implicitly suggests that melancholy traditions in Western writing since antiquity and writing on the legacy of the Holocaust circumscribe two separate kinds of literary aesthetics, one that belongs to a distant and archaic world untainted by knowledge of the Holocaust, and one that emerges in the post-1945 world that is overshadowed by the legacy of Auschwitz. As I show in the following, German and German-Jewish writers after 1945 often adapt the melancholy traditions of a pre-Holocaust world to address, broadly speaking, from the perpetrator and victim perspectives, the problems of representation, literary language, and epistemology that the Holocaust poses. In so doing, they reinvent the invented traditions of melancholy in order to create a novel ethical poetics for a new historical context in which, from the 1960s on, the victim's perspective becomes paramount. They thus undermine the concept of a, to paraphrase historian Dan Diner, "Zivilisationsbruch" (rupture in civilization) after 1945, suggesting instead the importance—and not the bankruptcy—of established Western cultural traditions for a postwar literary ethics of memory.[3]

One name for the new aesthetics of ethical literary engagement after the "caesura" of Auschwitz is "Vergangenheitsbewältigung." A contested term that emerged initially in the West German political sphere of the mid-1950s and that soon spread to the cultural milieu, *Vergangenheitsbewältigung*, which today presides over its own complex discourse history, delineates the ongoing struggle to come to terms with the Nazi past and the Holocaust and generally designates questions of remembrance in postwar (West) Germany from the end of the Second World War to the present. In the following, I trace tendencies in literary *Vergangenheitsbewältigung* from the 1960s to the present through the analysis of melancholy traditions across an exemplary set of texts by writers Günter Grass, Wolfgang Hildesheimer, Peter Weiss, W. G. Sebald, and Iris Hanika. First, however, I frame the understanding of literary *Vergangenheitsbewältigung*, in Eric Hobsbawm's sense, as an *invented* tradition that reflects the political and ethical demands of the postwar intellectual sphere, for example, the signification in the text of the "unspeakablity" of the Holocaust and of the ethical memory of Holocaust victims. Then I will show how these writers' use of melancholy in postwar German literature demonstrates that the invented tradition of literary *Vergangenheitsbewältigung* itself relies on the reinvention of established traditions to produce different ethical resonances.

Invented Tradition

Hobsbawm defines invented tradition as "a set of practices . . . which seek to inculcate certain values and norms of behavior by repetition."[4] His seminal insight is that societies do not just passively inherit traditions: they also actively invent them. Tradition defined in this way challenges the simplistic idea of inheritance as something that we merely receive. In a given contemporary context, tradition can be a stabilizing force: images from the past—which might be mythical—are mobilized to anchor the present. In this spirit, Hobsbawm's concept of invented tradition asserts humans as strategic agents in the creation of their own pasts and shows how traditions attempt in a *selective* manner to establish continuity with the past. This reinforces the sense that invented traditions are creations of the present: they aim to establish affiliations "with a suitable historic past," yet continuity with the past need not stretch "back into the assumed mists of time."[5] This is the peculiarity of invented traditions: they look old but they are often expressions of contemporaneity.

It is just this sense of contemporaneity that, appearances to the contrary, emerges in iconic images from two melancholy traditions that recur in postwar texts by Grass, Hildesheimer, Weiss, Sebald, and Hanika: the Renaissance tradition of heroic melancholy genius, or *melancholia generosa*, on one hand, and the older tradition of *acedia* or monk's melancholy of early Christian monasticism, on the other.[6] Arguably, *melancholia generosa* in texts such as Grass's *Aus dem Tagebuch einer Schnecke* (From the Diary of a Snail, 1972), Hildesheimer's novels *Tynset* (1965) and *Masante* (1973), and Peter Weiss's *Die Ästhetik des Widerstands* (The Aesthetics of Resistance, 1983) initially guaranteed the explicitly noble pedigree of the postwar artist who performs ethical memory work. Sebald continues in this vein in the late 1980s with saturnine self-references in his prose poem *Nach der Natur* (After Nature, 1988). In later works such as *Die Ringe des Saturn* (The Rings of Saturn, 1997) and *Austerlitz* (2001), however, he began gently to parody the image of the postwar artist as a dignified melancholy genius, instead taking recourse to the overtly "emotional" language of melancholy sentimentality. In Hanika's novel *Das Eigentliche* (The Quintessence, 2010), the *acedia* of the fallen monk supersedes the concept of ethical memory as a noble, melancholy, postwar task with grand cultural-historical predecessors. Instead, Hanika shows how *Vergangenheitsbewältigung* in the Berlin Republic of the present has been downgraded to the big—but ethically vacuous—business of what she bitingly terms *Vergangenheitsbewirtschaftung* (the management of the past).[7] Demonstrating that "novelty is no less novel for being able to dress up easily as antiquity,"[8] these texts and the melancholy traditions they invoke for the postwar context are the subject of the final section of this chapter. For now it is appropriate to give a brief overview of the origins and development of the concept of *Vergangenheitsbewältigung* understood as an invented tradition

Vergangenheitsbewältigung as Invented Tradition

Viewing *Vergangenheitsbewältigung* as a recently invented tradition reveals the extent to which writers and thinkers contributed to the creation—and eventual decline—of a new postwar literary aesthetic that was characterized increasingly by the ethical imperative to engage in the ongoing labor of the memory of catastrophe with a particular focus on the victims of the Holocaust. The victim was not always central to the memory concept of *Vergangenheitsbewältigung*, however. When the term came into use in the 1950s, its original domain was the political arena of the perpetrator collective: under the conservative West German government led by Konrad Adenauer, *Vergangenheitsbewältigung* signaled the official guilt of the West German collective and its willingness to take responsibility, in monetary and political terms, for the crimes of National Socialism.[9]

Critical voices soon began to note, however, that the verb "bewältigen," "to overcome," contained the inappropriate medical connotation that the past could be overcome, much as an illness might be, implying that once laid to rest in financial and political terms, the sickly contagion of the past would no longer spread its disease through the now healthy West German social body of the present.[10] By the end of the 1950s and into the early 1960s this critical perspective had evolved in intellectual circles; thinkers such as Hans Magnus Enzensberger and Walter Jens began to expand the meaning of *Vergangenheitsbewältigung* to include something other than West German guilt and responsibility articulated at the level of political and economic expediency: the memory of the Jewish victims of the Holocaust came to the fore here. On top of the high-profile trial of Adolf Eichmann in Jerusalem (from February to December 1961) and the Auschwitz trials in Frankfurt am Main a few years later (from December 1963 to August 1965), which publicly underscored the experience of victims in the Holocaust, the translation into German of seminal Holocaust survivor accounts during this period also helped conceptually to expand the meaning of *Vergangenheitsbewältigung* to include the perspective and experience of the victims.[11] The critical reconsideration of the concept was also profoundly influenced by Frankfurt School intellectual Theodor W. Adorno, who in an essay of 1959, "Was bedeutet: Aufarbeitung der Vergangenheit?" (What Does It Mean: Working through the Past?), addressed the insufficiency of West German memory culture.[12] Here Adorno critiqued the idea of "overcoming" or "mastering" the Nazi past that was implicit in the verb "bewältigen," proposing instead the critical concept of "Aufarbeitung der Vergangenheit" (working through the past), which emphasized that for postwar memory to be ethical, it should avoid closure and instead strive to be an ongoing and open-ended process. In 1967, the insufficiency of *Vergangenheitsbewältigung* that did not take account of the victims was given lasting expression in Alexander and Margarete Mitscherlich's famous psycho-sociological thesis concerning the inability of the perpetrator collective to mourn the crimes of the past.[13]

Perhaps the most pivotal moment in the genesis of *Vergangenheitsbewältigung* is Adorno's epochal and much misconstrued statement of 1949 that to write poetry after Auschwitz was barbaric. This is known as his famous "prohibition" on literary language after the Holocaust; it was published for the first time in 1951 and began to be received more widely by the West German intellectual milieu toward the end of that decade.[14] Initially, it was understood to mean that the only appropriate response to the trauma of the Holocaust was silence: literary language and aesthetics, viewed as complicit with the post-Enlightenment culture of instrumental reason that had facilitated the rise of National Socialism, and more broadly capitalism, was ethically compromised in representing the memory of the Holocaust. In fact, Adorno never intended to establish a prohibition on artistic representation; nor did he mean to silence the voices of the victims, as Hans Magnus Enzensberger suggested in 1959.[15] Rather than asserting that the impossibility of representation was a problem immanent to the postwar work of art and therefore inescapable, Adorno's "dictum" addressed the "unknowability" of the Holocaust as an *epistemological* problem that post-Auschwitz literary writing should aporetically reflect. In other words, the language of the postwar text should dialectically thematize its limitations. As Charlotte Ryland notes, however, with the widespread misunderstanding of Adorno's statement the idea of the unprecedented nature of the Holocaust and the "impossibility" of representing it culturally had been established.[16] In the cultural imaginary of caesura and silence, *Vergangenheitsbewältigung*, understood as "Aufarbeitung der Vergangenheit," could emerge as a new tradition of ethical writing featuring the Holocaust victim.

The idea of caesura is still pervasive in the contemporary discussion about the representation of historical catastrophe, as some theories of trauma reveal, yet caesura cannot account for apparent continuities in postwar German literature with the invented traditions of earlier epochs and the writerly creativity that underlies such engagement.[17] In the case of postwar literary melancholy, the examination of texts in light of the influence of their "archaic" predecessors has been further obscured, arguably, by the strikingly negative positioning of melancholy in psychoanalytical theories of postwar memory that have influenced the discourse of *Vergangenheitsbewältigung* since the 1960s. In key texts on memory ethics by the Mitscherlichs, Eric Santner, and Dominick LaCapra, for example, melancholy provides the dark foil of an ethically dubious mode of memory against which the labor of mourning work may shine.[18] In these discourses, furthermore, melancholy has no rich cultural heritage and demarcates an obscure, psychopathological state. By contrast, its putative opposite, the ability to mourn, indicates the morally right kind of postwar memory work that strives toward an ideal of healing and upholds the distinction between non-victim self and victim other, something that melancholy, which is often associated with self-obsessive wallowing and narcissistic disturbances, does not.[19]

Against this one-sided view of melancholy as a problematic mode of post-Holocaust memory, I propose the broader understanding of it as performative, that is, as a postwar literary discourse that writers establish by citing tradition and convention to stylize, in typological fashion, an erudite aesthetics of memory that, to paraphrase Hobsbawm, stretches back into the assumed mists of time. As Thomas Pfau argues, melancholy thus understood "unravels the project of an authentically expressive poetics," which suggests that distance, and not the immediacy of affect, constitutes the representation of memory in these postwar texts.[20] This goes against theoretical readings of melancholy that view it as the overly emotional, and therefore ethically inferior, memory mode for the post-Holocaust era: narcissistically defunct, it paves the way for the usurpation of authentic victim experience by those who are not victims.[21] On the contrary, melancholy understood as a distancing language of emotion in the literary text—taking "emotion" to mean primarily the sociocultural and historically variable expression of feeling—addresses the very problem of knowledge and representation that Adorno's "dictum" raised.[22] Indeed, the self-reflexive focus on the limitations of language in discourses on and about melancholy from antiquity to the present suggests a certain structural kinship between the age-old task of writing about melancholy and the more recent task of writing about the Holocaust. In both cases, the effort to find words that capture the object without distorting it raises the issues of knowing and representation and determines that these are central concerns of the signifying process. Melancholy as performative thus reveals how the language of "inauthenticity" or citation can be adapted to great ethical effect, as the works of Hildesheimer and Weiss demonstrate. Equally, however, citation, or as Jacques Derrida terms it, iterability, which is founded on the repeatability of all linguistic signs within language, also opens the way to irony and parody, as texts by Sebald and Hanika show.[23] To view melancholy as performative is to understand it as a series of evolving, and often competing, intellectual and cultural discourses in history; to analyze literary melancholy in postwar texts from this historical angle is to understand these texts as inheritors not just of the ethical strictures of *Vergangenheitsbewältigung* and the legacy of Auschwitz, but of much older iconic traditions that designate the unresolvable dialectical tensions of a condition between illness and empowerment.

Melancholy Dialectics in Postwar German Literature

This overview of the evolving discursive features of *Vergangenheitsbewältigung* suggests that postwar ethical literature should poetologically indicate the problems that the representation of catastrophe poses—the redundancy of language and the threat of silence—while at the same time conveying the necessity of literary memory work and the otherness of the victim. This endeavor outlines a dialectical struggle in which the reification of language compromises critical thought as well as the articulation of trauma, guilt, and contrition. Nevertheless, postwar writing must attempt "dialectical thought as the only mode of dealing with the aporia of modern society"—that is Adorno's message.[24] Melancholy as performative readily maps onto this requirement of literary *Vergangenheitsbewältigung*: throughout cultural history melancholy circumscribes, in iconic terms, extremes of behavior from the lows of mute and catatonic despondence to the highs of ecstatic creativity and exceptional insight. Albrecht Dürer's early modern engraving *Melencolia I* (1514) famously articulates the paradoxical co-dependency of these extremes: he surrounds the inactive figure of the winged genius at the center of the image with the symbols of intellectual industry—the geometrical tools of artistic and scientific inquiry with which the figure might, at any moment, re-engage, thereby recommencing the work of genius. The putto, perched on the winged figure's shoulder and busily writing, reinforces the melancholy dialectics of incapacitation and empowerment, silence and articulation.

When Dürer created the image, he was drawing on centuries of commentary on melancholy, from Aristotle, who first advanced the notion of melancholy as a sign of exceptional talent, to the Renaissance, when the Florentine philosopher, Marsilio Ficino, revived the Aristotelian text on melancholy, thus transforming melancholy into the marker of Renaissance genius.[25] In the medieval period, melancholy had been associated with demonic possession and the cardinal sin of *acedia*, or lacking faith in the divine good, thus Ficino and Dürer, in reanimating Aristotle's theory of melancholy genius, ushered in, in Jean Starobinski's words, "the golden age" of melancholy as the optimistic signifier of a new humanist subjectivity.[26] Dürer's image expresses the conundrum of the gifted humanist intellectual who has at her / his disposal the instruments of scientific inquiry but who nevertheless is confronted time and again with the limitations of her / his finite mind. The engraving captures one such moment of limitation and despair; for this reason, Klibansky et al. suggest that in *Melencolia I* Dürer presents us with a psychological theory founded on epistemology.[27]

This dialectical quality of melancholy genius between despair and hope, language and silence, and its problematization of the limitations of the human imagination, renders it a useful template for a literary discourse of *Vergangenheitsbewältigung* that establishes its ethical credentials by self-reflexively flagging its own limitations while nevertheless straining to imagine the impossible: the Holocaust. Equally, the citation of melancholy traditions as part of this effort also attests to the erudite cultural credentials of the evolving literary discourse of *Vergangenheitsbewältigung*. Melancholy of this aesthetic appearance and dialectical nature is at work in the aforementioned texts by Hildesheimer, Grass, Weiss, and Sebald; however, each writer encodes the humanist melancholy icon differently because the contexts—the moral worlds of perpetrator and victim—into which they transfer the "Renaissance episteme" vary considerably.[28]

Grass and Hildesheimer present us with an interesting case study for examining the role of melancholy traditions in the evolving discourse of *Vergangenheitsbewältigung* of the 1960s. While their texts reveal a predilection for the image of male melancholy genius, the message that emerges from their respective bodies of writing could not be more different, often subtly revealing the moral pressures of belonging to the victim or perpetrator collective. In *Tagebuch einer Schnecke*, which was written while Grass was on the campaign trail in support of SPD politician Willy Brandt's election campaign in 1969, he subverts images from genial melancholy to create for West German consumption an ideal memory model of ethical *Vergangenheitsbewältigung* based on a sober concept of the imagination that acknowledges its limitations but persists in writing, thinking, and reflecting despite the problem of limitation. Grass thus converts Dürer's figure into the titular snail, a humble, postwar incarnation of the winged genius: the snail's slow trek through time and history captures in an earthy and deliberately non-genial manner the idea of ethical memory as a difficult and open-ended process that everyone—not just intellectuals—must engage with. The symbol of the snail thus reflects Grass's ideal of a democratic society governed by the constitutional politics of consensus rather than the political extremes that, in his view, led to the rise of National Socialism and were, at the time that he composed the *Tagebuch*, resurfacing in the student revolution. As a palatable artistic-intellectual persona and dedicated citizen, his narrator embodies the snail's qualities of patience, tenacity, and periodic retreat. The dialectics of melancholy between political action and the contemplative "inaction" of the intellectual circumscribe this vision of ethical memory. Divided between political activism and artistic reflection, the narrator repeatedly attempts to overcome himself, demonstrating the idea of melancholy *Vergangenheitsbewältigung* as an open-ended process in a paradoxical mode of limited geniality. However, this adaptation of melancholy dialectics has its ethical limitations, too. In the fictional strand of his hybrid text, Grass tries to tell the story of Jewish victims in the Holocaust, yet the Jewish victim is not a central figure of the *Tagebuch*: the diary is essentially preoccupied with the legacy of German guilt. Thus it is questionable whether Grass manages to think past the guilty but genial German postwar artist self (his narrator) in order to empathize with the Jewish victim other.

By contrast, Hildesheimer, a German Jew who escaped to Palestine in the 1930s and worked as a translator during the Nuremberg trials at the end of the war, uses melancholy traditions in order to evoke, from the *victim* perspective, the victim experience. Where Grass emphasizes time and again that the optimistic goal of *Vergangenheitsbewältigung* as performed by the melancholy snail is a West German society based on political consensus (but curiously devoid of Jewish victims), Hamlet, one of the tragic icons of Renaissance melancholy genius, and the ghost of his murdered father, are central to the ethical poetics of Hildesheimer's novels *Tynset* and *Masante*. The narrator of both of these works is a kind of postwar Hamlet who escaped destruction in the Holocaust, while others, including his father, did not. Hildesheimer thus invokes details from *Hamlet* in order to convey a sense of the victim survivor's trauma and guilt: the ghost of the narrator's murdered father, an Elizabethan incarnation of the dead Holocaust victim, keeps appearing on his nocturnal perambulations. In contrast to Grass, who adapts melancholy genius in an apologetic manner for the (guilty) postwar German artist, Hildesheimer draws on the "Renaissance episteme" of genial melancholy first and foremost to signal, from the victim survivor's perspective, an ethics of memory dedicated to the dead victims of the Holocaust. Second, while the narrator is an intellectual and an aesthete—Hamlet too is a scholar, having recently returned from a period of study in Luther's Wittenberg[29]—Hildesheimer's adaptation emphasizes the passivity of this character, his lethargic and depressive moments, which reinforces the negative dimension of the melancholy dialectic between illness and empowerment and conveys the pathological consequences of victim trauma. Significantly, he further darkens the "Renaissance episteme" of Hamlet by codifying the narrator as a sinner: both novels contain several images of *acedia*. Through this combination of genial melancholy with *acedia*, the accolades of nobility, intellect, and artistic sensibility ultimately give way to the guilt and self-recrimination of the slothful melancholy sinner. In this highly original way, Hildesheimer conveys the torment of the Holocaust victim survivor; moreover, his combination of different traditions engages with Adorno's "dictum" that poetry after Auschwitz is barbaric, and debates, in *poetic* fashion, the tension between literary language and historical representation. In this political sense, we might say that Hildesheimer's use of melancholy, as well as expressing the trauma of the marginalized victim, also signals circumspection, on the meta-narrative level, about the problems facing literature after Auschwitz.

The third volume of Weiss's *Die Ästhetik des Widerstands* also uses Dürer's engraving to reflect on the ethical memory of the Holocaust and the problem of the representation of historical catastrophe. Written at the end of the 1970s, the language of *Vergangenheitsbewältigung* we encounter in this volume goes beyond Grass, and even Hildesheimer, in terms of the problems of ethical memory it presents us with. Where Hildesheimer articulates the guilt of the German-Jewish victim survivor and Grass treats the memory of the victims only superficially, Weiss explores tensions in the emotional expression of ethical memory, from the debilitating identification of non-Jews with the Jewish Holocaust victim to the transformation of this mute identification into political resistance through the "anesthetic" or distancing effect of language. Arguably, Weiss establishes a literary template for what LaCapra two decades later describes as "empathic unsettlement": a way of identifying with the victim that acknowledges the experiential difference between non-victim self and victim other.[30] Thus Weiss advances the literary discourse of *Vergangenheitsbewältigung* by reflecting on emotion and ethical memory and by searching for a form of literary narrative that could contain identification and critical distance, a quest that Sebald pursues further in his works on Holocaust memory, *Die Ausgewanderten* (The Emigrants, 1992) and *Austerlitz.*[31]

Through the figure of the narrator's mother, Weiss uses the gendered history of melancholy to address the role of affect in memory. A member of the antifascist resistance, the narrator—and before him his parents—had to flee Germany in the early stages of the war. The third volume commences when the narrator arrives at his parents' home in Stockholm. There he encounters his mother in a mute, vegetative depression that came about because she witnessed the murder of Jews on the journey from Germany into Swedish exile. Her catatonic state expresses an unwillingness to give up the lost object—the melancholy narcissistic incorporation of the Jewish victim other—and outlines identification as a key stage in the development of an ethical memory of Holocaust victims. She cannot therefore be considered to be cut off from the masculine sphere of political relevance: within the novel as a whole she stands for a burgeoning affective ethics of identification and empathy that is catastrophically lacking among the male resistance fighters. Their inability to envisage the Holocaust as she does is presented as a failure of the empathetic imagination.

Despite the ethical commitment it mutely expresses, however, Weiss does not put forward the mother's pathology as a solution to the problem of how to commemorate the victims. While his presentation of her silent condition in a problematic masculine intellectual-political milieu suggests that madness is the only possible response to traumatic history, he also explores through the narrator, the chronicler of this historical period, a means of developing an ethical memory of the victims that is not pernicious for the witness/thinker and yet preserves the victim other. The written word is central to the narrator's memory work, yet in a dialectical twist he indicates that his writing is powered by his mute mother: revealingly, he imagines himself as Dürer's infantile putto, whose incessant scribbling can only occur in the context of Melencolia's (his mother's) incapacitation. In this way, Weiss cites the "Renaissance episteme" to show how language and silence must be thought together dialectically in the postwar era: writing complements the position of identification with the victims that the mother represents. Thus Weiss bypasses the dichotomy of mourning work—typically associated with narrative processes— as a better alternative to melancholy, suggesting instead that melancholy (the mother) and mourning (the narrator) each mark out an ethically valid emotional position on the past.

The mother is therefore not just a sick person. She embodies a melancholy dialectics between illness and a kind of *ethical* empowerment that remains obscure to the men of the anti-fascist resistance who refer to *Melencolia I* in an effort to understand her. In this scene, the mother's empty gaze returns to the men a distorted reflection of the post-1945 artistic imagination, here encoded as a limited *masculine* imagination. Through her, Weiss's melancholy performative overturns in the postwar context the gendered history of the "Renaissance episteme," in which male melancholics are exceptional, while melancholy women are merely depressed.[32] His play on the dialectical tension between illness (the depressed woman) and empowerment (the male genius) cites the gendered tradition in a new and terrifying era in order to pinpoint the origins of contemporary suffering in violent patriarchy and to suggest the necessity of developing an alternative existential modus not based on masculine hegemony. His intervention in gendered melancholy traditions also underscores the need for a different concept of memory after the Holocaust and, through the mother's muteness, alludes to the problem of a caesura in postwar representation and language.

Sebald too uses melancholy traditions to negotiate the place of affect and emotion in post-Holocaust memory. His adaptation of melancholy lies between Grass, whose attempt to foreground Jewish victims recedes behind the melancholy of the perpetrator collective and the solipsism of the narrator's artistic melancholy, and Hildesheimer, whose melancholy radicalism expresses the moral stringency of the victim survivor. Narratologically, Weiss exerts the greatest influence on Sebald—his careful rendering of the victims' voices continues Weiss's exploration of the role of identification and empathy in ethical memory. One of the differences between these two writers, however, lies in the different times in which they were writing. While Weiss wrote his magnum opus during the Cold War, it was especially in the nineties and after that Sebald became known as an international literary name, the decades in which the memory of German experiences of victimization and trauma during the Second World War began to re-emerge as a discourse alongside the globalization of Holocaust memory.[33] The discourse of "Germans as victims" and the related problem of "victimology," or the internationalization of the trauma idiom, threatened to blur the historical specificity of Holocaust victims.[34] Ethical literary *Vergangenheitsbewältigung* was thus obliged to discriminate carefully between these different "memory contests."[35] Sebald's narrative poetics signal a keen awareness of this situation: he is at pains to protect the integrity of the Jewish victim's voice. Melancholy, as a form of occasionally self-ridiculing *Weltschmerz*, helps distinguish the postwar German penitent from the Jewish other. Yet Sebald does not just parody the emotional awkwardness of the "good German" after 1990.[36] His concept of the postwar German artist also elevates this figure, consciously drawing on the "Renaissance episteme" of melancholy genius. In *Nach der Natur* he aligns himself with genial melancholy by stating that he was born under Saturn, the planet that during the Renaissance became the astrological marker of thinkers and artists. Like Grass and Hildesheimer he presents himself in a longstanding noble intellectual tradition, while focusing this broad tradition historically by mentioning his year of birth, 1944.[37] Through this juxtaposition of mythology with contemporary history he self-reflexively alludes to the problems of post-Holocaust representation: he integrates the saturnine tradition into a poetic discourse that reveals the power of myth to afford insight into history and the subject's place within it. Like Weiss, however, Sebald also combines the image of melancholy genius with mental illness, a theme that recurs across his work, thus endorsing the basic principle of Aristotle's seminal coupling of the pathological with genius to produce a dialectical figure between illness and empowerment, language and silence.

Set in contemporary Berlin, Hanika's satirical novel *Das Eigentliche* announces the decline of the project of *Vergangenheitsbewältigung* and the demise of the melancholy genius of ethical memory. An employee of the "Zentrum für Vergangenheitsbewirtschaftung" (Center for the Management of the Past), the main protagonist, Hans Frambach, has fallen prey to the affliction of *acedia*, the hermit's melancholy of early Christian monasticism that in the Middle Ages became one of the Seven Cardinal Sins. Reviled by the extent to which the once noble project of *Vergangenheitsbewältigung* has been degraded in the Berlin Republic to "Shoah business," Frambach opines that his particular *acedia* is not of a theological nature.[38] Rather, he has lost his ability to extract joy from the good works of *Vergangenheitsbewirtschaftung* because this project has become separated from authentic feeling and ethical memory in unified Germany.

Hanika's depiction of this paradigm shift in memory from individual subject to anonymous bureaucratic collective renders even as recent a writer as Sebald somewhat a relic of the past. His work makes a case for the importance of subjective memory and careful empathy for the victim other. Frambach, by contrast, seems to have become trapped in the world of mechanical "Shoah business." Hanika tragicomically dresses up in the theological hair-shirt of *acedia* this paradigm-shift in German memory culture since unification. In so doing, she rejects the post-Holocaust ideal of a normalized collective emotional afterlife that testifies to the successful task of working through the past. She does this by cleverly reanimating one of the most negative motifs in the history of melancholy, the sin of *acedia*, in order to undermine the ideal of successful mourning work in the post-Holocaust present of the Berlin Republic. By contrast with Hildesheimer, who combines the melancholy genius of the Elizabethan era, Hamlet, with the iconography and imagery of *acedia*, Hanika's choice of source texts on *acedia* in *Das Eigentliche* explicitly argues against the cult of melancholy genius and nobility.[39] The crisis in faith of the desert monks of early Christianity parallels the scandalous loss of faith in the sacred memory of Auschwitz and the precedence of bureaucracy in the management of attitudes to this past. Frambach's crisis is a secular variant on the theme of the absent God, but in the early twenty-first century, this absent God is none other than Holocaust memory. Frambach laments the absence of authentic feeling in the memory discourses of contemporary Germany. In the era of post-postmemory, the state has appropriated collective memory and fashioned it into an automatized business with little space for subjective initiative: individual and collective memory are thus out of synch, and, accordingly, Frambach appears to mourn not so much the historical event of the Holocaust as an imagined past ability to mourn. *Das Eigentliche* ironically lays bare the paradoxical situation of guilty feeling about the inability to feel guilty.

The novel thus marks the endpoint of a development in literary commemoration that began in the 1960s with the emergence of melancholy as a literary discourse of ethical *Vergangenheitsbewältigung*. At the end of the first decade of the new millennium it is no longer possible, Hanika suggests, to use melancholy for this purpose, because the greater project of postwar ethical memory is in decline. Worse still, she presents the emotional dependence of a generation of postwar West Germans on the wider sociopolitical project of *Vergangenheitsbewältigung* as deeply problematic: Frambach's very identity depended on the authenticity of *Vergangenheitsbewältigung*. Now he questions whether *Vergangenheitsbewältigung* ever meant anything: was it merely a version of Adorno's concept of "Jargon," the language of inauthenticity and reification?[40] The novel seems to confirm this suspicion, casting a shadow over decades of German mourning work: the demise of the image of melancholy genius, along with its dialectical force, drives home that the reification of language, culture, and memory has won out. The capitalist concept of *Vergangenheitsbewirtschaftung* thus neatly conveys the continuing contemporaneity of Adorno's impression of "the barbaric depths that late capitalism has reached."[41]

With its dramatic cultural history, its dialectics between illness and empowerment, and not least its rich iconicity, melancholy offers writers interested in commenting on the legacy of the German past a treasure-trove of materials with which to co-create the literary discourse of *Vergangenheitsbewältigung*. If melancholy traditions help sculpt an ostentatious version of *Vergangenheitsbewältigung*, then these archaic-contemporary images from the distant mists of time ultimately produce a sense of disharmony, pointing to the absence of consensus on how the past should be remembered, uncertainty around post-Holocaust identities, and in Hanika's case, the question of whether the Holocaust will continue to be remembered in a meaningful way at all. Simultaneously, however, the reinvention of existing traditions for the renewal of literary language in the postwar era endows the literature of that period with archaic atmosphere and intellectual authority, features that, in cementing the historical and cultural caliber of a given work, can also compromise its ethical objectives. Whether framed as the tragedy of the noble outlook, cardinal sin, or parody, however, melancholy traditions in postwar literary works can tell us much about trends in postwar German memory discourses.

Notes

[1] Klibansky, Saxl, and Panofsky, *Saturn and Melancholy: Studies in the History of Natural Philosophy, Religion, and Art* (London: Nelson, 1964). Because it is still in print, I refer to the later German translation: *Saturn und Melancholie*, trans. Christa Buschendorf (Frankfurt am Main: Suhrkamp, 1992). Examples of scholarship on melancholy and literature since then include: Klara Obermüller, *Studien zur Melancholie in der deutschen Lyrik des Barock* (Bonn: Bouvier, 1974); Hans-Jürgen Schings, *Melancholie und Aufklärung: Melancholie und ihre Kritiker in Erfahrungsseelenkunde des 18. Jahrhunderts* (Stuttgart: Metzler, 1977); Franz Loquai, *Künstler und Melancholie in der Romantik* (Frankfurt am Main, Bern, New York: Peter Lang, 1984); Günter Blamberger, *Versuch über den deutschen Gegenwartsroman* (Stuttgart: J. B. Metzler, 1985); Martina Wagner-Egelhaaf, *Die Melancholie der Literatur: Diskursgeschichte und Textfiguration* (Stuttgart: Metzler, 1997); Burkhard Meyer-Sickendiek, *Tiefe: Über die Faszination des Grübelns* (Munich: Fink, 2010).

[2] An exception is Blamberger's study, *Versuch über den deutschen Gegenwartsroman*. However, Blamberger is concerned more with the role melancholy plays in the crisis of the novel during existentialism than with its potential as a memory discourse after Auschwitz.

[3] Diner, ed., *Zivilisationsbruch: Denken nach Auschwitz* (Frankfurt am Main: Fischer, 1996).

[4] Hobsbawm, "Introduction: Inventing Traditions," in *The Invention of Tradition*, ed. Hobsbawm and Terence Ranger (Cambridge: Cambridge University Press, 1983), 1–14, here 1.

[5] Ibid., 1–14, here 2.

[6] On melancholy genius in antiquity, the Renaissance, and Romanticism, see Klibansky et al., *Saturn und Melancholie*, respectively 55–92, 351–94, 347. On *acedia* see Siegfried Wenzel, *The Sin of Sloth: Acedia in Medieval Thought and Literature* (Chapel Hill: University of North Carolina Press, 1960).

[7] Grass, *Aus dem Tagebuch einer Schnecke* (Munich: Deutscher Taschenbuch Verlag, 1998); Hildesheimer, *Tynset* (Frankfurt am Main: Suhrkamp, 1965), *Masante* (Frankfurt am Main: Suhrkamp, 1973); Weiss, *Die Ästhetik des Widerstands* (Frankfurt am Main: Suhrkamp, 1983); Sebald, *Nach der Natur: Ein Elementargedicht* (Frankfurt am Main: Fischer, 2008); *Die Ringe des Saturn: Eine Englische Wallfahrt* (Frankfurt am Main: Fischer, 1997); *Austerlitz* (Frankfurt am Main: Fischer, 2001); Hanika, *Das Eigentliche* (Vienna: Droschl, 2010).

[8] Hobsbawm, "Introduction: Inventing Traditions," 5.

[9] West Germany's reparations agreement with Israel in 1953 is central here. See Robert G. Moeller, *War Stories: The Search for a Usable Past in the Federal*

Republic of Germany (Berkeley: University of California Press, 2001), 27; Eitz and Stötzel, *Wörterbuch der Vergangenheitsbewältigung,* 684–89.

[10] Eitz and Stötzel, *Wörterbuch der Vergangenheitsbewältigung,* 604–5.

[11] For an overview of *Vergangenheitsbewältigung* in the 1960s see Fischer and Lorenz, *Lexikon der "Vergangenheitsbewältigung,"* 125–85. Victim testimonies include: Primo Levi, *Ist das ein Mensch* (Frankfurt am Main: Fischer, 1961); Elie Wiesel, *Die Nacht zu begraben, Elischa* (Munich: Bechtle, 1962); Tadeusz Borowski, *Die steinerne Welt* (Munich: Piper, 1963).

[12] Adorno, "Was bedeutet *Aufarbeitung der Vergangenheit* (1959)," in *Gesammelte Schriften,* 20 vols., ed. Rolf Tiedemann (Frankfurt am Main: Suhrkamp, 1977), 10:2: 555–72.

[13] Mitscherlich and Mitscherlich, *Die Unfähigkeit zu trauern: Grundlagen kollektiven Verhaltens* (Munich: Piper, 2007).

[14] Adorno, "Kulturkritik und Gesellschaft (1951)," in *Gesammelte Schriften,* 10:1:11–30, here 30.

[15] Enzensberger, "Die Steine der Freiheit," *Merkur* 13 (1959): 770–75. For an overview of how Adorno's "dictum" was misconstrued in this first wave of reception, see Stefan Krankenhagen, *Auschwitz darstellen: Ästhetische Positionen zwischen Adorno, Spielberg und Walser* (Cologne, Vienna: Böhlau, 2001), 83–120, here 90–91.

[16] Ryland, "Re-membering Adorno: Political and Cultural Agendas in the Debate about Post-Holocaust Art," *German Life and Letters* 62:2 (2009): 140–56, here 147.

[17] For a discussion of some of the problems of contemporary trauma theory see Mary Cosgrove, "Narrating German Suffering in the Shadow of Holocaust Victimology: W. G. Sebald, Contemporary Trauma Theory, and Dieter Forte's Air Raids Epic," in *Germans as Victims in the Literary Fiction of the Berlin Republic,* ed. Stuart Taberner and Karina Berger (Rochester, NY: Camden House, 2009), 162–76.

[18] Mitscherlich and Mitscherlich, *Die Unfähigkeit zu trauern;* Santner, *Mourning, Memory, and Film in Germany* (Ithaca, London: Cornell University Press, 1990); LaCapra, *Writing History, Writing Trauma* (Baltimore, London: Johns Hopkins University Press, 2001). For more on this topic see Mary Cosgrove, "Introduction," in *Born under Auschwitz: Melancholy Traditions in Postwar German Literature* (Rochester, NY: Camden House, 2014).

[19] For a historical perspective on the negative view of melancholy as a form of self-indulgence see Schings, *Melancholie und Aufklärung,* parts II and III.

[20] Pfau, *Romantic Moods: Paranoia, Trauma and Melancholy, 1790–1840* (Baltimore: Johns Hopkins University Press, 2005), 326.

[21] LaCapra uses the term "negative sacralization" to describe this phenomenon. *Writing History, Writing Trauma,* 23. Historian Charles S. Maier equates post-1990 global identity politics with "sweet melancholy." "A Surfeit of Memory? Reflections on History, Melancholy and Denial," *History & Memory,* 5:2 (1993): 136–51.

[22] See Jan Plamper, *Geschichte und Gefühle: Grundlagen der Emotionsgeschichte* (Munich: Siedler, 2012), 11–50.

[23] Derrida, *Limited Inc*, trans. S. Weber (Evanston: Chicago University Press, 1988). Also Derrida, *Without Alibi*, trans. P. Kamuf (Stanford: Stanford University Press, 2002).

[24] Ryland, "Re-membering Adorno," 144.

[25] *Aristotle: Problems II, Books XXII–XXXVIII*, trans. W. S. Hett (Cambridge, MA: Harvard University Press, 1957), book XXX, 155. The text on melancholy is widely attributed to a follower of Aristotle, Theophrastus or "pseudo-Aristotle." See Hellmut Flashar, *Melancholie und Melancholiker in den medizinischen Theorien der Antike* (Berlin: de Gruyter, 1966), 61 and *Marsilio Ficino: Three Books on Life*, trans. Carol Kaske and John Clark (Binghamton, NY: Center of Medieval and Renaissance Studies, 1989), book I, chapts. 3–5.

[26] Starobinski, *Histoire du traitement de la mélancolie des origines à 1900* (Basel: Actapsychosomatica, 1960), 38.

[27] *Saturn und Melancholie*, 485–512.

[28] The term "Renaissance episteme" comes from Henning Mehnert's study: *Melancholie und Inspiration: Begriffs- und wissenschaftsgeschichtliche Untersuchungen zur poetischen "Psychologie" Baudelaires, Flauberts, und Mallarmés* (Heidelberg: Winter, 1978), 82–83.

[29] *Hamlet* I, 2.

[30] La Capra, *Writing History, Writing Trauma*, 41.

[31] Sebald, *Die Ausgewanderten: Vier lange Erzählugen* (Frankfurt am Main: Fischer, 1994).

[32] See Julia Schiesari, *The Gendering of Melancholia: Feminism, Psychoanalysis, and the Symbolics of Loss in Renaissance Literature* (Ithaca, NY: Cornell University Press, 1992).

[33] The "Germans as victims" discourse after 1990 was not new. See Bill Niven, "Introduction," in *Germans as Victims: Remembering the Past in Contemporary Germany*, ed. Bill Niven (Basingstoke, UK: Palgrave Macmillan, 2006).

[34] Aleida Assmann, *Der lange Schatten der Vergangenheit: Erinnerungskultur und Geschichtspolitik* (Munich: Beck, 2006), 76.

[35] See Anne Fuchs, Mary Cosgrove, "Germany's Memory Contests and the Management of the Past," *in German Memory Contests*, 1–21.

[36] Brad Prager, "The Good German as Narrator: On W. G. Sebald and the Risks of Holocaust Writing," *New German Critique* 96 (Fall 2005), special issue: *Memory and the Holocaust*, 75–102.

[37] Sebald, *Nach der Natur*, 76.

[38] Hanika, *Das Eigentliche*, 123. On "Shoah business" see Norman Finkelstein, *The Holocaust Industry: Reflections on the Exploitation of Jewish Suffering* (London: Verso, 2000). In coining the term "Vergangenheitsbewirtschaftung" Hanika put her finger on the pulse of contemporary critical thinking about Germany's formulaic and commercialized memory culture among literary scholars and historians. See Erhard Schütz, "Zweitgeschichte? Gegenwartsliteratur zwischen

Vergangenheitsbewirtschaftung und Geschichtsermunterung," *Zeitschrift für Germanistik* 23:3 (2013): 592–606. Hanika's novel inspired the title of Christoph Kühberger and Andreas Pudlat, eds., *Vergangenheitsbewirtschaftung: Public History zwischen Wirtschaft und Wissenschaft* (Innsbruck: StudienVerlag, 2012).

[39] Hanika quotes from Michael Theunissen's essay on melancholy in antiquity and the *acedia* of the Middle Ages. *Das Eigentliche*, 96–98. Theunissen, *Vorentwürfe von Moderne: Antike Melancholie und die Acedia des Mittelalters* (Berlin: de Gruyter, 1996).

[40] Adorno, *Jargon der Eigentlichkeit: Zur deutschen Ideologie* (Frankfurt am Main: Suhrkamp, 1964). "Jargon" is a particularly strong kind of identity thinking in Adorno's view, a reified mentality that tries to press difference into uniformity; it becomes manifest in language through the choice of words that reinforce an ideology of universal humanity.

[41] Ryland, "Re-membering Adorno," 143.

"Even the word 'und' has to be re-invented somehow": Quoting the Language of the Perpetrators in Texts by Anne Duden

Teresa Ludden, Newcastle University

> When I listen to Hitler's or Goebbels' speeches I am still shocked that I speak the same language, inevitably have to use the same words they use. And I have to re-use them, there aren't other words. So I have to re-invent them; even the word 'und' has to be re-invented somehow.[1]

THIS STATEMENT BY Anne Duden suggests not only the need to be constantly aware of the connections with the language of the National Socialist past but the self-imposed task of re-writing *German* itself, an endeavor that Duden recognizes as not really possible, and one that places her writing at times on the boundary of incomprehensibility. For Duden, existence is *Schreibexistenz*,[2] only possible in language, in her German mother tongue, so the ethical questions surrounding how to inhabit the German language in the post-Holocaust world are fundamental to her oeuvre. This essay analyzes the different techniques and approaches she used in texts written in the 1980s and 1990s, from her short story collection *Übergang* (1982), and the novel *Das Judasschaf* (1985), to her poetry collection *Steinschlag* (1993).[3]

Übergang: Using Words with History

Übergang comprises eight short texts that all have in common a crisis or breakdown of the narrating self. For instance, in the first text, "Das Landhaus," the narrator is isolated in a country house and experiences terror as boundaries collapse. In the central text, also called "Übergang," the narrator is attacked and her face smashed; the writing interrogates the pain and experiences of the body. It is here that historical connotations are evoked in flashbacks, printed in italics, which represent the narrator's memories while she is in her hospital bed. In these italicized sections clues as to the nature of and reason for the narrator's sensitivity and breakdowns occur. There is a mixture of personal anecdotes, which appear to be personal and fragmented memories, and cultural memories in the form of quotations from contemporary films and popular music. One of the techniques that emerges is the use of words that we associate with genocide, but which are not applied to direct representations of specific historical realities:

> *Ich war gerade dreiunddreißig Jahre alt geworden, als ich mir endlich eingestehen konnte, was ich lange schon geschluckt hatte, nämlich daß es um Ausrottung ging. Die Spezies, zu der ich gehörte, kam allerletzt dran; es war zugleich die Spezies der Verantwortlichen.* (Ü 63–64)

The use of the word "Ausrottung" evokes National Socialist terminology, as it activates memories in the reader of the notorious speech by Heinrich Himmler to the senior SS leadership in Poznań on October 4, 1943:

> Ich meine jetzt die Judenevakuierung, die Ausrottung des jüdischen Volkes. Es gehört zu den Dingen, die man leicht ausspricht. Das jüdische Volk wird ausgerottet, sagt ein jeder Parteigenosse, ganz klar, steht in unserem Programm, Ausschaltung der Juden, Ausrottung, machen wir.[4]

Duden's next sentence introduces the word "die Spezies," which adds potentially further meanings, making the word "Ausrottung" reverberate with scientific meanings by referencing ecological connotations, for example the eradication of animals, plants, and diseases. Through this she intimates that such words have a history that precedes their use by the National Socialists. The scientific meanings are widened when the next sentence refers to the "Spezies der Verantwortlichen," a phrase that brings an ethical dimension into play. Who is responsible for the "Ausrottung"? Up until this point in the text, the narrator appears as victim, so her positioning of herself with those responsible is confusing. But referring to herself as a member of a species also jars, as the scientific terminology has no obvious referent in the text. A possible reading could suggest an encapsulated environmental critique; this "Ausrottung" may indeed refer to the eradication of a species of animals and may be referencing human destruction of the environment. Adorno and Horkheimer also use the word in relation to Enlightenment hegemony and the scientific demystification of nature: "Die Entzauberung der Welt ist die Ausrottung des Animismus."[5] In this way it can be seen that the writing introduces multiple levels of meaning, keeping them all in play without finally settling on clarity. It is a technique that is intensified in her poetry, as we will see below. A further passage in italics relates more specifically to the Holocaust, but confusingly the narrator positions herself differently when the memory of watching early documentary footage of the camps is introduced: "*Dann sah ich das Wegbaggern der Leichenberge in 'Nacht und*

Nebel'—und wußte, wenn das einmal passiert ist, kann es jederzeit wieder passieren, eigentlich allen, je nachdem. Auch mir" (Ü 64). Here the memory is visual, not primarily linguistic, and is an image that has become almost iconic—the mountains of corpses being bulldozed into piles from the film Nuit et Brouillard.[6] The compound nouns chosen to re-write the image from the film, "Wegbaggern der Leichenberge," are succinct and precise, as if the recreation of the visual image in words needed to avoid sentimentalizing metaphors. The introduction of this image in conjunction with the meanings associated with the word "Ausrottung" makes the general threat of violence inherent in the word more specifically related to the Holocaust, which now becomes the primary referent. Other acts of violence may be alluded to as well, but this places the Holocaust within a cultural spectrum of violence, oppositional conflict, and oppression. In the quotation the idea is raised that any group could potentially be victims of genocide. This literary-philosophical critique runs the risk of relativizing the Holocaust or of narratorial appropriation of extreme experiences of victimhood that do not belong to her own history.[7] However, through references to stock cultural images of the Holocaust, the narrator signals that she belongs to the post-war generation that does not remember the actual events of the Holocaust but remembers the histories, memories, novels, photographs, and films that they have seen over the years.

In "Übergang," the murdered bodies of the past are figured as generally silenced: "Die Heere der Toten, die Gemordeten und so oder so Um-die-Ecke-Gebrachten wurden einfach verschwiegen" (Ü 74). In order to counteract this forgetting of absent dead bodies, the narrator focuses her gaze on the corpses that are visible in the everyday—such as dead bodies of animals at the side of the road or in paintings—and resonances with the Holocaust are produced by the text through repetition of the words associated with the genocide:

> Wenn sie nicht weggeräumt würden oder verwitterten, läge da schon Schicht auf Schicht totgefahrener, totgeklatschter Tiere. Ein stündlicher, minütlicher, sekündlicher Krieg, ein Ausrottungsprogramm . . . Jedes tote Tier auf der Straße mußte ich in mir selber begraben . . . als wir abends in Bozen ankamen, war ich ein einziges Massengrab. (Ü 86)

The repetition here of the word "Ausrottungsprogramm" recalls the earlier use of the word in the text, but is applied here in a different everyday context that reinforces the extraordinary nature of the image of the animal corpses lining the edge of the road on the car journey. The use of the word is highly provocative. It suggests firstly perhaps the scientific connotations of the word "Ausrottung," as in the eradication of species of animals, because the number of animals killed along this stretch of road appears to be very high. But, of course, it also recalls the association with Himmler's speech and the passages about *Nacht und Nebel* and thus appears to be a way of bringing the memory of the Holocaust into the everyday. The way the text does this is through the association with the German words, which have been used in a very different context. When the word "Massengrab" occurs in the text "Übergang" for the first time (though not for the first time in the collection *Übergang* as a whole: it also occurs in the opening text, *Das Landhaus*)[8] this is not necessarily a reference to the Holocaust: it could allude to unspecified massacres. But the choice of the word in close proximity to the other words and phrases associated with the Holocaust ("Ausrottungsprogramm," "Nacht und Nebel") compounds the evocation of the genocide of the Jews. This striking image portrays the narrator as both implicated in the deaths by dint of simply seeing the corpses, and yet she is also represented as a resting place for the dead bodies. She becomes a memorializing figure but is also aligned with the perpetrators. The narrator's ambiguity points to the dilemma of the second-generation German writer who needs to find, within the language of the perpetrators, a way of remembering the suffering of the victims while not speaking for them.

What of the ethical dimensions of the literary re-using of these words which are loaded with specific historical meanings? These questions may be addressed by turning to further examples of repetitions of the words of the perpetrators and the practice of quotation in Duden's second novel, *Das Judasschaf*.

Das Judasschaf: Quotation from the Words of Perpetrators and Survivors

Fundamental to *Das Judasschaf* are the quotations from historical documents from Auschwitz and Dachau and the speeches and diary entries of the perpetrators. These are all in German, the same language as the fictional text that they appear alongside, and so linguistic continuity between past and present is highlighted. There is one quotation from a survivor of Auschwitz, Kitty Hart, whose words are quoted in German, although Polish is Hart's mother tongue.[9] However, the style and tenor of the fictional German is also completely different from all of the quotations. Even without the references at the back of the book and the use of italics within the text, it is impossible to read the quotations from the historical documents as the narrator's words. The documents flash into the text amidst descriptions of the narrator's everyday life, of bodily sensations or memories of travel, but are not engaged with by the narrator in the text—she is not represented as reading them or interpreting them. Nevertheless they perhaps function as fragments of memory—her cultural/historical knowledge—which is not merely personal. Their status in the text is not clear; the way they appear in relation to the narrator's other thoughts could suggest that they are ideas in her own mind, memories of knowledge, but also, because they are quotations from documents of the camps or memories of survivors' speeches, they appear as cultural memory or as remnants of German history.

The strategy of re-presenting original documents from Auschwitz and Dachau signals textual awareness that we only have representations of history. The narrator and the reader do not have access to history "as it really was" or to the experiences of the victims. Indeed the quoted originals contain the voices and perspectives of perpetrators, with the exception of one survivor, and this doubly underscores the absence of representations of the voices of the victims—their suffering is not heard in the perpetrators' words and is not voiced again when these are quoted in *Das Judasschaf*. There is a double bar to accessing the voices of the dead. The text highlights over and over again through the reconfiguring of the documents, the *silences* of the victims that are not translated into speech but resonate as gaps. The text reminds us that the trauma of the victims cannot be accessed, and it is this gap that the text helps us experience, not the suffering of the victims themselves. This is nowhere more apparent than in the quotations from a letter written by S. Rascher describing the torture of prisoners during scientific experiments at Dachau.[10] The letter is printed in full so that the shockingly scientific and distancing style of the language in relation to what is being described can be encountered.[11] The victims are termed "Versuchpersonen" (*DJ* 50–52). In another quotation from a different but related document, one of the victims is named but then abbreviated to VP W: "*Die letzte VP Wagner ließ ich nach Atemstillstand durch Druckerhöhung wieder ins Leben kommen.*" Then further on the quotation continues: "*setzte ich einen neuen Versuch an, den die VP W nicht überstand*" (*DJ* 70).[12] The violence done to the victims is reflected in the words that survive to describe the torture. They are the words of the perpetrators, not the victims. Duden includes them in the literary text to highlight that she uses the same language. The intent, however, is not primarily to shock, but to allude to a critical need to develop modes of reading history against the grain to avoid the unthinking repetition of the voices of the perpetrators. The words of the perpetrators from the documents of history must be read in a way that remembers the silences of the victims, even while the words of those responsible are re-quoted. Although Duden does not change the words of Rascher's letter, the very act of quotation, by taking the original out of context, appears to alter the meanings of the original.[13]

Thus although the quotations appear in the text as an involuntary return of the cultural repressed, the choice as to which quotations to include must have been a conscious one, based on what the author might want to critique. Take, for instance, the quotation from Himmler's speech to the SS at Poznań, the same speech in which the word "Ausrottung" was used. Its appearance in this *Das Judaschaf* as well as oblique references in "Übergang" shows Duden's ongoing interest in the speech. It was, of course, important, as we have already seen, at the war-crimes trials in Nuremberg as constituting proof of the high-level organization and planning of the Holocaust. The quotation references the whole of Himmler's speech and the text relies on the reader to know the well known next sentence, which is not quoted in *Das Judaschaf*: "Dies ist ein niemals geschriebenes und niemals zu schreibendes Ruhmesblatt unserer Geschichte." In *Das Judaschaf* the part where Himmler praises the qualities of the SS is quoted:

> *Von euch werden die meisten wissen, was es heißt, wenn 100 Leichen beisammen liegen, wenn 500 daliegen oder wenn 1000 daliegen. Dies durchgehalten zu haben und dabei—abgesehen von Ausnahmen menschlicher Schwächen—anständig geblieben zu sein, das hat uns hart gemacht.* (*DJ* 74)[14]

The quotation is not commented on, so is not explicitly being used to make a specific point, but it comes in the middle of sections in which the narrator expresses that she is experiencing continual breakdown and an inability to fit into a norm of carrying on. There is an implicit comparison between her breakdown and the "durchhalten" mentioned by Himmler; indeed any kind of "durchhalten" is implicitly suspect in the light of the quotation. The text appears to be using the perpetrators' words against themselves to highlight the barbarity and to question what an ethical response might be to the sight of—or memory of—the piles of corpses. The reactions of the SS as described by Himmler, "hart" and "anständig," appear abhorrent, and this raises the question as to how the narrator is able to process images of the murdered victims of the Holocaust. The work of the text, then, is to promote a dismantling of the boundaries between the observer and the victims in order to counteract the distancing stance expressed in Himmler's words. However, this does not result in the narrator identifying with the victims. Rather the text signals its distance from the victims through the repetition of the words of the perpetrators. The continuity between the German fictional text and the historical quotation in the same language highlights a discomfort with the use of German and also prompts the question as to how the murdered can be remembered by means of the repetition of the words of the perpetrators. Who remains to write the history and whose perspective it is re-told from?

Similar questions are also posed by the quotation from Kitty Hart. It is an anomaly in the book, as it is the only one from a survivor: "Ich könnte Ihnen, meine Damen und Herren, wenn Sie das wollten, auf den Kopf zusagen, wer von Ihnen überleben würde. Ich habe dafür in

Auschwitz einen Blick bekommen" (*DJ* 26). As already noted, Hart is a survivor of Auschwitz whose mother tongue is Polish and who has lived in England since 1946. The quotation is not marked as a translation but it is possible that Duden translated it into German herself after listening to an educational talk.[15] The fact that this is quoted in German might suggest linguistic appropriation, but the care with which the quotation is used in the text signals instead awareness of the loss of original homeland and language through exile and translation. That the survivor's memories are now rendered in the language of the perpetrators in a third foreign country highlights the issues of submergence and distance from the original events. The formality of the words "meine Damen und Herren" evoke the time in which they were said—the performativity of the original speech. The statement is provocative, because it would make the audience connect with the experience of the camps by encouraging them to imagine their being there, bringing this experience into their everyday rather than encountering it as an objective historical topic. Hart's imagery seemingly consciously repeats the division and selection of victims on arrival at Auschwitz, and also suggests that personality, rather than luck, played a role in who survived and who did not. There is no discernible stance taken by the narrator on the content of the speech. The words appear to occur to the narrator as she is traveling in Venice and looking at a Tintoretto painting of the corpse of St. Mark (although this is not made clear and is only made apparent when the painting is reproduced at the back of the book and the reader can connect the images she has read to what she sees in the reproduced painting).[16] The painting portrays people fleeing from the dead body with a striking dividing line down the middle of the canvas, which the text links to Hart's division of survivors and non-survivors.

In a chapter in which there is little other geographical or semantic orientation, Kitty Hart's words about Auschwitz are the only clear statement. The quotation even functions as a kind of key to decipher previously opaque images. The words "wuchtige Rauchsäulen," "Qualmfaden," and "ein Scheiterhaufendickicht, das schnell und heiß gebrannt hätte für den ohnehin Toten, um ihn in fettige Asche zu legen" take on clearer allusions to the camps when juxtaposed with Kitty Hart's statement. At the same time they are concrete descriptions of images from Tintoretto's painting, which depicts the stealing of the corpse of St. Mark before it can be burned.[17] It is as if the narrator needs the images in the painting in order for the images to be created in words, and the reader is confronted with both the visual and linguistic images alongside the statement from Kitty Hart. They evoke the smoke and fire and dead bodies being burned on open pyres, which functions as a reminder of the fate of thousands of corpses in the camps. This remembering is encouraged without actual representation of the victims. It is as if the montage of quotations and

visual references is needed precisely in order to avoid direct representation. However, although representation is avoided, the text is nevertheless making a critical point. When read alongside Kitty Hart's quotation,
the seemingly opaque line earlier on, "Der Tod muß so schnell wie
möglich unsichtbar werden" (*DJ* 26), suddenly resonates with meanings
and questions: historical meanings such as the destruction of the victims'
corpses to hide the crimes; and questions such as how to remember the
dead bodies who do not have a final resting place. Thus the text is capable
of eliciting ethical responses not through explicit historical content but
by reconfiguring material and images—including German words—which
already contain sediments of history within them.

It might be problematic that we need Hart's clarity to decipher
the non-referential words if the text set up an implicit dichotomy of
modes of language: words about the camps need to be clear and precise whereas post-fascist literary German is difficult, impenetrable, non-
representational. However, a quotation in the second chapter from an
autobiographical text by Rudolf Höß, the Kommandant at Auschwitz,
introduces the idea that the perpetrators also used metaphorical and
poetic language. This, of course, is not a new idea, but it underlines that
the quotations from historical documents in the text are being used to
highlight what Sigrid Weigel terms a "Kontinuität der Sprache um und
nach Auschwitz."[18] This suggests an interest in the German that was used
in, around, and about the death camps, a language that survived into the
post-Holocaust era. And what happens to language itself as a result of its
past uses and its present activity of writing about the atrocities? Höß's
words are quoted in the text at one of the places in the text where the
narrator's *German* identity comes to the fore (albeit obliquely) as she
conjures up intense and sensual memories of landscapes she inhabited as
a child. The concentration of geography, history, and language in this
chapter suggest the most intimate aspects of the self, of perception and
being-in-language. The narrator is represented as re-visiting the area and
house in which she was born, and the quotation from Höß interrupts the
vivid re-painting of the landscape:

> *Im Frühjahr 1942 gingen Hunderte von blühenden Menschen unter
> den blühenden Obstbäumen des Bauerngehöftes, meist nichtsahnend, in
> die Gaskammern, in den Tod. Dies Bild vom Werden und Vergehen
> steht mir auch jetzt noch genau vor den Augen.* (*DJ* 39)

The note at the back of the book states (erroneously) that this comes
from a diary entry; the language conveys an unpalatable sentimental-
ization of the genocide; the comparison with natural processes appears
to be a way of covering up mass murder and in so doing distancing the
writer from it. The metaphor of becoming and passing away is redolent
of German Romantic thought. It foregrounds the dilemma of re-using

the perpetrators' words: can an author write the words "die blühenden Obstbäumen" without being aware of the way Höß used them and what he has compared them to? It is this connection to the language of the perpetrators that I would argue results in the breakdown of the narrator represented in this chapter. Although the quotation is again not directly commented on, the context in which it is placed suggests that the narrator cannot remember some childhood memories without recalling other events that were taking place nearby at around the same time.

The date in the quotation underlines that the Holocaust is not an actual memory, for the narrator would have been a small child at that time. But it is hinted in this section that she is connected to Höß through their shared language, landscape, and culture. Bodily relations with nature feature strikingly here (and elsewhere in the text),[19] evoking pre-linguistic experiences of sensuous childhood connections with the natural environment. Such early, intimate, repeated connections between self and environment are constitutive of the self and produce what George Eliot called in *The Mill on the Floss* the "mother tongue of the imagination."[20] But for the narrator, the pre-linguistic is already always marked by knowledge and history, and is thus a space not outside of time and language. The most intimate aspects of self and perception are profoundly affected by the shared nature of her *Muttersprache.* the narrator is depicted as walking under trees and watching the leaves fall "wie zur Erinnerung," which results in a shattering of her stability: "die Blätter fielen überall, ohne Taumel, ohne Windzug, Tropfen, schwer und geradlinig. Lieber Gott. Laß sie. Es ist zuviel" (*DJ* 40). It is hinted then that the text does not turn its back on German poetic language but instead needs to find a way of re-using it to remember the silences left by the quotation from Höß. Although narration in the idiom of the murdered is not present in the text, which instead stresses their loss to history, the text signals its own silences, allowing the silence of the unheard stories to weigh heavily for the contemporary reader.

Steinschlag: What Can German Words Do?

The cycle of poems *Steinschlag* (1993) appears to have at its heart the desire to re-invent the German language. The number of neologisms in the cycle is frequently commented on in the criticism,[21] and the extreme difficulty of the poetry is often seen as rejuvenating rather than alienating.[22] The six poems that make up the cycle include many quotations (which are identifiable as such through the use of capital letters throughout the cycle), ekphrastic treatments of Renaissance paintings, and a patchwork of others' words, some identifiable, some not. For instance, the lines from the final poem 'Mundschluss' "WEHE DU VOGEL TÖTEST MICH" (*S* 55) is not given a specific attribution but

is marked as someone else's words through the use of capital letters.[23]
"WO DIE AUGEN ZUGEDECKT" (S 61), on the other hand, is identifiable as Hölderlin.[24]

The "re-invention" of German perhaps entails a sewing-together
of a patchwork of others' words from different historical periods but
the use of foreign languages is limited to English and Latin, which I
take to be an allusion to their cultural dominance as "world languages
of empires (ancient and modern) and their role in the historical disap-
pearance or drowning out of "minor" languages. There are many words
from Latin, for instance "Trifolium Tetrachord" (the title of the fifth
poem and a reference to the cloverleaf-shaped windows in cathedrals
and to music theory) and Latin phrases of religious origin "noli me tan-
gere" (the Latin version of the words Jesus said to Mary Magdalen after
his Resurrection: John 20:17). Quite frequently English phrases appear
as a re-writing of slogans or phrases seen in everyday life: "DO NOT
TALK OUTSIDE THIS AREA" (S 59) evokes the phrase "Do not
walk outside this area" on an airplane's wings. Some lines, for example,
"HARROWING OF HELL" (S 41) use the English term for theological concepts—here Christ's descent into Hell between crucifixion and
resurrection is referenced along with the genre of Renaissance paintings
that depicts this. "DESCENT INTO LIMBO" (S 41) is the title of a
specific painting by Andrea Mantegna. The predominance of Latin and
English in a German poem suggests the profound difficulties associated
with acknowledging the silences of history when writing in the language
of the perpetrators. Some of the German words, such as "Genickschuß"
(S 15), cannot be written without "hearing" their National Socialist
connotations ("allein in der tagsüber geheizten Einöde / wo die Festen
am Hinterkopf nur durch Genickschuß zu sprengen wären"). Some
words have many levels of meaning, such as "sich abspritzen" (S 52),
which can mean wash oneself down or to ejaculate, but as a transitive
verb "abspritzen" means giving someone a lethal injection: "übersieht
sie den Rest / der nur lauern / beischlafen / sich abspritzen kann / wie
die toten Augen des Sommers" (S 51–52).

However, for all of the abstraction of the poems, the opening of
Steinschlag seems to straightforwardly refer to the camps. This marks a
shift in literary technique, as it appears possible that the Holocaust may
be evoked directly by the poetic imagination itself rather than having to
be alluded to via a montage of quotations as in *Das Judasschaf:*

Kein Weg geht am Arbeitslager vorbei
und nur einmal pro Schicht darf der Abtritt benutzt werden.
Die aus dem steinernen Karree mit den schweren Eisentoren
werden bei einsetzende Abenddämmerung gewaltsam geweckt
zusammen in die Auferstehung getrieben

und unverzüglich nach nebenan in die
Strumpfhosenproduktion geschickt
obwohl sie unbedingt liegen müßten.
Die Worte krümmen sich nach innen
und stecken gebückt in den Verstorbenen
nach einer solchen Nacht.[25]

The difficulties with such passages are manifold: they evoke a real historical experience of forced labor at night in factories adjoining the camps, but this real experience is imaginatively re-created in the poem. The impact on the reader is an impression of what it was like for the inmates physically and psychologically. This is achieved through the intimate bodily images of exhaustion and defecation. ("Abtritt," amongst other meanings, is also an old word for toilet, like privy in English).[26] There is a mixture of concrete detail of the "Strumpfhosenproduktion" and the religious and metaphorical connotations associated with the word "Auferstehung." To describe being forced to get up as "in die Auferstehung getrieben" suggests that in the poem, the victims of such treatment are somehow being resurrected, brought back to life, and maybe even redeemed. Words themselves are profoundly affected, the image suggesting the victims' inability to speak about these experiences but also that words turn in on themselves and reside with the dead; they are hiding within these spaces, and the hope remains, created through the word "Auferstehung," that they might be brought across again into audibility. Part of the utopian work of the poetry, it is intimated, is to create a polyphony of voices, perhaps even including those of the lost victims.

Such poetic evocation of the camps in *Steinschlag* is different from quotation of the words of the perpetrators, and runs the risk of poetic appropriation of the experiences of the victims, especially as the poet is depicted in 'Steinschlag' as struggling to find words for bodily sensations, experiences of liminality, and having intense bodily connections with boundary-figures.[27] Indeed, Margaret Littler has argued, with reference to an earlier *Prosagedicht*, "Arbeitsplätze," that there is confusion between the "reality of the death camps [and] the *jouissance* of the poetic encounter with the Real."[28] There are frequent images of speechlessness and ecstasy in *Steinschlag* that, when juxtaposed with images of unspecified violence or more direct references to the camps, may suggest alignment of the experience of the poetic "I" and the victims of the camp that the poem remembers. However, I would argue that we could read such juxtapositions as evidence of a dilemma: how does a contemporary German poet write about experiences of beauty and moments of epiphany when the memory of the German past intrudes? For instance in the first poem, "Steinschlag": "Natürlich ALLES ist Ekstase / letztendlich / und vom Asphalt bis zum Horizont / würden sich keilförmig ausbreiten / klaffende Schluchten wenn man es ließe. / Jedoch: immer an den Lebenslänglichen vorbei [. . .] / die sich nichts wünschen als nie wieder aufstehen zu müssen / nackt und kahl wie sie sind / mit nichts als ihrer ungefütterten Haut bekleidet . . ."; S 8–9) Here it is as if the poet is embarrassed about moments of poetic encounter with the sublime and has to force her imagination away from such moments. This is reprised over and over throughout the cycle: if experiences do not include remembrance of past atrocities, they are somehow suspect. This is also alluded to in sections, such as the one quoted below from the poem "Steinschlag," where the poet is walking next to a motorway and observing the effect of the heat on the surface. The final line reminds the reader that meteorological phenomena are abstractions, not participating in history:

> Aufschluchzen
> einiger Kilometer Landschaft
> entlang der Autobahn
> der Autobahn selbst
> wo die Landschaft flimmernd vor Hitze
> sich bis auf sie gelegt hat.
> Eigentlich nichts weiter als die Regung
> ganz alltäglicher Mischungsverhältnisse
> Licht Luft Farbe und Form
> die sich immer schon herausgehalten haben. (S 8)[29]

In the fifth poem, "Trifolium Tetrachord," a particular work camp is mentioned by name: "In Esterwegen zum Beispiel. Mittagszeit / und wieder nur Strichwolken / und einige Schießbefehle" (S 51). Esterwegen is in the Ems region in Lower Saxony and was the site of a "Strafgefangenenlager" from 1923, a decade before the Nazis took power. During the war non-Jewish prisoners, German "Zivilstrafhäftlinge" and foreign "Zwangsarbeiter" were kept in this camp.[30] By mentioning the camp by name in the poem perhaps signals that it is remembering violence in camps prior to the National Socialist era and to many types of victims; the poem suggests that it does not intend to re-create or appropriate *specifically* Jewish suffering.

Furthermore, there are ways of reading *Steinschlag* more politically. In the last poem in *Steinschlag*, "Mundschluss," Duden self-referentially thematizes the struggle involved with wresting the German language from its association with violent masters:

> Entsichert
> bereit für die Querung
> lösen sich aus dem Salaamkrampf
> Worte
> enthoben dem Bellwerk

der Aufseher und Abwürger
entwichen den Fettzapfern
Fallmeistern von heute und morgen (*S* 58)

The words escape from the barked orders of the "Aufseher und Abwürger" and become dangerous themselves ("entsichert"). We can link the word "Fettzapfern" to the rumours of making candles from the fat of corpses in Auschwitz, and it is deliberately meant to evoke this. The German neologism actually does the opposite of obfuscatory Nazi rhetoric by creating a new term for the perpetrators in their own language, a term that makes their activities extremely concrete.

But the main focus of the poet's attention is the words and what they can now do. Throughout the *Steinschlag* cycle words themselves have an uneasy status vis-à-vis the images of violence. They are evoked as victims of violence (it is constantly suggested that something has killed words, although the hope remains they may be resurrected: "Engellose Flügel / am Todwort / geräderten Horizont," *S* 55), but they are also capable of inflicting violence by mindless repetition. A problem with words and types of words is frequently evoked: the clichéd repetition of stock phrases signals at best an unthinking attitude to language and at worst responsibility for patterns of violence and oppression. The "Leichtfüßiger," the "Vertreter der leisure class" (*S* 9) are depicted as unreflective, not seeing the whole picture of the destruction of the environment and of exploitation and misery. The lines "DAWNTRADERS /—Garantien Gebrauchsanweisungen / ihre einzige Lektüre—" (a reference to market traders or shopkeepers) evoke an impoverishment of language, which is reduced to a set of instructions. The problem of unthinking repetition is evoked through quotation of stock phrases such as "in all fairness and if I may say so" (*S* 15), English idioms which mean next to nothing, probably quoted by Duden because these conversational "padders" stand out more in a language that is not one's mother tongue.

This criticism of modes of language use would sound more general were it not for the references to the camps in the poems. The implicit comparison is made between such everyday uses of language and the modes of language used in the camps. If the German language was reduced to shouted orders in the camps, any contemporary "reduction" of language by eradicating ambiguity and multiplicity and reducing it to a set of instructions seemingly repeats this sort of violence to words. There seems to be a connection between how words are used and how humans treat other humans.

Another problem with words is the use they have been put to in late capitalism. Phrases from advertisements are alluded to in quite a humorous tone—for example, "VORSPRUNG DURCH TECHNIK" (*S* 14). This German phrase in capitals signals a quotation in the poem and is of course the famous slogan from Audi adverts. *Steinschlag* appears critical again of these modes of using language persuasively to hoodwink people into believing certain things about material goods and to get them to buy the product. It seems that this type of language use is linked to other ways in which language has been used as a means to an end. It appears a short step from advertisement to propaganda. Given the criticism of modernity made explicit in other sections of the cycle, the phrase states the exact opposite of the poetic vision. In the wrong hands technology can lead to Auschwitz.

Images of the work camps in the first poem, "Steinschlag," give way to images of destruction and misery in contemporary Africa in the last poem, "Mundschluss." The latter poem can be read as an extended environmental critique employing images of pollution of the oceans and destruction of species of birds for culinary purposes. In the third section of the poem the mention of a real place name again helps to decipher previously opaque images and encourages more concrete political interpretations: "Botswanas Zäune / kreuz und quer / in Drahtverhaue / sich einfolternde Tiere / die unverbesserlich lauf- und trinkbesessenen" (*S* 58) alludes to real fences that trap and torture animals in Botswana.

These fences have been built by the Botswana government to prevent the spread of cattle disease, thus protecting the beef industry, an important source of income for elite groups. Environmentalists say that the fences have been erected in the path of ancient migratory routes to water sources and so have become a death-trap for many animals, which run into the fences and get trapped or die of thirst and starvation when their routes to water are blocked off.[31] Many images in the poem directly relate to Botswana's geography. The environmental problem is the loss of habitat for the black rhino, roan antelope, oribi, waterbuck, sable antelope, klipspringer, white rhino, mountain reedbuck, and puku. The nomadic life of the local bushmen and bushwomen is also disrupted.[32] Images of free movement in the poem are replaced by evocations of entrapment and containment: "eingepfercht in den Korral einiger Söhne" (*S* 55); "zum Schlußatem auf die Seite gelegte / Populationen" (*S* 59).

The final sections of "Mundschluss" imply that speech is so fraught with difficulties that allusions to a paradoxical "silent" language abound. References to the genre of paintings of the severed head of John the Baptist position the writing poet inside the gaping mouth of the dead saint:[33] "Schrieb / den Kopf auf der Schüssel / angerichtet / wie im Schlaf" (*S* 59). In this image the idea of a speech which cannot be deciphered or heard converges with evocations of the violent suppression of subversive political opinions. In its highly allusive style the poem continues:

sprach
mit eingeklemmten Organen
schickte schwimmende Steine aus
befispelte
mannlöcher Gullis
kratzte Scharten Kuhlen
in den Boden
mit zersplissenen Nägeln
und las abgemurmelt
DO NOT TALK OUTSIDE THIS AREA

The suggestion is that the poet cannot "speak for" oppressed groups or the victims of history but a critical vision is nevertheless discernable through the images of pollution and suffering in contemporary Africa.

Duden's struggle with writing in the "language of the perpetrators" has been traced in her modernist prose works, where resonances from the past are made palpable through connotations inherent in the words and through quotations from the historical documents. In the poetry cycle *Steinschlag*, through a web of more oblique and diverse quotations, and imaginative and direct references to the camps, her ongoing concern to signal the memory of National Socialism and its effects on contemporary literary German can be seen. However, the poetry intimates a wider-ranging cultural critique: the movement of the cycle away from the camps in the first poem to contemporary Botswana in the last one suggests that German words can be freed from the atrocities of the past only by confronting catastrophe and injustice in the present.

Notes

[1] Anne Duden, unpublished interview with Teresa Ludden, 2002.

[2] Duden develops this idea of identity constituted in written language in *Zungengewahrsam* (Cologne: Kiepenhauer and Witsch, 1999).

[3] Anne Duden, *Übergang* (Berlin: Rotbuch Verlag, second ed. 1996) with an afterword by Uwe Schweikert; *Das Judasschaf* (Berlin: Rotbuch Verlag, second ed, 1997); *Steinschlag* (Cologne: Kiepenheuer & Witsch, 1993). All references will be given in the text using the abbreviations *U*, *DJ*, and *S* plus page numbers. All quotations refer to the second editions.

[4] Internationaler Militärgerichtshof Nürnberg (IMT), ed., *Der Nürnberger Prozess gegen die Hauptkriegsverbrecher*, vol. 29: *Urkunden und anderes Beweismaterial*, Document 1919-PS (Munich: Delphin Verlag, 1989), 145. In the speech Himmler uses an extended biological metaphor when he calls the Jews "Bazillus" in the "Volkskörper." This document was used in the Nürnberg trials, as it constituted proof that that the Final Solution was planned at the highest level of the National Socialist hierarchy.

[5] Theodor W. Adorno and Max Horkheimer, *Dialektik der Aufklärung* (Frankfurt am Main: Fischer, 1969), 11. They also use the word in the essay "Juliette oder Aufklärung und Moral" in *Dialektik der Aufklärung*, in the context of the creation of a barbaric side of culture through eradication of ties to the natural world: "Die verhaßte übermächtige Lockung, in die Natur zurückzufallen, ganz ausrotten, das ist die Grausamkeit, die der mißlungener Zivilisation entspringt, Barbarei, die andere Seite der Kultur" (119).

[6] *Nuit et Brouillard*, dir. Alan Resnais (with script by Jean Cayrol and Paul Celan, music by Eisler), Argos Films, France, 1955.

[7] This is the interpretation of Stephanie Bird in *Woman Writers and National Identity* (Cambridge: Cambridge University Press, 2003), 95–123.

[8] "Das Landhaus" depicts a breakdown that the isolated narrator suffers while house-sitting for an acquaintance. When she opens the freezer, the narrator sees hunks of dead meat, which is said to resemble a "Massengrab" (*Ü* 12).

[9] See *Das Judasschaf*, 26. Kitty Hart-Moxon (b. 1926) is a survivor of Auschwitz. She is from Poland originally but moved to England in 1946 after liberation. She is a dedicated educator about the Holocaust. The notes at the back of *Das Judasschaf* tell us she is the author of *Return to Auschwitz* and that the quotation comes from a "Gespräch, London, 1981."

[10] This refers to Dr. Sigmund Rascher, one of the Nazi doctors working at Dachau who conducted medical experiments on camp prisoners. In another letter he had previously requested from Himmler the use of inmates of Dachau for his experiments on altitude and hypothermia, and in this letter he is reporting some of his findings.

[11] The notes at the back of the book give the source as "Dokument Nr. 294 aus dem Katalog: Konzentrationslager Dachau 1933–1945."

[12] The source is given as "Dokument Nr. 297 aus dem Katalog: Konzentrationslager Dachau 1933–1945."

[13] This is Walter Benjamin's argument about the role of quotation in "Karl Kraus" in *One Way Street* (London: Verso, 1997), 244–58.

[14] Speech given on October 4, 1943. "Der Prozess gegen die Hauptkriegsverbrecher vor dem Internationalen Militärgerichtshof, Nürnberg 14. November 1945–1. Oktober 1946," Band XXIX, Dokument 1919-PS, Nürnberg 1948. Internationaler Militärgerichtshof Nürnberg (IMT), ed., *Der Nürnberger Prozess gegen die Hauptkriegsverbrecher*, vol. 29: *Urkunden und anderes Beweismaterial*, Dokument 1919-PS (Munich: Delphin Verlag, 1989), 145.

[15] As the note at the back of *Das Judasschaf* tells us, the talk took place in London, it is unlikely that Hart was speaking German.

[16] On the relation between words and paintings in the text see Anna Parkinson, "Aptitudes of Feeling; Ekphrasis as Prosthetic Witnessing in Anne Duden's *Judas Sheep*," *New German Critique* 38 (Winter 2011), 39–63.

[17] See Jacobus de Voragine, *The Golden Legend: Readings on the Saints*, trans. by William Granger Ryan, vol. 1 (Princeton University Press, 1993), 242–48.

[18] Sigrid Weigel, "Zum Bild- und Körpergedächtnis in Anne Duden's "Judas-schaf", in *Bilder der kulturellen Gedächtnisses. Beiträge zur Gegenwartsliteratur* (Dülmen-Hiddingsel: tende, 1994), 26.

[19] The importance of relations with the landscape is discussed by Duden in *Zungengewahrsam*, where she is careful to stress that its importance is not linked to the idea of *Heimat* or "Ortsgebundenheit sondern Landschaft als Erzeugerin eines Überschusses [. . .] Auslöserin von Intensitäten." Duden, *Zungengewahrsam* (Cologne, Kiepenheuer & Witsch, 1999), 30.

[20] George Eliot, *The Mill on the Floss* (London: Wordsworth Editions, 1993), 36. Originally published 1860.

[21] See, for instance, Uwe Schweikert, "Schlacke mit geladenem Gedächtnis," *Frankfurter Rundschau*, April 24, 1993.

[22] See Ute Ruge, "Mennigrot in kleinsten Portionen," *tageszeitung*, April 22, 1993. Ruge writes of the poetry giving "Wortnahrung."

[23] This is spoken neither by a victim nor by a perpetrator but by a young German schoolchild, a quotation from a workshop Duden did in a school in Berlin (interview with Teresa Ludden, 2002). We are not expected to know this, however, so the lines suggest an undeterminable and unspecific threat of violence from nature.

[24] There are many quotations from the late Hölderlin in *Steinschlag*: see in particular page 15, where quotations and titles of his poems interrupt the flow of the lines.

[25] An obvious intertext is Celan's "Todesfuge" in *Mohn und Gedächtnis* (Stuttgart: DVA, 1952), 37.

[26] There is a whole group of words throughout the cycle with the ab- prefix. See "Trifolium Tetrachord" (S49–53) in particular.

[27] In an earlier poem, "Arbeitsplätze," which can be read as an extended poetological statement, Duden describes her work as developing a vision from the point of view of the excluded, which, in images in the poem of remnants of bodies from paintings, sounds like writing from the perspective on the boundary between life and death. "Dämmerzustand Zwitterwesen Traumfigur / die seit eh und je / in ihrem eigenen Narkosezustand nach schwerer Krankheit überlebt. Sie träumt sich auch selbst garantiert so ihr Fortbestehen oder ist im Koma / gleich weit entfernt von allem. / Ich muss ein Gehör entwickeln für das was sie hört / einen Blick für das was sie sieht / und Buchstaben, Silben, Worte für das / was sie unhörbar sagt." See Anne Duden, *Wimpertier* (Cologne: Kiepenheuer & Witsch, 1995), 103.

[28] In Margaret Littler, "Traum and Terrorism: the problem of violence in the work of Anne Duden," in Heike Bartel and Elizabeth Boa, eds., *Anne Duden: A Revolution of Words. Approaches to Her Fiction, Poetry and Essays*, German Monitor 56 (Amsterdam: Rodopi, 2003), 43–61, here 56.

[29] See also the lines "Schwer klumpt das Gedächtnispack / verkappt die Vision aufs Allernotwendigste / kappt die kleinste Verklärung ab" (*S* 60).

[30] See Gudrun Schwarz, *Die nationalsozialistischen Lager* (Frankfurt am Main: Campus Verlag 1990), 89.

[31] See Fred Pearce, "Botswana: Enclosing for Beef," *The Ecologist* 23, no. 1 (1993): 25–29.

[32] Fred Pearce, "Beef for Europe Threatens Botswana's Wildlife," *The New Scientist* 134, May 23, 1992, 10.

[33] The genre is known in German as *Johannesschüssel*, literally the head of John the Baptist on a plate.

"Reden ist Silber, Schweigen ist Gold": German as a Site of Fascist Nostalgia and Romanian as the Language of Dictatorship in the Work of Herta Müller

Jenny Watson, University of Swansea

Throughout her oeuvre Herta Müller has returned to the question of language: its insufficiency, its power, its potential to surprise, its personal significance to her, and how as an author she makes use of it. She has also often discussed language in historical context, examining the use of language in the Ceauşescu regime and the abuse of language as a means of manipulation by political leaders more generally. Through her fiction and non-fiction writing a picture develops of Müller as someone who is deeply suspicious of language but at the same time uses it to great effect, and for whom language has provided a means of liberation. I will bring together Müller's relationship with German and with Romanian against the backdrop of established discourses of postwar German *Sprachkritik* in order to draw conclusions about her attitude regarding language's potential to be damaged by dictatorial regimes. With reference to both representations of language use within the Banat-Swabian community of Müller's childhood and the author's claims regarding her relationship with Romanian I will argue that, although interested in the idea of language tainting, Müller does not go so far as to suggest that the contamination of language by ideology inhibits free expression, instead demonstrating that the historical associations of language add to its impact and meaning-creating potential. Unlike members of Gruppe 47, who tried to escape from the connotations of the past through their use of language, Müller embraces the difficult relationship between language and memory as something fundamental to her creative approach.

The practice of analyzing language for its ideological content and identifying ways in which regimes manage their own linguistic activity and that of their citizens is well established within German literature and cultural criticism. Since the early postwar period writers and cultural theorists as well as linguists have tried to quantify the extent to which the German language was "tainted" by the National Socialist regime.

Some authors, including members of Gruppe 47, tried to use language in a new way, resorting to absolute simplicity of expression in an attempt to escape the shades of associated meaning created by the Nazis' abuse of German.[1] Like many other more recent German writers Herta Müller displays a suspicion towards that which can be read as part of this post-war trend towards *Sprachkritik*. However, Müller grew up in a regime where another language, Romanian, was the language of a dictatorship. Her position as someone massively influenced by the West German dis-courses of guilt and *Vergangenheitsbewältigung* yet external to their set-ting mean that her work is of particular interest for those considering creative responses to language and oppression. Her awareness of the Nazi past is constantly present in her perception of language both within the German community and within Romanian society, with her descriptions of the language of the village in which she grew up informed by but not entirely compatible with ideas of language tainting such as those explored by German intellectuals of the *Stunde Null*.

Critics have discussed both Müller's relationship with language and the influence of Romanian on her writing for many years. Generally, how-ever, this critical discussion has been restricted to a recognition of Müller's distrust of language and its sufficiency for expression (her writing as post-modern or as the consequence of traumatic experience) or, with regard to Romanian, to the level of intertext and metaphor.[2] Notable instances in which critics have drawn attention to Müller's emotional or personal relationship with Romanian are Lyn Marven's explorations of the rela-tionship between Romanian and Müller's persecution by the Securitate, the Romanian secret police, and Alex Drace-Francis's observations about Romanian being something that Müller appears to regard as at once alien and familiar.[3] Her attitude to German in particular, as opposed to lan-guage in general, has been more noticeably overlooked, especially given the numerous instances in which Müller has discussed her feelings sur-rounding it. The troubled relationship that several of her literary influ-ences, such as Jorge Semprún, Georg-Arthur Goldschmidt, and Paul Celan had with language and, in the case of the latter two, with German specifically, is the central focus of the 2006 essay volume *In der Falle*, for example.[4] Müller's heightened awareness of German as the language of National Socialism is clearly visible throughout her work and demands further exploration.

Language as a Means of Creating Reality

The most famous proponent of the idea that German was tainted dur-ing the years 1933–45 is Victor Klemperer, whose book *LTI: Notizbuch eines Philologen*, based on extensive notes made during the Nazi regime, remains seminal if not uncriticized within scholarship and public debates on National Socialist language since 1945.[5] Klemperer believed that the consciously-created "LTI," or "Lingua Tertii Imperii," language of the Third Reich, had been successful in manipulating the inhabitants of the Third Reich. He identified certain traits within state publications and political speeches such as the dehumanization of Jews and other political enemies, the promotion of instinct and emotional knowledge over rationality and intellectualism, and the repetition of slogans and individual words which were loaded with new meaning under the Nazi system. Analyzing everything from obituaries to overheard conversations, Klemperer became convinced that the language of the National Socialist party was "infecting" the vocabulary of normal people and determining the nature of their reality.[6] He also believed that this change remained in effect in the postwar era and that the German language had been fundamentally damaged by National Socialism.[7]

Müller shows a similar concern with the potential for language to affect communal ideology and behavior. She discusses the power of the word "normal" through descriptions both of how it was used by the Romanian regime and in everyday life in the village, where the word appeared innocent but its implied opposites, such as "irr" and "verrückt," were instant markers of the outsider:[8] "Die ungeschriebenen Gesetze regierten die Köpfe als öffentliche Meinung. Sie trennten alles, was es gab, in: richtig und falsch. Aber diese öffentliche Meinung kam auch aus den Köpfen, die sie regierten. Sie stellte sich immer gegen den einzelnen . . . Es drückt den Zwang, zur Gemeinschaft zu gehören, tief in den Verstand."[9] Through this process of uncritical internalization by the villagers, the concept of "normal" enforces a particular worldview and model of behavior. For Müller the word becomes a metonym for all forms of mutual surveillance, social exclusion, and self-restriction, a word that leaves people vulnerable to exploitation by parties who seek to control its meaning.

More recently, Müller has argued against what she sees as the ideologically-loaded description of ethnic German refugees in public discourse as "Heimatvertriebene," contrasting this emotive word with the standard choice of "Emigranten" to describe those who were forced to emigrate (or as Müller points out, were "vertrieben") by Hitler during the fascist period. Arguing that the contrast exposes a difference in ideological value judgment between the two groups and their experiences, that is, that the ethnic Germans who fled Poland and other occupied territories were forced to do so but that the Jews and left-wing intellectuals who left Germany in the 1930s did so by choice, she suggests, "Das Wort 'Heimatvertriebener' hat einen warmen Hauch, das Wort 'Emigrant' hat nur sich selbst. Man könnte sagen, einem Herzwort steht ein Kopfwort gegenüber. Man muss sich doch fragen, wurden die 'Emigranten' nicht aus der Heimat vertrieben?"[10] This idea of *Herzwörter* and *Kopfwörter* is a further example of Müller's *Sprachkritik*, in this case expressed in a distrust of speech that seeks to solicit sympathy by using words with an ideological subtext. By trying to expose a hidden agenda behind such linguistic choice and hinting at the danger of substituting the rational for the emotional, Müller places herself within a tradition of Klempererian discourse analysis.

In the next section, I will examine how Müller represents the linguistic production of reality in the Banat-Swabian village and how this relates to the idea of language as a conduit for ideology. In order to do so I will focus on several aspects of National Socialist language that were identified by Klemperer and have since been analyzed by various scholars and writers. By looking at *Dorfsprache* through the lens of his LTI I aim to demonstrate that Müller's criticisms of the villagers' mentality are rooted in a similar kind of *Sprachkritik*, which takes aim at the way language can be used to discourage independent thought, create a sense of group identity, and influence the worldview of individuals.

LTI in the Banat-Swabian Village

The setting of the Banat-Swabian village is one to which Müller has returned throughout her writing career. The communities she portrays are conservative, xenophobic, oppressive to those who live within them, and display a particular collective concern with the recent German past (most being set in the 1950s and 1960s). The link between Banat-Swabian conservatism and the National Socialist regime is central to Müller's portrayal of her village, in which characters of her parents' generation express nostalgia for the Nazi era, when Banat-Swabians were part of Hitler's pan-German community, and their children struggle to come to terms with the authoritarian, unreconstructed attitudes of the community in which they grow up. Most critics discussing this setting have alluded to the village's fascistic tendencies, but to date no thorough analysis of the linguistic dimensions of this characteristic of the village has been offered. As I will demonstrate, Müller uses conversations between her characters to present a *Sprachkritik* of the Banat-Swabian community and its unapologetically xenophobic, conservative, and repressive attitudes.

Throughout her representations of the village Müller portrays relationships in which there is little communication. The child protagonists who feature in *Niederungen* (1982), *Drückender Tango* (1984), *Barfüßiger Februar* (1987), and *Herztier* (1994) are discouraged from asking questions and interpret their parents' wishes mainly through isolated statements regarding what is and is not acceptable within the community; what represents moral and immoral conduct; and how a child should behave. Müller overdetermines some of these platitudes, such as "der Teufel sitzt im Spiegel," and "Reden ist Silber, Schweigen ist Gold" so that they become shorthand for complex ideas about the nature of village life and the repression of individuality.[11] Others she uses to provide an ironic commentary on events in the village, such as in *Niederungen*, where the mother, whose marriage is characterized by antagonism and drunken violence on the part of her husband, makes a wall-hanging that reads, "Lieber Mann, ich rate dir, meide Gasthaus, Wein und Bier. Sei beim Nachtmahl stets zu Haus, lieb dein Weibchen, sonst ist's aus."[12] The false impression of light-heartedness and choice (divorce was socially unacceptable) contrasts bitterly with the reality.

More relevant to the present discussion are the ideas Müller expresses in her poetics essays about the associations various proverbs provoke in her, specifically in relation to the legacy of fascism:

> Zerbrochene haben zum Unterschied von Intakten ein Ohr für jeden Hinterhalt der Worte . . . Für die Dreistigkeit der Redewendungen und Sprichwörter. *Arbeit macht frei*, sagten die Mörder. *Reden ist Silber, Schweigen ist Gold*, sagt man noch heute in dieser Sprache, die den Toten das Zahngold stahl. *Leben und leben lassen*, sagten die Mörder mitten im Handwerk des Tötens . . . Redewendungen verabsolutieren. Vielleicht sollte man in jeder Sprache, und besonders in der deutschen, ohne diese Treffer auskommen und Worte finden, die im eigenen Mund entstehen.[13]

Müller criticizes the reliance on phrases that obscure complexity and are easily repeatable, reflecting an idea Klemperer expounded in *LTI*: that "certain characteristic expressions" can become a substitute for individual thought.[14] However, she also adapts this argument by suggesting that sayings that predate the National Socialist era are also suspect, both in their simplicity and absolutism. Although like Klemperer she recognizes the importance of simplistic, memorable phrases, it is not just propaganda slogans that remind her of the crimes of the Third Reich. Words that were said during that time without reflection and that continue to be seen as harmless proverbs carry with them—in Müller's hyper-aware perspective—the memory of an era in which their repetition became an abomination. All simplistic expressions are filled with dangerous potential.[15]

One concept that offers insight into Müller's extreme reactions to German *Sprichwörter* is that of the "Irrlauf im Kopf," which she first explored in her *Leipziger Poetikvorlesung*.[16] She explains this concept as the sudden chaos of associations, emotions, and insights that are the desired product of literature, something that words can provoke even as they fail to express it directly: "Die Hälfte von dem, was der Satz beim Lesen verursacht, ist nicht formuliert. Diese nichtformulierte Hälfte macht den Irrlauf im Kopf möglich, sie öffnet den poetischen Schock, den Mann als Denken ohne Worte gelten lassen muß."[17] The shock that comes from effective literature is related in the case of these sayings to the shock of historical perspective; the "Hinterhalt" of words created by an awareness of history. Knowledge of the Holocaust, which cannot be unknown, infiltrates the network of associations surrounding phrases like "Gold im Mund."

Müller also describes how individual words can take on meaning through a subject's experiences (or acquisition of knowledge), carrying these associative meanings into different contexts. Taking the example of the word "Taschentuch," she spoke in her Nobel Prize speech about the development of meaning that began in her mother's daily reminder to take one with her, accompanied her through her attempted recruitment as an informer and harassment by the Securitate, then resurfaced in her relationship with the Romanian-German poet Oskar Pastior; the banal object had become a site of multiplied meaning and an island of safety amid chaotic and frightening experiences.[18] Thinking in terms of associations, knowledge of the National Socialist past saturates Müller's perception of the village and its inhabitants' speech patterns. She is, as I have said, hyperaware of the potential meanings of each word, which can nevertheless ambush her at any time. This potential for intrusions of meaning is arguably what lies at the heart of Klemperer's LTI, and the criticisms that have so often been levelled at it. Klemperer's response, like Müller's, is an intuitive, personal response to the contamination of language, at odds with scientific approaches to linguistics.

As well as ill-chosen sayings, the Banat Swabians of Müller's texts use quasi-slogans that appear even more directly fascistic than the proverbs discussed above. When the night watchman in the novel *Der Mensch ist ein großer Fasan auf der Welt* (translated as *The Passport*, 1986) voices the opinion that "die Juden verderben die Welt," he could be directly repeating Nazi rhetoric.[19] Prejudicial statements against Romanians and "Gypsies," which set off alarm bells to the reader, are expressed as if they were established sayings in their own right: "Ein Walach ist ein Walach, mehr gibt's da nicht zu sagen" and (of Gypsies) "sie sammeln Speck, und Mehl, und Eier ein . . . Und Kinder."[20] Müller makes it clear that these pieces of "wisdom" (presented as reported speech) are transmitted from one villager to another and cement collective attitudes. Clear examples of this can be seen in *Der Mensch ist ein großer Fasan auf der Welt*, where the villagers repeat the bad things they have heard about West Germany. "Die schlechteste Schwäbin ist . . . noch mehr wert, als die beste Deutsche von dort," reports the emigrant Kürschner in a letter from the Federal Republic.[21] Later, a statement from his friend Windisch demonstrates how this opinion is spread through the community by means of repetition and being received as categorical fact, "'Das mit den Weibern in Deutschland stimmt,' sagt Windisch, 'Der Kürschner hat's geschrieben. Die Schlechteste von hier ist immer noch mehr wert als die Beste von dort.'"[22] Kürschner also reports back about the racial make-up of

Germany, alarming Windisch and the Nachtwächter, to whom he relates Kürschner's findings: "Dort sind Türken und Neger. Die vermehren sich rasch."[23] Once again the means of expression; the use of a biological word like "vermehren" (like the ideologically-marked "verderben") conveys a sense of racism and xenophobia tipping over into typically fascist ideas. While declarations like this potentially reveal the ideological influence of fascism on language, through the manner in which difference is responded to, Müller also exposes fascistic tendencies—the promotion of instinct over rationality, absolutism, the creation of dichotomies—in the everyday vocabulary choices of her characters. I will explore this issue in greater detail in the next section.

Attachment to the Past and Resistance to the Present in "Dorfchronik"

Müller's debut novel-length work *Niederungen*, from 1982, is a collection of interlinked stories and sketches of varying length that combine to give an autofictional account of a Banat-Swabian childhood. One story from the collection, "Dorfchronik," is directly concerned with the question of language within the context of the German community. The text is structured around the repetition of a formulaic sentence exposing differences between how objects and ideas are described in the German of the communist regime, of West Germany, and the German of the village. Over seventy times the sentence "X, was im Dorf Y genannt wird" is repeated, with everything from animal names to what they call net curtains ("Nylonvorhänge" versus "Spitzenvorhänge"—a euphemism to disguise the quality of the curtains) listed.[24]

The tendency of the villagers to hold on to their past and specifically the era of the Second World War is exhibited very prominently in the story in a way that demonstrates the centrality of that era to their worldview and the lingering effects of fascist thinking. At the level of plot this connection is exhibited in the way the men sing songs from their days in the SS and reminisce about the war, whilst in the speech of the characters their word choice suggests the influence of Nazi ideology. The phrase "Vorfahren, was im Dorf Ahnen genannt wird" may be a reference to Nazi rhetoric, which made use of archaic words such as *Ahnen* in terms like *Ahnenpass*, the document with which citizens of the Third Reich proved their racial purity.[25] In other less direct examples the contrast between the words demonstrates the nostalgic, unreconstructed attitudes of the villagers, who glorify the war. Müller's alternatives to the villagers' words open up a chasm that is at once poignant and bitter because it exposes the difference between the reality of what happened (from Müller's perspective) and the way the villagers choose to see it.

Thus "erschossen" becomes "gefallen," "vergebens gestorben" becomes "den Heldentod gefunden," and "im Massengrab liegen" becomes "im Krieg geblieben sein."[26] The villagers employ euphemisms about the war as a means of distancing themselves from what happened and of painting the village itself in a positive light but also display an ideological devotion to war that seems at odds with acceptable public discourse within post-fascist Europe and, crucially, overlooks the devastating effects of the National Socialist era.

The linguistic choices made by the villagers are a means by which they communicate and perpetuate their collective ideas concerning their place in the world, their preferred behavior, and their opinion of other individuals. As such, language is a crucial part of defining themselves as a group. They call "Banater Land" "Inland," suggesting that they regard their immediate area as a country in itself, separate to the rest of Romania, while the term "Ausland" replaces "im Westen": when it comes to thinking about abroad or the possibility of going there, the West is their only possible destination. The villagers' judgemental views on behaviour are also touched on in this passage so that "nach Parfum riechen" becomes "nach Parfum stinken," conveying their opposition to vanity and social airs, and the (much-hated) "Milizmann" is known simply as "der Blaue."[27] The examples of word-choice used in 'Dorfchronik' suggest that Müller follows the example of *Sprachkritiker* like Klemperer in reading the use of certain words and sayings as expressive of a particular mentality and that the villagers' ideology is one of xenophobia, rigid social expectations, and militaristic or even revanchist views. All in all, Müller's depictions of language use in the village appear to share commonalities with Klemperer's views on the language of National Socialism. The words the villagers use are shown to be a product of and an influence on their perspective, while their vocabulary is marked by a reliance on "Herzwörter" (see above) such as "Heldentod," "gefallen," "Enteignung," which highlight the inflexible boundaries of their worldview.

However, Müller does not show their language and vocabulary choices to be solely a means by which the inhabitants of the village express their nostalgia for the past and hatred of difference; instead she demonstrates the potential for resistance through self-expression in the way the villagers refuse to adopt the language of the Romanian Communist regime. Although their vocabulary selection is partially the choice of each individual and partially the product of the discourse in which they are immersed the fact that the Banat-Swabians choose to say "Geschäft" instead of "Konsumgenossenschaft," "Gemeinderat" instead of "Volksrat," and most provocatively "Enteignung" rather than "Verstaatlichung" demonstrates a resistance against the Romanian authorities.[28] That the villagers' attachment to the past is further entrenched through their opposition to communism in the present (communism also being the historical enemy from the Nazi era) adds an interesting layer of complexity to Müller's portrayal.

She also shows the villagers developing sayings of their own that are thematically unrelated to overarching ideologies such as National Socialism and that work against the impression of the *Dorfsprache* as solely restrictive and conservative. Prime examples of this are expressions like "Eine warme Kartoffel ist ein warmes Bett," which come from the experience of Müller's mother Katharina in the Soviet labor camp to which she was deported in 1945.[29] Phrases that her mother brought back from the camp seem to have provided Müller with an alternative perspective on the kinds of reflexively-repeated sayings that she criticizes so vehemently elsewhere; that is, she sees that they can be a means of survival.

Müller's portrayals of the village undoubtedly owe a great deal to postwar German discourses on language tainting. Her characters speak in absolutes; black and white conceptions that discourage independent thought, reinforce group prejudices and rigid social expectations, and rely on emotion over rationality. However, Müller goes beyond the idea that the changes to people's perception of the world produced by Nazi rhetoric were solely responsible for their modes of expression, revealing the importance of the communist present, as well as the Nazi past, in creating the villagers' discourse. By doing so she combines the approaches of *Sprachkritiker* like Klemperer with ideas expressed by scholars such as Krauss, who suggested that *postwar* conditions had a determining impact on modes of communicating. Krauss suggested that the continued use of what he terms "Landsersprache," a kind of slang that was a product of the conditions of the Nazi era, was not evidence that a fascist mindset endured in postwar Germany but "a specific manifestation of a general mistrust of Establishment values, ideology, and public rhetoric, a mistrust sharpened for this generation by its particular experience of Nazi Germany."[30] Similarly, although the *Dorfsprache* portrayed by Müller is shown to be a product of the Nazi era, the fact that it remains unchanged, as do the structures and attitudes of the village, is linked to the community's feeling of beleaguerment in communist Romania.

Romanian as the Language of Dictatorship

The role of Romanian in Müller's creative process, and especially her creation of metaphors and intertextual references, has been discussed elsewhere (see note 2), and there is no doubt that the language is an important resource for her writing. However with regard to Müller's personal relationship with Romanian, critics have tended to focus on the 1995 essay "Und noch erschrickt unser Herz," in which she pointed out that "In Rumänien . . . jede ausgesprochene Drohung auf rumänisch (war)."[31] The perceived disparity between that remark and the absence of Romanian as a language of narration or dialogue in Müller's writing has led Marven to suggest that "the use of German in the place of Romanian both acts as dissociation and enables representation" and that German functions for Müller as a "screening-device" for writing through her trauma.[32] Although Marven's argument that Müller's increasing use of Romanian, such as in the collage collection *Este sau nu este Ion* (2005), represents a move towards a more direct articulation of her experiences of interrogation is convincing in the sense that Müller is now writing in the language in which those specific interrogations were conducted, I would argue that this does not necessarily mean either that Müller's view of Romanian is wholly affected by that trauma or that she is (only) now adopting it "as a language of communication."[33]

Although she has only published a limited number of texts in Romanian, Müller has been using Romanian since she was fifteen, and has spoken about her experiences of interrogation and harassment in interviews conducted in Romanian.[34] Müller has also consistently claimed that she writes in German because it is her mother tongue, the language that is and has always been automatic to her. In a 1998 interview with Brigid Haines and Margaret Littler she explained that although the Romanian language is closer to her than a foreign language, she learned it "viel zu spät" for it to be "eine zweite Muttersprache," implying that it will always naturally be a secondary form of communication.[35] The phrase that she uses in connection with Paul Celan to explain why he continued to write in German despite *his* multilingualism, and that perhaps best summarizes her own position is that German "war das in den Kopf gewachsene Sprache und musste es bleiben."[36] Seen in this light, the question of whether writing in Romanian is a more *direct* approach to writing trauma is less straightforward. Müller is bilingual but German is her mother tongue; she does not see Romanian as a viable alternative, and in the written form at least, it has less potential for immediacy and precision in expression.

In an interview with *Der Spiegel* in 2012, Müller was asked whether her relationship to Romanian had been damaged by its role as the language of Ceauşescu's power. She denied this emphatically, saying, "ich habe viel mit den einfachen Leuten gesprochen, den Arbeitern in der Fabrik, in der ich war. Als ich die Sprache gelernt habe, war ich schon 15, es war als würde ich sie essen. Sie hat mir geschmeckt, ich kann es nicht anders sagen."[37] This distinction between the state and the "einfachen Leuten" echoes the distinction made by Krauss and some members of Gruppe 47, such as Hans Werner Richter and Nicolaus Sombart, between the *Heeressprache* and the *Landsersprache* in the Third Reich.[38] In various ways, these critics and authors argued that the language of the common soldier had a liberating potential in both the wartime and postwar period because, although affected by its speakers' exposure to Nazi rhetoric, it was a group idiom based on shared experience of being subordinates within the regime and "provid(ed) a defense mechanism against the ideological demands of State and Party."[39]

Despite (or perhaps because of) being a member of the German-speaking minority, Müller was very much aware of the effects of the Romanian regime on everyday behavior and language. She has described her disgust with the language she heard day-to-day in a manner reminiscent of Klemperer's diary entries on LTI, describing it as he did, and as she does at times in the case of the *Dorfsprache*, as a separate language. As she put it: "In Bezug auf die Wirklichkeit der Tage war die *Staatssprache* doch in jedem Wort zynisch, eine Provokation im Ganzen. Und die war überall, wie faule Luft."[40] She also recognizes, like Klemperer, the need to guard against adopting aspects of the regime's vocabulary into one's own idiom; the risk that that language could "sich hineinnisten."[41] However, unlike Klemperer, who argued that "supporters and opponents, beneficiaries and victims all conformed to the same models,"[42] Müller articulates a distinct and stable difference between the language of the common people and the language of the regime in terms of there being a *Staatssprache* that differs from that used normally, an idiom that is tainted by its use by the state. She describes this elsewhere as "die Untertanensprache":

> Wenn man die Untertanensprache hörte, tat sich angesichts der Misere im Land ein Abgrund auf. Die Untertanensprache war Lüge und Hohn bis zum letzten Atemzug. Ihr Anspruch war, von allen wiedergekäut zu werden. Sie forderte kein Ideal. Sie forderte nur Selbstverachtung und blinde Wiederholung, bis das eigene Denken gelähmt, geschrumpft und vergessen war . . . Das eigene Denken wurde von der Untertanensprache verwandelt in eine Art schlechtes Gewissen.[43]

In contrast to this, Müller sees the common Romanian language as inherently liberating, particularly with regard to politeness and directness of expression. Unlike the language of the state, which she describes as prudish, Romanian "as used by the people" makes constant use of rude words and references to bodily functions are a means of expressing true emotions outside the bounds of the regime's worldview. Swearing in particular was something that Romanian offered Müller, who described good Romanian swearing as a "eine halbe Revolution am Gaumen":[44]

> Im Wörterbuch der rumänischen Sprache kommen diese Wörter und Redewendungen nicht vor. In den offiziellen Medien, für die Zensur gehörten diese Wörter und Redewendungen in die Schublade der Pornographie. Sie waren verboten. Im Alltag waren diese Wörter und Redewendungen für die Menschen, die die leeren Gänge und den Blicken trugen, die einzige Leichtigkeit.[45]

Like the villagers in her fiction, the people Müller describes having come in contact with use vocabulary that expresses their opinions about the communist state. They call cockroaches "Russen," bare light bulbs "russischer Kronleuchter" and sunflower seeds "russisches Kaugummi."[46] Unlike the euphemisms used in the German used in the village, which were aimed at least partially at self-deception, these jokes, which Müller calls "pfiffige, verachtliche Sprachspiele," are an act of defiance in which the gap between phrase and meaning open up a space to laugh at the regime.[47] Romanian as spoken by the people was a means to step outside the reality created by the communist state, and it is this Romanian to which Müller expresses an attachment. It is a colloquial style separate and distinct from the language of the Ceaușescu state, which stifles self-expression and rejects the everyday (bad) language of its citizens; the workers' jokes and directness cut through the euphemistic and wooden speech of the public sphere.

As well as providing relief from the rhetoric of the regime, Romanian functioned as a means by which Müller could step outside the linguistic boundaries and therefore the worldview of the village in which she grew up at an early age. These positive effects of exposure to Romanian are the ones to which Müller lays claim; they can be seen as the ultimate reason for her repeated use of Romanian expressions and proverbs rendered into German. Müller's choice of language is determined by German being the one in which she is best able to express herself, "das in den Kopf gewachsene Sprache," but Romanian's constant presence in her German as "das in den Blick gewachsene Sprache" suggests a comfortable familiarity with the language that persists despite its association with Ceaușescu.[48]

Conclusion

As I have demonstrated, Müller exhibits a deep interest in language and meaning-creation throughout her oeuvre. She describes the tendency of regimes to try to control their subjects' mentality and shows in her village stories how language is determined by and reinforces particular perspectives. In this awareness of the dangerous potency of words, Müller follows the tradition of *Sprachkritiker* such as Klemperer. However, unlike Klemperer Müller remains optimistic about the possibility of "state language" and "the people's language" remaining discrete and identifiable, making a distinction between *Staatssprache* and the colloquial language of the everyday in the Romanian context, and imitating the latter in some of her Romanian collages.[49] She also implicitly affirms the possibility of remaining untainted through her criticism of the *Dorfsprache*, in that she is able to identify and analyze it, thereby transcending the linguistic world of the community in which she grew up.

The fact that Müller claims to have witnessed untainted Romanian even in the midst of extremely invasive state policies and the constant broadcasting of ideology would appear to suggest that she regards this as having been a possibility for German also, and that the idea of a language of a people within an oppressive regime (such as the *Landsersprache* described by Krauss) is one to which she subscribes. However, her attitude towards German appears pessimistic by comparison, and although the language of the village can also be read at times as resistance to Romanian *Staatssprache*, Müller does little to mitigate the sense that the *Dorfsprache* and by connection German is irretrievably marked by its association with fascism. This may be due to her greater intimacy with that language or her fixation on the Nazi past and its impact on her family, but the most important thing to recognize is that this tainting is not seen by Müller as a barrier to creative expression. As Müller writes in her essay collection *Der König verneigt sich und tötet* (The King Bows and Kills, 2003), the power of language is ultimately wielded by the individual: "[Die Sprache] . . . lebt immer im Einzelfall, man muß ihr jedesmal aufs neue ablauschen, was sie im Sinn hat. In dieser Unzertrennlichkeit vom Tun wird sie legitim oder inakzeptabel, schön oder häßlich, man kann auch sagen: gut oder böse."[50] Müller is keen to expose those who seek to manipulate people using language and the dangers of using language without reflection, but she also expresses optimism that there can always be another perspective. Her writing alerts the reader to the limitless potential, the layering of meaning and counter-meaning, and the mingling of history and present within everyday words and phrases as well as overt propaganda. She is sensitive to the "tainting" of language in all contexts, but her response is to embrace rather than avoid the historical connotations of words both as part of the web of meaning she perceives and as one cause of the powerful "Irrlauf im Kopf" that words can (and good literature should) unleash.

Notes

[1] Siegfried Mandel, *Gruppe 47: The Reflected Intellect* (Carbondale, IL/London: Southern Illinois University Press/Feffer & Simons, 1973), 16; "Georg Guntermann, "Einige Stereotype zur Gruppe 47," in *Bestandsaufnahme: Studien zur Gruppe 47*, ed. Stephan Braese (Berlin: Erich Schmidt, 1999), 11–34, here 17; "Der 'Ruf' als Vorläufer der Gruppe 47," in *Text + Kritik Sonderband: Die Gruppe 47*, ed. Heinz Ludwig Arnold et al. (Munich: text + kritik, 1980), 11–70, here 46–47; Hans Werner Richter, "Wie entstand und was war die Gruppe 47?" in *Hans Werner Richter und die Gruppe 47*, ed. Hans A. Neunzig (Munich: Nymphenberger, 1979), 41–176, here 76–77, 80–81.

[2] Katrin Kohl, "Beyond Realism: Herta Müller's Poetics," in *Herta Müller*, ed. Brigid Haines and Lyn Marven (Oxford: Oxford University Press, 2013),

16–31, here 28–29; Valentina Glajar, "Banat-Schwabian, Romanian, and German: Conflicting Identities in Herta Müllers Herztier," *Monatshefte* 89, no. 4 (1997): 521–40, here 537; Grazziella Predoui, *Faszination und Provokation bei Herta Müller* (Frankfurt am Main: Peter Lang, 2001), 183–87; Herta Haupt-Cucuiu, *Eine Poesie der Sinne: Herta Müllers "Diskurs des Alleinseins" und seine Wurzeln* (Paderborn: Igel, 1996), 140–44; Paola Bozzi, *Der Fremde Blick: Zum Werk Herta Müllers* (Würzburg: Königshausen & Neumann, 2005), 122–24.

3 Lyn Marven, "Herta Müller's *Herztier* (*The Land of Green Plums*)," in *The Novel in German since 1990*, ed. Stuart Taberner (Cambridge: Cambridge University Press, 2011), 180–94, here 181; Lyn Marven, "'So fremd war das Gebilde': The Interaction between Visual and Verbal in Herta Müller's Prose and Collages," in *Herta Müller*, ed. Brigid Haines and Lyn Marven, 135–52, here 152. Alex Drace-Francis, "Beyond the Land of Green Plums: Romanian Culture and Language in Herta Müller's Work," in *Herta Müller*, ed. Brigid Haines and Lyn Marven (Cardiff: University of Wales Press, 1998), 32–48, here 38–48.

4 Herta Müller, *In der Falle* (Göttingen: Wallenstein, 2006).

5 John Wesley Young, "From *LTI* to *LQI*: Victor Klemperer on Totalitarian Language," *German Studies Review* 28, no. 1 (2005): 45–64, here 52; Roderick H. Watt, "'Landsersprache, Heeressprache, Nazisprache?': Victor Klemperer and Werner Krauss on the Linguistic Legacy of the Third Reich," *Modern Language Review* 95, no. 2 (2000): 424–36, here 426–27.

6 Watt, "'Landsersprache, Heeressprache, Nazisprache?'", 426.

7 Victor Klemperer, *The Language of the Third Reich: LTI Lingua Tertii Imperii: A Philologist's Notebook*, trans. Martin Brady (London: Continuum, 2006), 9. Not all of Klemperer's contemporaries shared this opinion, Werner Krauss for example arguing that the effects of Nazism upon German had been minimal. However, although subsequent linguistic investigations have generally discredited Klemperer's approach, it is certainly the most widely-known and understood study of National Socialist language. For an illuminating discussion of various differing contemporary views see Watt, "'Landsersprache, Heeressprache, Nazisprache?'"

8 Müller, "Das Ticken der Norm," in *Hunger und Seide* (Hamburg: Rowohlt, 1995), 88–100, here 88, 90–91.

9 Müller, "Das Ticken der Norm," 88.

10 Herta Müller, "Herzwort und Kopfwort," *Der Spiegel* 4 (2013), January 21, 2013, accessed June 9, 2014. http://www.spiegel.de/spiegel/print/d-90638332.html.

11 For the connection Müller makes between the saying "Der Teufel sitzt im Spiegel" and the avoidance of facing the collective past see: Karin Bauer, "Tabus der Wahrnehmung: Reflexion und Geschichte in Herta Müllers Prosa," *German Studies Review* 19, no. 2 (1996): 257–78, here 267.

12 Herta Müller, "Niederungen," in *Niederungen* (Frankfurt am Main: Fischer, 2011), 42–103, here 74.

13 Müller, *In der Falle*, 36–37.

14 Victor Klemperer, *The Language of the Third Reich*, 13.

[15] For an intriguing discussion of the Nazis' focus on proverbs as a source of *Volkswissen* and mainstay of propaganda see Wolfgang Mieder, "Proverbs in Nazi Germany: The Promulgation of Anti-Semitism and Stereotypes through Folklore," *The Journal of American Folklore* 95, no. 378 (1982): 435–64.

[16] Herta Müller, *Lebensangst und Worthunger (Leipziger Poetikvorlesung)* (Frankfurt am Main: Suhrkamp, 2010), 55.

[17] Herta Müller, "Wenn wir schweigen werden wir unangenehm, wenn wir reden werden wir lächerlich," in *Der König verneigt sich und tötet* (Munich: Hanser, 2003), 74–105, here 87–88.

[18] Herta Müller, "Jedes Wort weiß etwas vom Teufelskreis" (Nobel Prize Lecture), December 7, 2009, accessed June 9, 2014, http://www.nobelprize.org/nobel_prizes/literature/laureates/2009/muller-lecture_ty.html.

[19] Herta Müller, *Der Mensch ist ein großer Fasan auf der Welt* (Frankfurt am Main: Fischer, 2009), 77.

[20] Herta Müller, "Die große schwarze Achse," in *Barfüßiger Februar* (Berlin: Rotbuch, 1990), 6–24, here 7, 12.

[21] Müller, *Fasan*, 42.

[22] Müller, *Fasan*, 72.

[23] Müller, *Fasan*, 80.

[24] Herta Müller, "Dorfchronik," in *Niederungen*, 125–38, here 134.

[25] Müller, "Dorfchronik," 138.

[26] Müller, "Dorfchronik," 125, 147, 138.

[27] Müller, "Dorfchronik," 133, 134, 130, 132.

[28] Müller, "Dorfchronik," 131, 128, 135.

[29] Müller, "Gelber Mais, keine Zeit," in *Immer derselbe Schnee und immer derselbe Onkel* (München: Carl Hanser, 2011), 125–45, here 127 quoted in Haines, Brigid, "Return from the Archipelago: Herta Müller's *Atemschaukel* as Soft Memory," in *Herta Müller*, ed. Brigid Haines and Lyn Marven (Oxford: Oxford University Press, 2013), 117–34, here 124. It is also interesting to note how Müller's narrators and sympathetic characters, such as Leo Auberg in *Atemschaukel* (2009), fall back on the creation of phrases as a means to rationalize and cope with their experiences. In the case of *Atemschaukel* this is also linked to Müller's friend and creative collaborator Oscar Pastior—the basis for the character of Leo—and the phrases he used to describe his time as a forced labourer. (Ibid, 127) In many cases across Müller's work the creation and repetition of set phrases serve a self-affirming function.

[30] Watt, "'Landsersprache, Heeressprache, Nazisprache?,'" 429.

[31] Herta Müller, "Und noch erschrickt unser Herz," in *Hunger und Seide*, 19–38, here 37.

[32] Marven, "Herta Müller's *Herztier (The Land of Green Plums)*", 183, 188.

[33] Marven, "Herta Müller's *Herztier*," 181; "'So fremd war das Gebilde," 151.

[34] Gabriela Adameşteanu, "Limba română participă la limba germană în care scriu, un interviu cu Herta Müller," *Revista 22*, October 28, 2003, accessed June 18, 2014,

http://www.revista22.ro/limba-romana-participa-la-limba-germana-in-care-scriu-653.html.

[35] Brigid Haines and Margaret Littler, "Gespräch mit Herta Müller" in *Herta Müller*, ed. Haines and Littler, 14–25, here 15.

[36] Müller, "In jeder Sprache sitzen andere Augen," in *Der König verneigt sich und tötet*, 7–39, here 27–28.

[37] "Ich habe die Sprache gegessen: Interview mit Susanne von Beyer," *Der Spiegel* 35 August 27, 2012, accessed December 31, 2013, http://www.spiegel.de/spiegel/print/d-87908042.html.

[38] Hans Werner Richter, "Wie entstand und was war die Gruppe 47?," 80–81; Watt, "'Landsersprache, Heeressprache, Nazisprache?,'" 428–29, 430.

[39] Watt, "'Landsersprache, Heeressprache, Nazisprache?,'" 429.

[40] Müller, *Lebensangst und Worthunger*, 13 (My emphasis).

[41] Müller, *Lebensangst und Worthunger*, 13.

[42] Klemperer, *The Language of the Third Reich*, 10.

[43] Müller, "Hunger und Seide," in *Hunger und Seide*, 65–87, here 77.

[44] Müller, "In jeder Sprache sitzen andere Augen," 31.

[45] Müller, "Hunger und Seide", 75–76.

[46] Müller, "In jeder Sprache sitzen andere Augen," 32.

[47] Müller, "In jeder Sprache sitzen andere Augen," 32.

[48] "das Rumänische schreibt immer mit, weil es mir in den Blick eingewachsen ist." Müller, *Heimat ist das was gesprochen wird* (Blieskastel: Gollenstein, 2001), 21.

[49] Drace-Francis, "'Beyond the Land of Green Plums': Romanian Culture and Language in Herta Müller's Work," 47.

[50] Müller, "In jeder Sprache sitzen andere Augen," 39.

The Power of Language and Silence: Reinhard Jirgl's *Die Stille*

Dora Osborne, University of Edinburgh

Introduction

REINHARD JIRGL (1953–) is an emphatically German author. He insists that German is "die Sprache in der ich denke, spreche und schreibe,"[1] and the award of several prestigious prizes (including the Büchner Prize in 2010) has confirmed his place in the German literary tradition. Yet Jirgl uses the German language in consistently and characteristically iconoclastic ways to challenge the authority of historical, political, and institutional discourse. Precisely because his work went against the ideological prescriptions of the East German state, it remained unpublished in the GDR, where Jirgl lived and worked. Since unification he has become a prolific author, but has also been criticized for his pessimistic, misanthropic view of history, his focus on German suffering (at the exclusion of the Holocaust), as well as his insistence on what some regard as little more than a linguistic tic, namely his idiosyncratic orthography.[2] His peculiar use of German is bound inextricably to the Third Reich and its legacy, specifically, the radical challenge this period of history posed to language as a mode of representation. Jirgl takes his cue from Arno Schmidt, who responded to the upheavals of war and fascism by rejecting conventional modes of writing and developing an idiosyncratic orthography.[3] Influenced by Michel Foucault, Roland Barthes, and Vilém Flusser, amongst others, Jirgl is also interested in language as a system, which, on the one hand, transcends history, but on the other, is made to function differently according to context. Fundamental to Jirgl's project is his concern for the role of language in the machinations of power and the subjugation of the individual: "Die Kommandohöhen allgemein bilden die *Sphäre der Parolen*; in den untergeordneten Schichten innerhalb der Gesellschaft verzeichnet man die *Wirkungen dieser Parolen*."[4] For Jirgl, the act of remembering is similarly subject to external control through language: in order to remember, the traces of the past must be made part of an objective, external order; but, being made to conform to the rules of language, this version of the past is no longer proper to the individual. In the act of retrieval, something is lost.[5]

As a literary author, Jirgl seeks to reclaim language for the individual by writing against what he calls the "verbindlichen Duden-Norm."[6] His texts are the product of his struggle to wrest language and memory (as necessary means of self-expression) from hegemonic discourse. Jirgl signals the effects of power in his writing through various linguistic devices, for instance, his use of capital letters.[7] Like the fragments uncovered at an archaeological dig, the visual elements of language remain, even outside their historical context, and can be used to make language function differently.[8] Jirgl's prose is experimental in form, but pessimistic in tone, and so oscillates between the two poles of language's liberation from, and enslavement to, the repetitions of history. On one level, the Third Reich represents for Jirgl (merely) another instance of the abuse of power across history, but on another stands out as an extreme instance of the imbrication of German language in mechanisms of power. This essay focuses on Jirgl's 2009 novel *Die Stille*, which, encompassing five generations of a family and five regimes, registers the eruption of violence across the long twentieth century. Yet National Socialism constitutes its undoubted epicenter and as such has far-reaching, detrimental effects that bring the power of language itself into question.

Die Stille is a family history, or rather the history of three families from the Eastern provinces (Niederlausitz and East Prussia).[9] The novel's main protagonist is the sixty-eight-year-old widower and retired doctor, Georg Adam, whose father, August, is murdered on Christmas Eve 1939 and whose mother commits suicide two years later. Together with his younger sister, Felicitas, Georg is taken first to an orphanage and then to live with a local pastor. At the age of twenty-five, he marries Henriette, who is also training to be a doctor; it is her family history that constitutes a substantial part of the narrative. Henriette's maternal grandmother, Hedwig, is the owner of a small estate in the fictional village of Thalow. She has to defend her property repeatedly against attempted appropriation (in the Third Reich for "war purposes" and in the GDR for brown-coal mining). But schooled by the pastor in the language of bureaucracy, she, and subsequently her daughter and grandson, fight for the family property. Whilst this struggle forms an explicit part of the family history, the novel also deals with a pervasive, noxious undercurrent, the source of which is an incestuous affair between Georg and his sister. Felicitas becomes pregnant as a result, and in order to conceal their illicit act, they have their son, Henry, registered as the twin sister of Corinna, the daughter born to Georg and Henriette only a few days earlier. The official documents betray nothing, but truth will out: rejected by his father, Henry attempts suicide as a teenager and Felicitas feels compelled to tell him that she is his real mother. Henry becomes a professor of German, moves to Frankfurt and marries Dorothea. In 2003, he takes up a post in the US, but before he leaves, Felicitas insists that Georg give him the family photo album compiled by Georg's mother-in-law, Johanna. The two men meet one sultry evening in Frankfurt, where, walking along the river, Henry confesses that three years previously he assisted his pseudo-mother's suicide as she lay terminally ill with cancer. Struck with rage, Georg attacks his murderous son. A fray ensues—possibly involving a nearby gang of youths—and Georg is badly beaten. He survives the attack, but his skull must be reconstructed. Although he recovers from the operation and retains normal brain function, he refuses to speak, retreating into a silent world.

In *Die Stille*, family history serves as an allegory for history writ large. Jirgl shows how the long twentieth century devours its children indiscriminately, but that it is overshadowed specifically and emphatically by the Third Reich. This can be seen in the photograph album that structures the narrative: almost half of its one hundred images were taken between 1933 and 1945. Jirgl's novel focuses on the story (*"Unsere=Geschichte"*; 22) of the siblings Georg and Felicitas, where this story is also their shared history, the historical moment into which they are born (the growing domination of the Third Reich), and the legacy they must bear.[10] Their family is marked by a fatal flaw ("Webfehler im genealogischen Stoff"; 136), which becomes visible at critical moments throughout the narrative. With the idea of genealogical fabric, Jirgl mediates between the familial and the sociohistorical, referring in a Foucauldian sense to the discursive structures that govern society and make up the texture of history. Thus the fatal family flaw in *Die Stille* is symbolic of the downfall of a nation in the twentieth century. Similarly, the "Logopathie" (324) affecting Georg Adam after his accident can be read as the post-traumatic symptom of the century's upheavals. *Die Stille* even describes an attachment to, and desire for, this aphasic state where the truth of events has been overwritten by official documents, silenced by the authorities, or displaced by the accounts of others. Indeed *Die Stille* centers on stillness and silence and encompasses both their positive and negative connotations: it refers to the calm that comes after conflict, but also the terrifying nothingness that echoes in the wake of catastrophe, in other words, to both contemplative solitude and the taboo and repression surrounding unspeakable events.[11] Yet Jirgl's five-hundred-page novel is anything but taciturn: like the paradoxically verbose *Sprachkrise* of Modernism, it uses a barrage of complex, elaborate German to circumscribe the absence or refusal of language at its center.[12] Considering the function of bureaucratic jargon, photography, and stillness in the novel, we can see how Jirgl seeks to articulate the legacy of unspeakable violence that underlies *Die Stille* through the interplay of language and its negation.

Official Language

Die Stille uses language to show the tyranny of the dominant regime in general and of National Socialism in particular. As in his other texts, Jirgl uses Fraktur, a typeface linked inextricably to the Third Reich, to signal ideological clichés associated with that regime:[13] "**kriegswichtig**" (important for the war), "**Auftrag=der=Geschichte=&=der=Rasse**" (34), "**Blitz=Sieg der=Wehrmacht**" (38).[14] These words and phrases proclaim the National Socialist regime's propagandistic rhetoric. Language, power, violence, and history converge in this symbolically loaded typescript, which, as Thorsten Erdbrügger notes, is not only a symbol of National Socialism, but a metaphor for collective memory: these phonetic reminders literally break or rupture (Fraktur = Lat. fractura) the text.[15] The use of the equals sign, meanwhile, signals the inseparability of Nazi actions and ideology, and moreover, the link—both constructed and extant—between National Socialism and German history.

The violent impact of the Nazi regime is also symbolized in the rupture of the family. Born on September 1, 1939, Felicitas stands in for the war and the misfortune it brings. Since she represents the absolute opposite of the happiness or good fortune her name signifies, she is also made to symbolize the radical overturning of the order of language. If Georg's sister is a personification of the Second World War,[16] his unwanted son embodies its burdensome legacy. Georg only wants to forget his unfortunate union with Felicitas, but Henry is the abject reminder of their incestuous affair, who cannot or must not be integrated into the familial and social order, and who remains a scornful monument to his disgraceful past (186). Also in the inauspicious year of 1939 Georg's father, August Adam, is murdered, and in his place comes the war, father of all things in a brutal century ("*Derkrieg als Dervater Allerdinge*"; 250). The death of the father signals the end of the family: suppressed by the authorities, Georg's mother is driven to suicide and her children are given over to the state. In the orphanage, they are confronted with the incontrovertible fact of war—"Jetzt war ER=!Hier: DER KRIEG" (49)—its presence in the here and now underscored by an exclamation mark; they are barked at in Nazi slogans—"ERZIEHUNG ZU ANSTAND ORDNUNG SAUBERKEIT" (47)—and threatened by punitive discourse rendered in Fraktur—"**Deine Strafe ist noch lange !nicht zuende**" (50). In a time of political turbulence, no one is interested in investigating August Adam's murder properly. Instead the German authorities use the official documents that remain to appropriate power and establish themselves as the ruling force: "**Blitz=Sieg der=Wehrmacht** in Polen schwemmte aus dem Himmel des Krieges den-Behörden die-Aktenflut an—denn jeder Sieger muß auch das-Gesetz des Besiegten besiegen. . . . ." And the crime is simply pinned on the enemy: "Und weils in die Zeitstimmung passte, schob Man kurzerhand Dietat-am-Fluß=dem-Pollack zu" (38). The language of bureaucracy and administration speaks the law. No matter if the documents are made to speak differently, more opportunistically, and the truth about a man's death is silenced.

The case of August Adam is no exception. Jirgl's starting point for *Die Stille* was his confrontation with the bureaucratic reduction of the individual to the sum of his uniformly recordable data ("dem verwaltbar Biographischen"; 86), a reduction necessary above all for the efficient administration of war (88).[17] Jirgl is concerned to show how those in power use official documents to control the individual. Such documents are the product of a particular historical era, which they survive in files and archives: "Die Staaten kommen und gehen, die Akten (Dokumente, Urkunden etc.) = die bürokratisch geronnenen Geschichtszeugen aber bleiben."[18] As such they can be appropriated and instrumentalized by the next regime. In this unending process, the fate of the individual is a matter of indifference, subsumed in the broader effects of power: "*In Zeiten wo Leben's Sicherheit nicht mehr garantiert ist von Papieren, denn Papier kann MAN mit Herrschaft's Pfoten zerreißen [. . .]. Unter den Zungen von Denunzianten werden Papiere zu Listen: Deportation Zwang's Arbeit Tod. Jeder Tote 1 Strich auf einer Liste—Millionen Striche [. . .] die Auferstehung der Akten. . . . .:Die bleiben*" (245). Jirgl's extended ellipsis (five dots) makes visible the construction of text as a kind of pixelation in the moment of its disintegration, and it appears in front of words that signal a threat (in the most extreme case, death) to the individual.[19] Here, the documents that remain and are resurrected under another regime represent a mortal danger to those not favored by the authorities.

Jirgl makes Hedwig's protracted struggle to keep her property emblematic for the latent, enduring, but indifferent power of bureaucratic language. Even when it seems the case is closed and Thalow will remain in the Baeskes' hands, the files remain, waiting to be retrieved by the next regime: "*Es fängt immerwieder an, die-Akten & die-Vorgänge; von Papier bist du zu Papier wirst du: die einzig=wirkliche Auferstehung heißt Bürokratie. . . . .Und mit ihr aufersteht die-Bosheit*" (193). The official notice Hedwig receives from the Wehrmacht informing her that her estate is to be appropriated by the state is shot through with the aggressive bureaucratic language of National Socialism: "Das *Heil Hitler!* zum Abschluß, der fettige Stempel sowie die steil=zackige Unterschrift des Bürgermeisters wie eine schwarze Wunde mit zerrissenem Verband" (198). Yet this language is merely a code like any other, which can be learned and used, and so the pastor, keen to see the mayor exposed for his underhand dealings in the matter of August Adam's murder, schools Hedwig in Nazi "Amtssprache" and empowers her to fight back (205). Hedwig's assault works: the unscrupulous mayor is sent to the front, where he disappears, and she is able to keep her property for the time being. But "*Die-Sprache-der-Ämter & des-Staatz [. . .] ist die Sprache des Todes*" and a threatening paper trail remains: "*-Doch bleiben wie=immer die-Akten. . . . .*" (214). The ideologically saturated rhetoric of NS administration is latent in the documents that remain and are re-inscribed in the next regime. A table with three columns, each containing the letter written in defense of Hedwig's property as a kind of template, shows how content and bureaucratic form do not change, only the various formulations, such as opening and closing greetings ("Heil Hitler!," "Mit sozialistischem Gruß," "Mit freundlichen Grüßen"), and the respective examples of good citizenship and service: in the Third Reich to Führer and Fatherland; in the GDR to world peace and the socialist society; in the Berlin Republic to Germany's economic status (343–44). For Jirgl, this is "kein Zeiten-, sondern ein Zeichenwechsel": the times do not change, only the dominant social and political codes.[20]

Photo Album

In contrast to her mother-in-law Hedwig, who from her subordinate position is forced to ape the language of the oppressors, Johanna goes against the grain of dominant discourse. As well as an official account book (for her husband's shop), she keeps an unofficial, secret diary, dubbed "Das Buch Johanna" (233). This is not an easily decipherable document, precisely because it is only meant to be read by its author: between its covers, Johanna expresses her feelings about a loveless and, for a long time, childless marriage, as well as her suspicions about her husband's infidelity. At first Georg fails to understand its significance, flicking through it like a "Daumenkino," but then, scrutinizing the tiny Morse code-like pencil markings, he discovers "im Telegrammstil die Leben's Bilanz 1 verheirateten Frau" (235). In the enigmatic, idiosyncratic form of "Das Buch Johanna" Georg sees the "Grundstock" for her most significant document, the photo album that is passed on to Henry (235). Using pictures, not words, and rejecting chronological order in favor of "einer in rätselhaften Zeitsprüngen zusammengestellten Abfolge" (14), the album is an unconventional family archive, governed by poetry, senility, or coincidence (181). Together with her diary, it resists the manipulations of power to which official documents both testify and contribute. As Dieter Stolz notes, the photograph album in *Die Stille* suggests links to Günter Grass's *Die Blechtrommel*, where the narrator also uses a family album to tell his epic tale.[21] Beyond this, it can be read as a part of a tendency in recent German literature to use photographic material (either as physical insert or narrative description) in the attempt to remember, recollect, or mediate the past, specifically the experiences—personal and collective— of the twentieth century (Marcel Beyer, Monika Maron, W. G. Sebald, Uwe Timm). For these authors, photographs function as a kind of textual supplement where language is found wanting in remembering an often traumatic past, and they allow for the belated or fantasy construction of family narratives in the face of loss.[22] Within *Die Stille* photographs testify to the women's attempts to keep the (illusion of) family together even when this is being torn apart by war and dictatorships: Hedwig tries to assert power over her fate by showing herself as matriarch with her family gathered round her (196). However, the album and its images have a very specific function for the narrative more broadly, namely, to objectify the process of memory.

With his photo album Jirgl adopts and adapts a Schmidtian device. The photo-album structure features in two of Schmidt's prose works, *Die Umsiedler* (1952)—which, as Julian Reidy has recently shown, forms a major point of dialogue with Jirgl's expulsion novel, *Die Unvollendeten* (2003)[23]—and *Seelandschaft mit Pocahontas* (1953), and is used to visualize and configure the process of remembering:

> man erinnere sich eines beliebigen kleineren Erlebniskomplexes, sei es "Volksschule," "alte Sommerreise"—immer erscheinen zunächst, zeitrafferisch, einzelne sehr helle Bilder (meine Kurzbezeichnung: "Fotos"), um die herum sich dann im weiteren Verlauf der "Erinnerung" ergänzend erläuternde Kleinbruchstücke ("Texte") stellen: ein solches Gemisch von "Foto=Text=Einheiten" ist schließlich das Endergebnis jedes bewußten Erinnerungsversuches.[24]

Jirgl develops this premise in *Die Stille*, using forty-five chapters to represent the forty-five pages of the album, and the descriptions of one, two, or three numbered photographs in each chapter to represent the images affixed to each page. Below each image description is a more elaborate text, the character count of which indicates the area (mm^2) of the photo.[25] "Writing" the surface of photographs in this way allows Jirgl to deconstruct and thus "decode" what Flusser, in his philosophy of photography, identifies as the assumed, ideologically predicated, link between the visual content and significance of the technical image.[26] Jirgl gives us these details about format and composition, but the pictures as such are not reproduced in the text. Moreover, the texts describe the preceding images only exceptionally (photographs 1 and 2 are described in the text following photo 2). Sometimes a text corresponds to the time and occasion of a photograph (for instance, descriptions of the time following Henriette's birth follow pictures of her as a newborn baby). But more often than not, the text does not correspond to the image, even describing a completely different era (for example, a picture from the First World War and a description of life in the Third Reich). Elsewhere, the text gives a detailed description of a photograph that refers to another image in the album, which the reader has to locate by cross-referencing. In addition to these irregular correspondences, arrows in the text direct the reader to another photograph elsewhere in the album, introducing an alternative to a linear mode of reading. These signs function like the hyperlinks in Jirgl's previous novel, *Abtrünnig* (2005), which produced a database structure, countering the linearity of narrative and allowing for different modes of maneuvering through the text.[27] This technique is developed in *Die Stille*, where the photo album—as Lev Manovich notes, a traditional form, but one already inscribed with a "database-like structure"[28]—with its alternative, non-linear structure, can also be seen as a family database.

Whilst the photo album in *Die Stille* shows possible new ways of structuring narrative, it also reveals its constitutional lack. According to Jirgl, remembering is Janus-faced: it is a process of externalization, objectivization, and thus archivization that allows for the retrieval of memory only in losing something of the past.[29] As it is passed between different people, the album produces acts of narrative, but it also reveals physical and metaphorical gaps in the memory and history of the family: "*als seien die chemisch erstarrten 4eck-Bilder stets nur angefangene, nicht zuende formulierte Sätze*" (420). The album as artefact feels soft to the touch (14), and is so fragile it threatens to fall to dust (122). Various pictures are missing from the album, but these are not accidental losses, rather forceful removals. Thus the absences symbolize not only the gaps in memory, narrative, and history, but, moreover, the violent effects of hegemonic discourse on the memory of the past. For the historian and philologist Henry, such gaps, read in relation to that which remains, are the stuff of history: "So können hier die beiden Photos, was die fehlenden verschweigen, uns vielleicht sogar besser, als wären sie noch da, erzählen" (136). But for Georg, the album symbolizes the burden of the past: it weighs heavily in his hands (16), and he hopes Henry will leave it behind to be cleared from his flat along with the other detritus (17). Felicitas, who only reminds Georg of his shameful past (and in a symbolic sense, the misdeeds of war and fascism), brandishes the album like a weapon (14). She forces it on her brother "*wie ein uraltes aus Ge&verboten bestehendes Gesetzwerk [. . .] getränkt mit Wut u Schande*" (67). For Georg, who desires the eradication of the family line—a veritable Bernhardian "Auslöschung"—the album, even or precisely in its incomplete form, is an unwanted provocation. Two photos have been removed, but "ebenso sind 2 Photos !geblieben. Wenn Vergangenheit !alles löschen will—?weshalb dann sind diese=beiden noch-?da" (136).[30]

The first book of *Die Stille*, "Aschenbrut," tells of the persistent traces of life that creep from the residues of destruction, of Georg's son who carries on living, reminding him of his shameful past, despite Georg's wish that he die. Georg wants every trace of his own existence to be eradicated: "Was mich betrifft, ich will, wenns mit mir vorbei sein wird, daß von mir nichts übrigbleibt" (286), and it seems this desire will be fulfilled when, at the end of this first part, he is left for dead following the brutal attack by the youths. The last photograph is one of those that have been torn from the album, although its center has been preserved. Exceptionally, Jirgl represents this with a black rectangle that fills the page beneath the photo's description. Seventeen lines of text, all but the last of which are set inside the box, read like a deeply pessimistic eulogy, which could refer to Georg, but equally to his unwanted son Henry. Despite the desire for eradication, life continues, and this unwanted, continued existence compels change—for Georg his retreat into silence:

> Du wolltest tot sein u: bist
> Unfähig zum Sterben
> Mußt noch immer dauern
> Dauern mußt du
> Anders. (311)[31]

Following the attack, Georg's skull is reconstructed using a pioneering implant technique. When the process has been refined, the body will generate its own tissue to replace this foreign body, resulting in complete recovery: "*Restitutio ad integrum*" (381). But for now, the implant will remain even when his own body has been returned to the earth: "Und wenner tot & verbrannt ist [. . .] dann bleibt immerhin noch Was von ihm" (381). Not only does Georg's treatment ensure his survival (thereby denying him the death that he wishes for), it also deprives him of the ultimate *restitutio ad integrum*, that is, eradication through decomposition. Try as he might, Georg cannot—and will not be able to—do away with the traces of the past. And in this sense, the impossibility of restitution to an original state might also indicate the persistence of past misdeeds: in a juridical sense, *restitutio ad integrum* means compensation that restores the claimant to the original position, but any kind of "Wiedergutmachung" remains elusive here. The failure of medical and organic restitution reminds Georg of his inability to do away with the past, and is an emblem in the novel for the impossibility of full, integral, juridical restitution following the injustices of history.

Silence/Stillness

Georg's death drive is expressed first and foremost in his desire for entropy, stillness, and silence, announced programmatically in the novel's title. As noted above, "Stille" can be read positively or negatively, as peaceful calm or threatening lifelessness: its ambivalence is embodied in the figure of Dorothea, Georg's daughter-in-law, who, both quiet and foreboding as a child, was known as "die Stille" (517). Referring not only to acoustic, but also physical stillness, to stasis, "Stille" contrasts with "Schweigen." Yet "Schweigen" occurs equally frequently in *Die Stille*, and both words carry a fatal significance: "Denn Schweigen u Stille bedeuten Tod" (285). *Die Stille*'s central theme of stillness/silence refers to the oppressive, but nonetheless desired, silence surrounding unspeakable events and unspoken feelings—war, murder, incest, infidelity, rejection (224, 244, 275, 285). Jirgl's title suggests a point of intertextual or intermedial reference with Ingmar Bergman's 1963 film *Das Schweigen*. Set in a fictional town threatened by war, *Das Schweigen* focuses on the intense, incestuous relationship between two sisters who do not understand the local language. With its sparse dialogue and sultry, oppressive atmosphere, the film corresponds to the themes of Jirgl's novel (war, incest, and the breakdown of communication), and both works are set during heat waves.[32] In 1973, Joseph Beuys redoubled Bergman's silence in his multiple piece of the same name, which casts five original reels of the film in zinc. Thus, Beuys preserves the reels, but only in making them unwatchable and obsolete. Beuys's version of *Das Schweigen* implicates Bergman's film in the postwar melancholy underlying his project and symbolized in his use of heavy, dampening materials like felt and lead. Jirgl's novel is equally cloaked in a heavy, melancholy silence and, like Beuys's galvanized film reels, redoubles this in its use of visual material: the photographs that structure the narrative and seemingly preserve (family) history cannot be seen; their factual, textual descriptions make them a tantalizing presence, proffered, but ultimately withheld. Indeed, *Die Stille* describes and reinscribes the silence that characterized the immediate postwar period and that has since been read as symptomatic of Germany's inability to mourn, that is, its resistance to an affective engagement with the Nazi past.[33] Whilst postwar silence is largely acknowledged to have given way to a more explicit and public discourse of memory, the return of the motif of silence in Jirgl's novel suggests, on the one hand, the more lasting effects of National Socialism on language, and on the other, the recurrence of this state of suppression and disavowal. In this context, *Die Stille* has a strong resonance with Gerhard Roth's seven-volume cycle, *Die Archive des Schweigens* (1991), which uses a kind of Foucauldian archaeology to cut through an even more pervasive and persistent silence to unearth the violent, fascist tendencies that underlie postwar Austrian society.[34] As in Roth's *Archive*, the motif of silence in *Die Stille* figures a "critique of language and its use in propagating and maintaining power structures."[35]

Whilst the links to Bergman, Beuys, and Roth underscore the more negative—oppressive and repressive—meaning of *Die Stille*, Jirgl's title might be read as a reference to John Cage's "silent" composition *4′ 33″* from 1952 (elsewhere, Jirgl writes in homage to the composer).[36] In this sense, silence suggests a model for the unburdened existence that the protagonist seeks. Georg's desire for stillness, his retreat into a speechless world, might correspond to the silence of Cage's composition, which is precisely not about the absence or erasure of sound, but about a mode of attention that allows us to hear what is not usually perceived. Georg seeks the visual correlative of this form of auditory stillness in photography. He initially rejects the family photo album he is supposed to pass on to Henry, but after Felicitas brings it to him on one of her hospital visits, he becomes obsessed with it. Yet the album does not arouse his interest because it serves as family archive, rather because it suggests to him a framework for his own anti-memorial, anti-genealogical project (476). Here attention shifts from the photo album as object, record, and legacy (bound up with memory, history, and family), which Georg rejects, to the act of photography as a means of resisting continuity.

Georg becomes a photographer, using a camera to record what happens around him (including the demolition of a nearby village, Rogow, for recently revived brown-coal mining). He not only sees everything through his camera lens, he experiences it at this remove. His eyes appear like "das kühle, unbestechliche Glas zweier Kameraobjektive" (476), and he becomes a kind of camera, merging, as Flusser describes, "into one indivisible function" with the apparatus.[37] Georg Adam uses his camera "in search of information": having rejected language, he finds in photography an extra- or post-linguistic mode of perceiving the world.[38] He is interested not in the superficial, social legibility of the family album, rather in the workings of the camera as perceptual apparatus. Abandoned, destroyed, forgotten, his own pictures are not to be instrumentalized in collective memory through infinite circulation. For Georg Adam, as for Flusser, photography is a posthistorical mode: it is "an act for which reality is information, not the significance of this information."[39] For Flusser, the photographic apparatus can only ever capture the socially codified and constructed meaning predestined for it. In order to decode these "cultural conditions," a photographer would have to "place within the image information that is not predicated within the program of the camera."[40] As photographer, Georg Adam certainly attempts to view the world more critically and objectively, but he does this by *erasing* that which is "predicated within the program of the camera." Georg Adam is "der Erfinder der *nichtorganischen Fotografie*" (496, emphasis in the original), meaning that he excludes organic, specifically human, figures from his photographs. Jirgl refers here to the Japanese photographer Naoya Hatakeyama (534), who, with striking detachment, photographs vast industrial and urban landscapes, highlighting the "dialectical relationship between nature and civilization," but always avoiding human presence.[41] We can imagine how Georg's pictures of the colonnade of industrial vehicles that arrive in Rogow to hollow out the village resemble Hatakeyama's wounded landscapes.[42] For the non-organic photographer Georg (as for Hatakeyama), these are not sorry sights, rather every image of the world at a standstill captures the very state of entropy he strives towards: "aus der Utopie des Verschwindens Die Stille" (496–97). Moreover, whilst these images are divested of human figures, the scenes they capture are not actually unpopulated. Like Hatakeyama, Georg uses long exposure times to ensure that any traces of human presence or passage will not be visible on the image. In this way, his photos *do* carry the presence of anyone there as the picture was taken, but this is not visible as such; rather, like Cage's silence, it must be perceived differently.

Whatever its utopian impulse, Georg's desire for erasure, for stillness, silence, and entropy is, however, deeply problematic. He strives towards the negation of history and language, and thus of the things that define us as human. Indeed Georg's rejection of the past—personal, familial, collective—is also a refusal of responsibility. The protagonist's logopathy is at the center of *Die Stille*, but it is not always clear whether Jirgl's narrative is critical of this failure of language or itself pathologically attached to the tacit condition of its protagonist. For Georg Adam, who sees how language is always implicated in the uses and abuses of power (of which the Nazi dictatorship is merely one example), withdrawing into a solitary, silent world is the only response. His behavior betrays a pessimistic and relativistic view of history, which converges in part with Jirgl's own and has thus invited renewed criticism of his work.[43] But Georg Adam's aphasia also marks point of contrast with the author, for whom the active use of language, despite or because of its compromised status, is an imperative: the violence of history erupts in every text, and it is the task of the author to ensure that this eruption is inscribed in and borne by literature.[44] Jirgl's protagonist desires erasure without trace, but the author knows there can be no "*Restitution ad integrum*": something will remain after all ("dann bleibt immerhin noch Was von ihm"). This remainder may be the "Webfehler im genealogischem Stoff," but it is the stuff of narrative.

Notes

[1] Reinhard Jirgl, "Natur und Gegen-Natur. Bemerkungen über Erinnern—Schreiben—Lesen," in *Land und Beute: Aufsätze aus den Jahren 1996 bis 2006* (Munich: Hanser, 2008), 210–30, here 211.

[2] See Jan Süselbeck, "Kein Vaterland!" *TAZ*, 12 March 2009; Clemens Kammler, "Unschärferelationen. Anmerkungen zu zwei problematischen Lesarten von Reinard Jirgls Familienroman *Die Unvollendeten*," in *Reinhard Jirgl. Perspektiven, Lesarten, Kontexte*, ed. David Clarke and Arne de Winde, *German Monitor* 65 (Amsterdam: Rodopi, 2007), 227–33, and Julian Reidy, "Reinhard Jirgls *Die Unvollendeten* und Arno Schmidts *Die Umsiedler*," *Orbit Literarum*, 67, no. 6 (2012), 494–524. For Katrin Hillgruber, Jirgl's writing manifests the symptoms of a kind of Tourette's syndrome ("Berge, Meere, deutsche Giganten," *Frankfurter Rundschau*, 17 March 2009).

[3] Jirgl, "Sprache ist Heimat oder 'Sind Sie auch allein?!' Arno Schmidt und sein Kurzroman 'Die Umsiedler,'" in *Land und Beute*, 165–82, here 165.

[4] Arne de Winde, Reinhard Jirgl, Bart Philipsen, "Über die Grenzen des Erträglichen. Briefgespräch mit Reinhard Jirgl," *nY: website en tijdschrift voor literatuur, kritiek & amusement*, 13 August 2010, accessed October 9, 2013, http://ny-web.be/transitzone/briefgesprach-jirgl.html.

[5] Reinhard Jirgl, "'Schreiben—das ist meine Art, in der Welt zu sein' Gespräche in Briefen mit Clemens Kammler/Arne de Winde," in *Land und Beute*, 125–62, here 143–44.

[6] Reinhard Jirgl, "Die wilde und die gezähmte Schrift. Eine Arbeitsübersicht," in *Land und Beute*, 92–122, here, 92.

[7] For an explanation of these different devices and their significance, see Jirgl, "Die wilde und die gezähmte Schrift" and Kammler, "Unschärferelationen," 229.

[8] Jirgl, "Die wilde und die gezähmte Schrift," 101.

[9] Reinhard Jirgl, *Die Stille* (Munich: Hanser, 2009). All references will appear in parentheses in the text.

[10] Jirgl's use of = and other linking punctuation counteracts grammar's rigid separation of linguistic elements by imitating in language the physical and symbolic connections between concepts ("Die wilde und die gezähmte Schrift," 117).

[11] Jirgl refers to the ambivalence of the word in his *Mutter Vater Roman* (1990): "es gibt zwei Arten der Stille; die Stille aus dem Nichts und die Stille aus dem ungeheurem Lärm" (Reinhard Jirgl, *Mutter Vater Roman* [Munich: dtv, 2012], 21).

[12] Oliver Jungen notes how Jirgl uses his mastery of language for acts of "phonetische[n] Terrorismus" ("Schluss jetzt mit dem ewigen Wiederkehr!" *Frankfurter Allgemeine*, 12 March 2009).

[13] Martina Meister, "Schauplatz Gedächtnis," *Die Zeit*, 31 March 2009.

[14] For ease of production, Jirgl's use of Fraktur has been rendered here as boldface type, though it should be noted that Jirgl uses boldface type in his prose for other purposes.

[15] Torsten Erdbrügger, "Die Ordnung des Erinnerungsdiskurses. Zur Kritik (phal)logozentrischer Erinnerung in Reinhard Jirgls *Die Stille*," in *Geschlechtergedächtnisse: Gender-Konstellationen und Erinnerungsmuster in Literatur und Film der Gegenwart*, ed. Ilse Nagelschmidt, Inga Probst, and Torsten Erdbrügger (Frank & Timme: Berlin, 2010), 135–159, here 154.

[16] Jungen, "Schluss jetzt mit dem ewigen Wiederkehr!"

[17] de Winde, Jirgl, Philipsen, "Über die Grenzen des Erträglichen."

[18] de Winde, Jirgl, Philipsen, "Über die Grenzen des Erträglichen."

[19] Jirgl, "Die wilde und die gezähmte Schrift," 120.

[20] Reinhard Jirgl, "Praemeditatio malorum—Schreiben am mitternächtigen Ort," http://www.deutscheakademie.de/druckversionen/DankredeBuechner.pdf (accessed 12 November 2013).

[21] See Dieter Stolz, "'45 Seiten aus dickem braunen Velourspapier beklebt mit 100 Mal geronnenem Tod'. Reinhard Jirgls Roman *Die Stille*," *Text und Kritik* 189 (2011): 57–68 and "Was auf dieser Welt, welcher Roman hätte die epische Breite eines Fotoalbums?" Photography and the Art of Modern Fiction in the

Works of Arno Schmidt, Günter Grass and Reinhard Baumgart," in *New German Literature: Life-Writing and Dialogue with the Arts*, ed. Julian Preece, Frank Finlay, and Ruth J. Owen (Oxford: Peter Lang, 2007), 23–35. Lothar Müller contrasts Jirgl's use of the photo album with its suturing effects in Gunter Grass's *Die Box* which appeared the year before ("Sturz in den Abgrund: Im Mahlstrom der Geschichte," *Süddeutsche Zeitung*, 18 April 2009.

[22] See Marianne Hirsch, *Family Frames: Photography, Narrative and Postmemory* (Cambridge, MA: Harvard University Press, 1997).

[23] Reidy, "Reinhard Jirgls *Die Unvollendeten.*"

[24] Arno Schmidt, "Berechnungen 1," *Bargfelder Ausgabe*, vol. III/3 (Zurich: Haffmans, 1995), 164.

[25] Stolz, "45 Seiten," 67.

[26] Vilém Flusser, *Towards a Philosophy of Photography*, trans. Anthony Mathews (London: Reaktion, 2000), 46–48. Jirgl's technique is reminiscent of that used by Gerhard Roth in his photographic project *Die Archive des Schweigens* and described by the author in "Reise durch das Bewußtsein. Ein Monolog von Gerhard Roth über *Die Archive des Schweigens*, aufgezeichnet von Kristina Pfoser-Schewig," in *Gerhard Roth: Materialien zu "Die Archive des Schweigens,"* ed. Uwe Wittstock (Frankfurt am Main: Fischer, 1992), 82–94, here, 92–93. The two projects resonate further through the motif of silence, which I go on to discuss.

[27] See Kristin Veel, "Maneuvering in Nervous Times: The Hyperlinks in Reinhard Jirgl's *Abtrünnig*," *German Quarterly* 85, no. 4 (2012): 455–71.

[28] Lev Manovich, *The Language of New Media* (Cambridge, MA: MIT Press, 2001), 219.

[29] Jirgl, "Schreiben—das ist meine Art, in der Welt zu sein," 143–44.

[30] At the beginning of *Auslöschung*, Bernhard's protagonist discusses at length the two photographs of his dead parents and brother, which remain where they (and other images) do not (Thomas Bernhard, *Auslöschung* [Frankfurt am Main: Suhrkamp, 1988], 21–31).

[31] The refusal of language as a response to a legacy of guilt suggests another link to Günter Grass's *Die Blechtrommel*, in which the anti-hero Oskar Matzerath causes himself to have an accident after which he refuses to grow. The three-year-old remains an infant (*in-fans*) who refuses language and makes his drum his mouthpiece. As well as the similarity to Jirgl's voluntarily mute protagonist, a link might be traced from Oskar's use of his drum as prosthetic mouthpiece to Jirgl's story of a refugee who arrives in Thalow after having been raped by Russian soldiers. Quite traumatized, she can only blow on a toy trumpet that has been hung round her neck by her aggressors (331–34).

[32] In Bergman's film, one of the sisters is dying of consumption, a fate possibly shared by Henry, who returns from America only to die following a short, intense illness that centers on his mouth, producing acute coughing fits and preventing him from speaking (489).

[33] Aleida Assmann notes how silence inflects the responses of both victims (as defense mechanism) and perpetrators (as disavowal); the difference can be understood in terms of the German terms "Schweigen" and "*Verschweigen*" (*Der lange*

Schatten der Vergangenheit: Erinnerungskultur und Geschichtspolitik [Munich: Beck, 2006], 82, 176–79). Ernestine Schlant has also shown how postwar silence is inscribed in literature (*The Language of Silence: West German Literature and the Holocaust* [New York: Routledge, 1999]).

[34] Gerhard Roth, *Die Archive des Schweigens*, 7 vols. (Frankfurt am Main: Fischer, 1991).

[35] Robert Halsall, "Language and Silence: Gerhard Roth's *Die Archive des Schweigens*," in *"Whose Story?": Continuities in Contemporary German-Language Literature* (Bern: Peter Lang, 1998), 133–47, here 135. Like Jirgl, Roth also uses textual devices to show these power relations. Bianca Theisen notes how Roth's use of italics "implies a latent violence in the way such a use of language appropriates the reality it describes" (Theisen, *Silenced Facts: Media Montages in Contemporary Austrian Literature*, Amsterdamer Publikationen zur Sprache und Literatur 152 [Amsterdam: Rodopi, 2003], 160).

[36] Reinhard Jirgl, "Hommage à John Cage," *Text und Kritik*, 3–13.

[37] Flusser, *Towards a Philosophy of Photography*, 39.

[38] Flusser, *Towards a Philosophy of Photography*, 27.

[39] Flusser, *Towards a Philosophy of Photography*, 17–18, 39.

[40] Flusser, *Towards a Philosophy of Photography*, 34, 84.

[41] Stephan Berg, "Foreword," Stephen Berg, Charlotte Cotton, Naoya Hatakeyama, *Naoya Hatakeyama* (Ostfildern-Ruit: Hatje Cantz, 2002), 7.

[42] Hanno Rauterberg, "Zerschlissen, zertrümmert," *Die Zeit*, 18 April 2002.

[43] See Süselbeck, "Kein Vaterland!" and Hillgruber, "Berge, Meere, deutsche Giganten."

[44] Jirgl, "Die wilde und die gezähmte Schrift," 116.

Words and Music

"Disrupted Language, Disrupted Culture": Hanns Eisler's *Hollywooder Liederbuch* (1942-43)

James Parsons, Missouri State University

FROM AMONG THE MANY German-speaking émigrés in 1940s Los Angeles it is difficult to imagine two with seemingly more different views on the time-honored Lied than Hanns Eisler and Thomas Mann.[1] What perhaps is most surprising is that Mann or Eisler gave the German art song any thought, for by the twentieth century's fifth decade the favored mode of musical expression of Hugo Wolf, Johannes Brahms, Robert Schumann, and, above all, Franz Schubert—nineteenth-century composers all—found its critical fortunes waning. The author of *Der Tod in Venedig* and *Der Zauberberg* simultaneously lauded the genre while holding it responsible for the Third Reich. Eisler traveled a different path. Then devoting most of his attention to film music, little by little he also began composing Lieder, the result of which is an anthology of forty-seven, most dating to his first fifteen months in California beginning in May 1942, known as the *Hollywooder Liederbuch* (see the appendix for an overview).[2] In this essay I make the case that German song provided Eisler with a medium to mediate a left-behind world and one that was at the time decidedly unsettled. I therefore part company with most scholars who have examined the composer's lyric omnibus. It is not an exile's outcry of despair, a retreat from life.[3] It is his sonic shield and sword.

In advance of his novel *Doktor Faustus* (begun 1943, published 1947) Mann, on May 29, 1945, previewed his views on German music in a speech he gave less than a month after Hitler's death. Calling his talk "Germany and the Germans," he asserts that "music is a demonic realm . . . Christian art with a negative prefix . . . calculated order and chaos-breeding irrationality at once, rich in conjuring, in incantatory gestures, in magic numbers, the most unrealistic and yet the most impassioned of arts, mystical and abstract." Laying a base for the equation that the German cult of music carries an unsuspected evil, the syphilitic infection of the fictional composer Adrian Leverkühn he will develop in *Doktor Faustus*, Mann charts "a secret union of the German sprit with the Demonic" through the plotline of a musical Faust. This bond has filled many a German "with arrogant knowledge that he surpasses the world in 'depth,'" the latter a concept Mann defines as "the musicality of the German soul, that which we call its inwardness, its subjectivity." Although inwardness is a German's "most notable" quality, defining it is not easy. Mann accordingly enlists "tenderness, depth of feeling, unworldly reverie, love of nature, purest sincerity of thought and conscience." These "are the characteristics of high lyricism," attributes that ensure that "even today the world cannot forget what it owes the German inwardness: German metaphysics, German music, especially the miracle of the German Lied—a nationally unique and incomparable product."[4]

In this essay, I do not defend the Lied from Mann's allegation or argue that because of Eisler's dedication to the genre it experienced anything other than a resplendent albeit fleeting rebirth. Focusing on three of the California songs, what I argue is this: Eisler does not bring more chaos into the world or engage in an "arrogant" display of knowledge. Without discarding the centrality Mann accords music in his "Germany and the Germans" address, Eisler may be said to invert one of its guiding principles, that "there are *not* two Germanys, a good one and a bad one, but only one, whose best turned into evil through devilish cunning."[5] With cunningness of a different kind, Eisler contemplates the challenges of expatriation and Germany's moral collapse, and yet—with one all-important caveat that I spell out at the end of this essay—uses music in the service of good. Eisler both embraces and eschews the traditional cyclic coherence by and large typical of a song cycle (for example Beethoven's *An die ferne Geliebte*), a stratagem that allows him to symbolize an existence formerly in possession of stability, now in search of its restoration. Acknowledging but just as often contravening the conventions of German song, the collection's cornerstone is constructive conflict. Eisler signals that characteristic in the work's title. With Lieder he bows to that most universalizing yet inner-directed of musical mediums. With the California *Traumstadt* he specifies the city's celluloid commodity, one that, as Eisler himself writes, rolls off an assembly line like an automobile: "whatever passes through the machinery bears its mark, is predigested, neutralized, leveled down."[6] Because German song enjoyed a long association with individual identity formation, it provides Eisler with a potent means to ponder the loss of a defining aspect of selfhood. What better way to treat the dispossession of home and self than by turning to a body of music with deep ties to those topics yet currently in the process of losing them?[7]

I first turn to Eisler's dual mediation of inclusion and exclusion in "Erinnerung an Eichendorff und Schumann." Composed April 19, 1943, the Lied is a setting of the first four lines of an 1833 single octave Joseph von Eichendorff poem, "In der Fremde," one Robert Schumann made the lead number of his 1840 Opus 39 *Liederkreis*. As Eisler's title confirms, words and music are equals. What he recollects is not one or the other but both. Whereas in many of his California songs Eisler, however subtly or overtly, alludes to past music, there is no such connotation here. Eisler's title promises just that, the very thing he withholds, and so the past is and is not present, suggesting again the exile's shattered link with what has come before. "Heimat" is a central element, yet the poet never makes known its location. He mentions a father and mother only to disclose that they are "lange todt." That those living in the unspecified locale once knew the poetic persona but no longer do only intensifies the broken connection to the past. Here is Eichendorff's poem with the second half bracketed to indicate Eisler's partial setting of only the first half.

> Aus der Heimat hinter den Blitzen roth
> Da kommen die Wolken her,
> Aber Vater und Mutter sind lange todt,
> Es kennt mich dort Keiner mehr.
>
> [Wie bald, wie bald kommt die stille Zeit,
> Da ruhe ich auch, und über mir
> Rauschet die schöne Waldeinsamkeit
> Und keiner mehr kennt mich auch hier.][8]

Given the time and place when Eisler composed the song, one understands his exclusion of the poem's second half, for it is there that Eichendorff envisions "the peaceful time" of "rest," one he emphasizes in the repeated "Wie bald, wie bald." In 1943 the return of "die stille Zeit" was something no one could have predicted. While omitting the poem's second half, Eisler's title plus the fame of Schumann's earlier setting encourages one to seek out the absent lines. Eisler's aim is for listeners to grapple with what is and is not included and so enlarge for themselves a song's expressive potential. Most importantly, naming but not quoting Schumann allows Eisler to expand a key element of Eichendorff's poem and Schumann's setting: "Heimat," a word German Romantics understood as the promise of home, never attainable but something one nevertheless should ever seek. Ludwig Tieck draws attention to this perpetual *Sehnsucht* when, in the first two lines of his poem "Ferne," he asks, "O alte Heimat süß! wo find' ich wieder dich?"[9] Experienced "beyond the red lightning" in Eichendorff's poem, the fact that Eisler avoids referencing Schumann's song allows him to accentuate the distance from home.

Does Eisler intend his Eichendorff truncation and silent citation of Schumann positively? Throughout the song (Ex. 1) he instructs the piano to maintain a *pianissimo* dynamic level and, in the left hand, as if machine driven, all twenty-two measures are staccato reiterated eighth notes. The voice does not diminish the song's brittleness, for Eisler heads the piece "mit bitterem Ausdruck, scharf." On the surface, then, the song gives

Ex. 1. Hanns Eisler, "Erinnerung an Eichendorff und Schumann,"
Hollywooder Liederbuch (Leipzig: Deutscher Verlag für Musik, 2008).
Copyright by Deutscher Verlag für Musik, Leipzig.

evidence of supporting the view of Eisler's friend Theodor W. Adorno, fellow California exile and one-time collaborator, who, in his *Minima Moralia: Reflexionen aus dem beschädigten Leben*, concludes that "Jeder Intellektuelle in der Emigration, ohne alle Ausnahme, ist beschädigt . . . Enteignet ist seine Sprache und abgegraben die geschichtliche Dimension, aus der seine Erkenntnis die Kräfte zog."[10]

Whereas Adorno may mean his aphorism dialectically, with Eisler there is little reason to doubt that what he leaves out of "Erinnerung an Eichendorff und Schumann" partakes precisely of dialecticism. Corroboration comes from a number of sources. One is the composer's own late-life statement when he describes himself as an "old Hegelian."[11] There also is the *Liederbuch*, above all "Nightmare," the only song for which Eisler wrote the music and text in its entirety.[12] Dating from late 1947, four years after most of the other California songs, it documents his ill-fated imbroglio with the House Un-American Activities Committee, an experience that Eisler characterized as "sinister and ridiculous" and that sparked a media frenzy that led to his forced departure from the United States on March 26, 1948.[13] "Nightmare" also clarifies his method of constructive conflict, one he distills from, among other sources, Hegel:

> The rat men accused me of not liking stench,
> Of not liking garbage, of not liking their squeals,
> Of not liking to eat dirt.
> For days they argued, considering the question from every angle,
> Finally they condemned me.
> You don't like stench,
> You don't like garbage, you don't like our squeals,
> You don't like to eat dirt.

What most draws the listener in is not Eisler's scorn when he calls his tormenters rat men—the English "rat" a clever play on the German "der Rat" (councillor)—or charges that they bandy their questions as do squealing animals. Nor is the highpoint the dialectically-rendered thought that those who reproach others for not liking stench and garbage enjoy those things themselves. The most arresting moment is the cross-cut change he reserves for his Hegel homage: "For days they argued, considering the question from every angle" (Ex. 2). With admirable economy Eisler sums up Hegel's dialectic in six words. Of course his HUAC examiners did nothing of the kind. Against the witch-hunt climate of the time, they posed their formulaic questions but had no interest in answers not conforming to what they already believed.

With the text set out in ABA form, the music follows suit. The quick-tempo outer sections are raucously percussive, the piano launching the Lied with four and a half measures of heavily accented repeated eighth-note F-G major seconds in an ear-assaulting high range in the right hand to which the left counters with D-E major seconds. The entrance of the voice with its rapid speech-like rhythms prods the piano into obsessive overdrive, both hands pounding out in octaves the D-E dyads for five measures before moving on to three measures of B-C minor seconds. Cacophony reigns over all. Following this, what measure 14 brings is extraordinary. Yapping discord abruptly acquiesces to the piano's

Ex. 2. Hanns Eisler, "Nightmare," *Hollywooder Liederbuch* (Leipzig: *Deutscher Verlag für Musik, 2008*). Copyright by Deutscher Verlag für Musik, Leipzig.

Ex. 2.—(concluded)

widely-spaced, predominantly consonant block chords, above which the voice lyrically soars. Song is now the crucible of justice previously denied. Not allowed to read a prepared text in Washington, DC, Eisler now speaks—sings—his piece.[14] With an ever-changing variety of syncopated rhythmic patterns the voice defies the piano's lockstep duple meter. It is in the central B section, lasting only eleven measures, where Eisler, like a sculpture carving in relief, places the words "considering the question from every angle." The word sustained the longest is "angle," an appropriate gesture given that questions should be subjected to a variety of perspectives, the thing lacking when Eisler's HUAC interviewers queried him. Highlighting the word "angle" and its Hegelian dialectic within the clatter of the A sections that frames it, Eisler transcends the vexations of 1947 and, if only in song, wins a victory for open-mindedness. Doing so, he provides a memorable example of Hegel's conviction that art aspires to knowledge.[15] Similarly, these eleven measures confirm a point Adorno makes in his 1949 *Philosophie der Neuen Musik*, published two years after "Nightmare." "Die neue Musik," he remarks, "nimmt den Widerspruch, in dem sie zur Realität steht, ins eigene Bewußtsein und in die eigene Gestalt auf. In solchem Verhalten schärft sie sich zur Erkenntnis."[16]

Sharpened knowledge suffuses the *Liederbuch*. Although loss tempers "Erinnerung an Eichendorff und Schumann" and indeed much of the collection, forfeiture is not the chief topic. Nor in "Nightmare" is Eisler a victim. In contrast to Adorno's *Minima Moralia* dictum, nowhere in the *Liederbuch* does Eisler give evidence that exile depletes the historical dimension nurturing understanding. His position is different. Another friend, German Marxist philosopher Ernst Bloch, who, like Adorno and Eisler, lived in the United States during the Third Reich, articulates that stance in a 1939 lecture. "The German writer," Bloch contends,

> brings his roots with him: a mature language, an old culture. He remains faithful to them not by making museum-pieces out of them, but by testing and quickening his powers of expression on the new stuff of life . . . It will remain, insofar as it succeeds, a deeply original creation, fostered by double but not divided loyalties—by memory and a vigorous faith in the future . . . We are creating on the frontier of two epochs. We, German writers in America, are frontier-men in a doubly legitimate sense—both temporally and spatially and we are working at the one necessary task: the realization of the rights of man.[17]

Bloch's thought that exile can inspire a duality leading to "the new stuff of life" is provocative. In "Erinnerung an Eichendorff und Schumann" Eisler mediates between a new and "an old culture," inclusion and absence, the fragment and the whole. Within a song collection most of whose texts are in German, "Nightmare" moves between adaptation and resistance, drawing on the disparity between English and German together with opposing musical styles to fight for "the one necessary task," "the rights of man."

Doubleness also informs the shared investigation Eisler wrote with Adorno while composing the *Liederbuch*, their book *Composing for the Films*, begun in 1941 but not published until 1947. Both the *Liederbuch* and the film music study consider creative contradictions, yet not according to either-or juxtapositions. Coherence and continuity have meaning only when conceptual opposites meet in lively interaction. In the section leading up to and including "Montage" in the film music study, Adorno and Eisler maintain that individual components "never coincide *per se.* If the concept of montage . . . has any justification, it is to be found in the relation between" constituent elements. That association "is not one of similarity, but . . . of question and answer, affirmation and negation, appearance and essence." "Montage," they continue, "makes the best of the aesthetically accidental . . . by transforming an entirely extraneous relation into a virtual element of expression." In film, music ought to create "a stimulus of motion, not a reduplication of motion." Therefore "the relation between music and film is antithetic at the very moment when the deepest unity is achieved."[18]

The two earliest songs, "Der Sohn I" and "Der Sohn II," illustrate antithetical unity with elegant simplicity, yet they prompt a question: should these Lieder begin the collection? More pressing, does Eisler conceive the *Liederbuch* as a totality? Eisler leaves the matter open-ended, a reality with implications for performers and listeners alike, for it is we who must determine order of performance and the number of songs to include. Complicating things is the fact that these two songs are linked by their titles, just as both are settings of Brecht poems. This too invites those inclined to come to terms with the *Liederbuch* to transform "an entirely extraneous relation into a virtual element of expression." With the titles "Der Sohn I" and "Der Sohn II" Eisler stresses these songs' close relationship, yet also their distinctness. Within Brecht's output these poems are related only to the extent that he wrote both of them during his Finnish exile in 1940.[19] What emerges is that Eisler takes two Brecht poems and brings them together because of their topical similarities. Whereas "Der Sohn I" treats a mother and son in the initial throes of exile, "Der Sohn II" deals with a father and son, who, slightly further on in their adjustment to their new situation, contemplate from dual perspectives what matters most to a person in flight. When in "II" the son asks "Soll ich Geschichte lernen?," the father responds "Wozu, möchte ich fragen, Lerne nur, Deinen Kopf in die Erde zu stecken."[20] Apparently but not categorically bestowing the same title on two distinct Lieder, Eisler avoids "aesthetic empathy." The two songs serve as mutual stimulants, accommodating beginning and not beginning, of "affirmation and negation."

Probing deeper into "Der Sohn I" affords insight into the ways Eisler negotiates contradictions. "Appearance and essence" manifest themselves in the song's outward division into strophic halves (see Ex. 3). Comparing the start of strophe 1, in measure 8, with the start of strophe 2, in measure 18, lays bare the artful illusion of strophic similitude. Both begin and end analogously, in each case with the voice initiating its strophe and the piano concluding it. The third measures of each strophe (mm. 10 and 23) advance differently, which is easily explained by observing that Brecht's two stanzas are dissimilar in length: the first contains twenty-three words, the second thirty-seven. While measures 8 and 18 are melodically alike, their time signatures are not. The first is in 3/4, the second in 2/4. The song begins with a seven-measure piano introduction, the first three measures of which herald the voice's entrance in measure 8. Throughout the song, the succession of triple, duple, and quintuple meters together with syncopation breed rhythmic ambiguity, another symbol of the uncertainties of exile. In the introduction the piano quickly traverses the chromatic scale, a gambit calling to mind Schoenberg's twelve-tone system—the older composer having been Eisler's teacher in Vienna from 1919 to 1923 and, since 1934 living in Los Angeles. Implying dodecaphonism but not employing it allows Eisler simultaneous "affirmation and negation." He had other reasons for intimating his teacher's compositional technique, the most obvious being their 1926 falling out at a time when Eisler was concerned about the insularity of the new music scene, one dominated in the 1920s by Schoenberg. In a March 1926 letter from Eisler to Schoenberg the disagreement reached the breaking point: "Mich langweilt moderne Musik," Eisler declares, "sie interessiert mich nicht, manches hasse und verachte ich sogar. Ich will tatsächlich mit der 'Moderne' nichts zu tun haben. Auch meine eigenen Arbeiten der letzten Jahre muss ich leider dazu rechnen."[21] On the eve of his departure for California mending fences with Schoenberg was a prudent move.

In the 1940s Eisler honored his teacher at least twice, the second time, as I explain below, in "Der Sohn I." To appreciate this reference it is necessary to know the much more overt Schoenberg homage Eisler made while still in New York in his film score for Joris Ivens's 1929 silent movie, *Rain*. Written in 1940 as part of his Rockefeller Film Music Project, Eisler's score is a manifesto of his belief that advanced compositional methods have a place in film, a belief that he and Adorno discuss in *Composing for the Films*. The score is entitled *Vierzehn Arten den Regen zu beschreiben: Variationen für Flöte, Klarinette, Violine, Viola, Violoncello und Klavier*, Opus 70, which Eisler dedicated to Schoenberg on his seventieth birthday. Whereas "Der Sohn I" only hints at the older composer's "complex composing technique," *Regen* is completely dodecaphonic.[22] The film music also calls for the same ensemble Schoenberg used in 1912 in *Pierrot Lunaire*, one of his most radically modern works, in which he dispenses with the normal resources of the singing voice, relying instead on *Sprechstimme*, a cross between speech and song. In *Regen* Eisler retains Schoenberg's ensemble but excludes the voice. While no thematic quotations link *Regen* and *Pierrot Lunaire*, Schoenberg's presence is palpable given that, as one reads in *Composing for the Films*, "at the beginning and at the end there is a cadenza-like 'monogram.'"[23] Using the German names of musical pitches, the sonic symbol is the name **Arnold Sch**oenberg: A–D–eS (=E-flat)–C–H (=B-natural)–B (=B-flat)–G. Schoenberg's name thus provides "a stimulus of motion" in *Regen* but "not a reduplication of motion."[24] Equally intriguing is the medium Eisler employs to esteem Schoenberg: film music. What precipitated their friction was Eisler's desire to compose music capable of reaching a broad audience and his claim that modern music bores him. How ironic that in saluting his teacher fifteen years later he does so in film music, cinema being almost always directed towards the widest possible public. Yet paradoxically, the compositional manner he adopts in *Regen* is Schoenberg's complicated "modern" style, one least likely to win Eisler broad listenership.

Eisler extends his idiosyncratic application of "affirmation and negation" in "Der Sohn I." In it he takes an idea from *Regen* and folds it into the Lied, a musical repertory long associated with high art. His previous allusion perhaps not having been noticed, Eisler evokes Schoenberg again in measure 24 of the song, when Brecht's poem states the word "Sohn" for the third and last time. There Eisler restricts himself to eight chromatic pitches, A–D–E-flat–C–B–B-flat–E-natural and G, and so, as in Opus 70, spells Schoenberg's name. Evoking Schoenberg while avoiding the twelve-tone method, Eisler respects the dislocation of Brecht's text in which a mother comforts her son with the thing that most disquiets her, water, while also maintaining the song's antithetical unification. One additional example of unity in conflict binds the first "Der Sohn" and *Regen*. One is a chamber work that sonically augments a motion picture that started as a silent film. The other includes a voice that is anything but quiet. The nexus of course is water. In the song, even though the mother dreads "der grimmigen See!," she is aware that it is what has brought her her son. She comforts him with the thing she most fears, flinging water on the wall behind which he rests so that he might sleep better, taking something from its usual context and refitting it for a new purpose. Designating Schoenberg in the song while avoiding the twelve-tone method, Eisler accomplishes something similar, and so establishes a productive tension between Lied and film score. The two Schoenberg allusions, the one explicit, the other anything but, reveal much. Eisler makes the first in an exceedingly public way: open the score of *Regen* and the first thing one sees are the words "Arnold Schönberg zum 70. Geburtstag gewidmet." In the second he incorporates the musical anagram in a genre

Ex. 3. Hanns Eisler, "Der Sohn I," Hollywooder Liederbuch (Leipzig: Deutscher Verlag für Musik, 2008). Copyright by Deutscher Verlag für Musik, Leipzig.

Ex. 2.—(concluded)

long coupled with intimacy and privacy. The difficulty in making out the song citation reflects Eisler's relationship with Schoenberg.

But in such chromatic music is this a true Schoenberg reference? In answering yes, I do so in view of the many other allusions Eisler incorporates throughout the *Liederbuch*, which, however fleeting they are, expand a song's expressive depth. At the mention of Bach in his setting of Brecht's "Unter den grünen Pfefferbäumen," Eisler spells B–A–C–H in the piano's left hand in measures 20–21. In setting another Brecht poem, "Über den Selbstmord," in the vocal line, Eisler, at the line "Und die ganze Winterzeit dazu, das ist gefährlich," invokes the opening of "Gute Nacht," the first song of Schubert's 1827 song cycle *Winterreise*. While Eisler scholars agree this is so, without help most listeners would not discern the allusion.[25] Occurring in measure 8, the borrowed motive lacks the primacy it has in Schubert's Lied, where, beginning in measure 1, it is the first thing in the piano's right hand, and, beginning in measure 7, the voice's first melody. Clearly Eisler wants us to have to work at detecting the citation. The line about winter's perils provides the clue, and that in turn leads to Schubert's "Gute Nacht," where the motive appears eight times as Schubert moves through the four strophes of Wilhelm Müller's poem. Tracking these passages, one gleans that the protagonist of *Winterreise* is a wanderer, a familiar *Aufklärung* figure recast for the new age of Romanticism. "Fremd bin ich eingezogen, / Fremd zieh' ich wieder aus," he states, "Ich kann zu meiner Reisen / Nicht wählen mit der Zeit," to mention two examples of the Schubert motive matching Eisler's appropriation. Scorned by love, Müller and Schubert's wayfarer embarks on a journey of self-discovery ending not in Enlightenment's sunny sanguinity but in deepest despair. As the concluding twenty-fourth song of Schubert's cycle "Der Leiermann" makes clear, snarling dogs and a barefoot hurdy-gurdy player join the journeyman on the ice, the latter playing ever on while never speaking a word, indications that the trek into desolation has no limits.

Does Eisler's *Winterreise* citation herald a similar destination in the *Liederbuch*? Since Eisler's engagement with the conventions of poetry and the Lied are as nuanced as they are intricate, ultimate answers are elusive. No matter a poem's date or its author, Eisler has no compunction in changing a title, omitting or substituting words, or, as he does in the 1943 "Der Mensch," assembling a textual montage of Old Testament verses from the Books of Job and Exodus. Such liberties are not capricious. As Eisler explained in 1961, less than a year before his death, "Das Merkwürdige ist: Es gibt da gar keine Prinzipien. Das ist keine wissenschaftliche Methode, das ist eine künstlerische. Das heißt, man liest ein Gedicht und versucht—ohne Barbar zu sein—, das zusammenzufassen, was einem heute wichtig erscheint."[26] The gathering of poets in the *Liederbuch*, eleven altogether, is likewise complex: the Bible, Brecht,

Eichendorff, Goethe, Hölderlin, Pascal, Rimbaud, Berthold Viertel, Eisler himself, and five Anacreontic fragments by way of Mörike. German is not the *Liederbuch's* sole language. Two poems are in English, translations of French works by the seventeenth-century mathematician-philosopher Blaise Pascal. "Rimbaud-Gedichte" is a setting of a French poem by Rimbaud. In sum, the *Liederbuch* encompasses three languages and a time frame extending from the Bible and ancient Greece to the 1940s. Eisler responds to these heterogeneous texts with music just as varied, with homages to Schoenberg, with allusions to the acknowledged master of German song, Schubert, and with echoes of his own *Kampflieder*, the latter a vital part of his musical output.[27]

If the *Liederbuch* is "the new stuff of life," Eisler's militant songs and dedication to antithetic unity provide the groundwork, placing the *Liederbuch* in a new light—not as a way to shut out the world but to live in it. A contributing factor to his rift with Schoenberg was his immersion in leftist politics and in the *Arbeitermusikbewegung*. He served as music critic for *Die Rote Fahne*, since 1919 the German newspaper of the Kommunistische Partei Deutschlands, collaborated with the agit-prop group Das Rote Sprachchor, and taught at the Berlin Marxistische Arbeiterschule from 1928. It was at this time that he began his almost thirty-year friendship with Brecht, one that, during the Weimar Republic, led to the "Lehrstück" *Die Maßnahme* (1930), the film *Kuhle Wampe* (1932), and the play with music *Die Mutter* (also 1932). It is Brecht, in one of the songs from *Die Maßnahme*, set memorably to music by Eisler, who best summarizes Eisler's goal as a composer at this time. "Versinke in Schmutz, umarme den Schlächter," Brecht proclaims, "aber ändere die Welt, sie braucht es." In an essay by Eisler and Ernst Bloch from 1938, the two acknowledge that the world is worth changing because "wir nicht nur in einer Fäulniszeit leben, sondern in einer dialektisch übergehenden, in einer Zeit und Gesellschaft, die von der künftigen schwanger ist."[28]

When above I asked whether Eisler's *Winterreise* allusion signals that his lyric journey is to end as direly as Schubert's I equivocated, stating that the question is demanding given the collection's many contradictions. In closing I do so again, for, it seems, this is one more thing Eisler did not wish to make easy. This is not to say he did not hold out the possibility of answers. In 1939 Bloch encouraged writers to join the old and the new, thereby quickening one's "powers of expression on the new stuff of life" in order to demonstrate "a vigorous faith in the future," an attitude I believe Eisler shares in his *Liederbuch*. Even though he confirms in his 1938 essay with Bloch that his time of exile, the time of Hitler, of concentration camps, is one of "obscene decay," he just as quickly affirms, through the exchange of opposing ideas, that it also is "pregnant with the future." Under California's sunny skies, parsing the difference between heaven and hell was a favorite exile concern. Brecht, in the fourth of what

Eisler names the Liederbuch's Fünf *Elegien*, reflects that Hollywood "hat mich belehrt, / Paradies und Hölle können eine Stadt sein."[29] Yet to take Brecht at face value, or Adorno when he asserts that damage is ever the exile's fate, denies the range of their émigré experience, just as it preempts the possibility that they agree with Bloch's idea of double loyalties. It may be that Brecht passes on to his reader the task of sorting out hell and heaven. While for Mann "music is a demonic realm," in his *Hollywooder Liederbuch* Eisler engages with both domains, harnessing them for good. But that outcome is not a given. In these songs Eisler extends an invitation, leaving it to performers and listeners to resolve, or not, the collection's many constructive conflicts.

Notes

[1] Between ten and fifteen thousand exiles from Nazi Europe settled in Southern California from 1933 to 1941, most in Los Angeles, the latter sometimes called "New Weimar" or "Weimar in Hollywood." Ehrhard Bahr presents "a collection of case studies" in which he examines the creative fallout of this exodus in his *Weimar on the Pacific: German Exile Culture in Los Angeles and the Crisis of Modernism* (Berkeley and Los Angeles: University of California Press, 2007).

[2] Born July 6, 1898, Eisler died September 6, 1962. For a life-works study, see Albrecht Betz, *Hanns Eisler: Musik einer Zeit, die sich eben bildet* (Munich: edition text + kritik, 1976). The appendix is a distillation of research I have carried out at the Hanns-Eisler-Archiv as well as information culled from the "Notes" section of Hanns Eisler, *Hollywooder Liederbuch*, corrected reprint of the first ed. with annotation by Oliver Dahin and Peter Deeg (Leipzig: Deutscher Verlag für Musik, 2008), 97–100. For an excellent recording, see Matthias Goerne, baritone, and pianist Eric Schneider, *Hollywooder Liederbuch*, London Records, 289 460 582–2, compact disc.

[3] While a comprehensive listing of previous investigations of the *Liederbuch*. In these terms exceeds this study's scope, a partial inventory includes Claudia Albert, *"Das schwierige Handwerk des Hoffens": Hanns Eislers "Hollywooder Liederbuch" (1942/43)* (Stuttgart: J. B. Metzlersche Verlagsbuchhandlung, 1991), Markus Roth, *Der Gesang als Asyl: Analytische Studien zu Hanns Eislers "Hollywood-Liederbuch"* (Hofheim: Wolke, 2006), and Horst Weber, *I am not a hero, I am a composer: Hanns Eisler in Hollywood* (Hildesheim: Olms, 2012).

[4] Thomas Mann, "Germany and the Germans," quoted in Mann, *Death in Venice, Tonio Kröger, and Other Writings* (New York: Continuum, 1999), 303–19, here 307 and 314. The full title of Mann's novel is *Doktor Faustus: Das Leben des deutschen Tonsetzers Adrian Leverkühn, erzählt von einem Freunde*. For a discussion of Mann, music, and German national identity, see Hans R. Vaget, "National and Universal: Thomas Mann and the Paradox of 'German' Music," in *Music and German National Identity*, ed. Celia Applegate and Pamela Potter (Chicago: University of Chicago Press, 2002), 155–77.

[5] "Germany and the Germans," 317–18.

[6] Hanns Eisler, *Composing for the Films* (New York: Oxford University Press, 1947), ix.

[7] The Lied as a sheltering space for subjectivity in the nineteenth century is the focus of my "At Home with German Romantic Song," in *Companion to European Romanticism*, ed. Michael Ferber (Oxford: Blackwell Publishing, 2005), 538–51.

[8] Multiple ambiguities pervade Eichendorff's poem, first published in his novella *Viel Lärmen um nichts* (1833) where the female character, Julie, speaks it. Yet the poem concerns a prototypically male figure, the Romantic wanderer. For the poem see *Sämtliche Werke des Freiherrn Joseph von Eichendorff: Historisch-Kritische Ausgabe*, vol. 1, book 1, ed. Harry Fröhlich and Ursula Regener (Stuttgart: Kohlhammer, 1993), 280.

[9] Quoted from *Gedichte von L. Tieck*, part 3 (Dresden: P. G. Hilscher, 1823), 79. My view of Heimat is in keeping with Celia Applegate's when, in her *A Nation of Provincials: The German Idea of Heimat* (Berkeley: University of California Press, 1990), 19, she calls the concept a "myth about the possibility of a community in the face of fragmentation and alienation."

[10] *Minima Moralia: Reflexionen aus dem beschädigten Leben*, in *Theodor W. Adorno Gesammelte Schriften*, ed. Rolf Tiedemann (Frankfurt am Main: Suhrkamp, 2003), 35. Adorno began the work in 1944 and finished it in 1949.

[11] Quoted in Albrecht Betz, "The Composer as Dialectical Thinker: Hanns Eisler's Philosophical Reflections on Music," trans. Jost Hermand, in *Sound Figures of Modernity*, ed. Jost Hermand and Gerhard Richter (Madison: University of Wisconsin Press, 2006), 232–43, here 232.

[12] This does not imply that Eisler did not intervene, and sometimes considerably, with the texts he set in the *Liederbuch*, a point I raise more fully below in my discussion of his citation of Schubert's *Winterreise*.

[13] The song's initial title was "The Hearing." Eisler assesses his HUAC appearances in the essay "Fantasia in G-men," originally published (in English) in *New Masses* (October 14, 1947), reprinted in *A Rebel in Music*, 150–52, here 150. Eisler appeared twice before HUAC, first in Los Angeles on May 12, 1947, and for three days in September 1947 in Washington, DC. For Eisler's full testimony from September 1947, see "Hearings Regarding Hanns Eisler: Hearings before the Committee on Un–American Activities, House of Representatives, Eightieth Congress, First Session, Public Law 601, Section 121, Subsection Q (2), September 24, 25 and 26, 1947" (Washington, DC: US Government Printing Office, 1947).

[14] Eisler subsequently published his statement as "Fantasia in G-men." See previous footnote.

[15] Georg Wilhelm Friedrich Hegel, *Phänomenologie des Geistes* (Leipzig: Dürr'schen Buchlandlung, 1907), 450, "Der Werkmeister vereint daher beides in der Vermischung der natürlichen und der selbstbewußten Gestalt, und diese zweideutigen sich selbst rätselhaften Wesen, das Bewußte ringend mit dem Bewußtlosen, das einfache Innre mit dem vielgestalteten Äußern, die Dunkelheit des Gedankens mit der Klarheit der Äußerung paarend, brechen in die Sprache tiefer schwerverständlicher Weisheit aus."

[16] Theodor W. Adorno, *Philosophie der neuen Musik* (Frankfurt am Main: Suhrkamp, 1959), 118–19.

[17] Ernst Bloch, "Disrupted Language, Disputed Culture," *Direction* 2/8 (December 1939): 16–17 and 36, here 36.

[18] *Composing for the Films*, 70–71, 78. When the book was first published, Adorno, the book's other author, opted to omit his name given Eisler's HUAC entanglement. I discuss the book's publication history and the complex issue of author attribution in my "The Exile's Intellectual Mission": Adorno and Eisler's *Composing for the Films*," *Telos* 149 (Winter 2009), 52–68.

[19] See the commentary in Hanns Eisler, *Hollywooder Liederbuch*, 97.

[20] Eisler amends certain aspects of Brecht's poem, particularly word choice. Here I quote Eisler's version. For Brecht's original see *Die Gedichte von Bertolt Brecht in einem Band* (Frankfurt am Main: Suhrkamp, 1981), 818.

[21] Quoted in Betz, *Hanns Eisler*, 46.

[22] *Composing for the Films*, 148.

[23] *Composing for the Films*, 148.

[24] *Composing for the Films*, 78.

[25] Wolfgang Hufschmidt, *Willst zu meinen Liedern deine Leier drehn?: Zur Semantik der musikalischen Sprache in Schuberts Winterreise und Eislers Hollywood-Liederbuch* (Dortmund: Pläne, 1986), 175.

[26] Hanns Eisler and Hans Bunge, *Gespräche mit Hans Bunge: Fragen Sie mehr über Brecht* (Leipzig: Deutscher Verlag für Musik, 1975), 218.

[27] Eisler sets forth his criteria for the mass fighting song, when, in his essay "Unsere Kampfmusik," *Illustrierte Rote Post* (Berlin, March 1932), 2, he writes: "Die erste Forderung, die der Klassenkampf an Kampflieder stellt, ist eine große Faßlichkeit, leichte Verständlichkeit und energische präzise Haltung." Quoted in *Hanns Eisler Schriften I: Musik und Politik, 1924–1948*, ed. Günter Mayer (Munich: Rogner & Bernhard, 1973), 169–70, here 169.

[28] "Die Kunst zu erben" (1938), quoted in *Hanns Eisler Schriften I*, 406–44, here 410.

[29] Eisler, *Hollywooder Liederbuch*, 43.

Appendix: Hanns Eisler's
Hollywooder Liederbuch

	Title	Date	Poet
1.	"Der Sohn I"	May 1942	Bertolt Brecht
2.	"Der Sohn II"	May 1942	Brecht
3.	"In den Weiden"	May 1942	Brecht
4.	"An den kleinen Radioapparat"	May 1942	Brecht
5.	"Frühling"	June 11, 1942	Brecht
6.	"Speisekammer 1942"	June (?), 1942	Brecht
7.	"Auf der Flucht"	June–July 1942	Brecht
8.	"Über den Selbstmord"	July 1942	Brecht
9.	"Die Flucht"	July 7, 1942	Brecht
10.	"Gedenktafel für 4000 Soldaten"	July 1942	Brecht
11.	"Epitaph auf einen in der Flandernschlacht Gefallenen"	July 1942	Brecht
12.	"Spruch"	July 1942	Brecht
13.	"Panzerschlacht"	Summer 1942	Brecht
14.	"Ostersonntag"	July 23, 1942	Brecht
15.	"Der Kirschdieb"	July 26, 1942	Brecht
16.	"Hotelzimmer 1942"	August 3, 1942	Brecht
17.	"Die Maske des Bösen"	September 1942	Brecht
	Zwei Lieder nach Worten von Pascal [*Pensées*, Nos. 169 and 171, trans. W. F. Trotter]		
18.	"Despite these miseries" (Sung in English)	September 12, 1942	Blaise Pascal
19.	"The only thing which consoles us" (Sung in English)	September 14, 1942	Pascal
	Fünf Elegien		
21.	"Unter den grünen Pfefferbäumen"	September 1942	Brecht
22.	"Die Stadt ist nach den Engeln genannt"	September 20, 1942	Brecht
23.	"Jeden Morgen, mein Brot zu verdienen"	September 25, 1942	Brecht

(continued)

	Title	Date	Poet
24.	"Diese Stadt hat mich belehrt"	Sept.–Oct. 1942	Brecht
25.	"In den Hügeln wird Gold gefunden"	Sept.–Oct. 1942	Brecht
26.	"Die letzte Elegie"	Begun September 15, 1942	Brecht
27.	"L'automne californien" (sung in German)	January 1943	Berthold Viertel

Anakreontische Fragmente by Eduard Mörike, ed. Eisler

28.	"Geselligkeit betreffend"	March–April 1943	Mörike/Eisler
29.	"Dir auch wurde Sehnsucht nach der Heimat tödlich"	March–April 1943	Mörike/Eisler
30.	"Die Unwürde des Alters"	March–April 1943	Mörike/Eisler
31.	"Später Triumph"	March–April 1943	Mörike/Eisler
32.	"In der Frühe"	April 18, 1943	Mörike/Eisler
33.	"Erinnerung an Eichendorff und Schumann"	April 19, 1943	Joseph Eichendorff

Hölderlin-Fragmente (Friedrich Hölderlin), ed. Eisler

34.	"An die Hoffnung"[1]	April 20, 1943	Hölderlin/Eisler
35.	"Andenken"	June 3, 1943	Hölderlin/Eisler
36.	"Elegie 1943"	June 10, 1943	Hölderlin/Eisler
37.	"Die Heimat"	June 21, 1943	Hölderlin/Eisler
38.	"An eine Stadt"	June 22, 1943	Hölderlin/Eisler
39.	"Erinnerung"	August 2, 1943	Hölderlin/Eisler
40.	"Der Mensch, vom Weibe geboren"	Mid 1943	Bible (Martin Luther trans.), textual montage from Job 14:1, Exodus 12:7 & 23
41.	"Vom Sprengen des Gartens"	August 1943	Brecht
42.	"Die Heimkehr"	August 1943	Brecht
43.	"Die Landschaft des Exils"	September 2, 1943	Brecht
44.	"Rimbaud-Gedicht" (Sung in French)	December 28, 1943	Arthur Rimbaud
45.	"Der Schatzgräber"	1944	Johann Wolfgang Goethe

(continued)

	Title	Date	Poet
46.	"Nightmare" (Sung in English)	1947	Eisler
47.	"Hollywood-Elegie Nr. 7" (Sung in English)	1947	Brecht
	Anhang		
	"Sprüche" (fragment; together with contrapuntal fragments)	1943	
	"In Sturmesnacht"	June 4, 1943	Brecht
	"Deutsches Miserere"[2]	June 1943	Brecht

Notes

Consecutive shaded Lieder indicate likely interior subgroupings.

[1] Eisler transforms this song with minimal alteration to the vocal line as No. 4 of his 1961-62 *Ernste Gesänge*, a song cycle of seven Lieder for baritone and string orchestra.

[2] Included by Eisler in music for Brecht's play *Schweyk im zweiten Weltkrieg* (1943–59; Warsaw, 1957), No. 19.

"and all of a sudden, in the middle of it, they began singing . . .": Languages and Commemoration in Arnold Schoenberg's Cantata *A Survivor from Warsaw* (Op. 46)

Ian Biddle and Beate Müller, Newcastle University

ARNOLD SCHOENBERG'S *A Survivor from Warsaw*, Op. 46, is a twelve-tone cantata for male narrator, male chorus, and orchestra, written in August 1947. The narrator recounts, in *Sprechgesang*, how, one day during an early morning reveille in an unnamed camp, the Nazi guards started viciously beating the Jews, killing many of them. Those surviving are ordered to repeat the roll call, and suddenly start singing the Jewish prayer *Shema Yisroel*. One of the most striking elements of the cantata is the fact that its libretto uses three languages: English, German, and Hebrew. The narrator tells his tale in English, citing Nazi commands in German, and the prayer is sung in Hebrew by the chorus; this tripartite linguistic organization is mirrored by the music, which is characterized by tripartite parallelisms.[1] The push and shove between English and German in the narrative section of the cantata and the use of Hebrew in the *Shema* raise questions about the relationship between languages: how is German (the language of the composer, an émigré German-speaking Jew living in Los Angeles) positioned as the perpetrator language in the figure of the Feldwebel? How is English (the then-emerging language of Holocaust memorialization, the dominant language of prosecution during the Nuremberg Trials, and subsequently the leading language of Holocaust Studies as a discipline) framed as the language of witnessing in the cantata? And finally, how is Hebrew (the language of liturgy, but also the language of political Zionism) enacted here and to what effect? These three languages, we will suggest, stage a range of subject positions and, in particular, invite the audience to make specific ideological and ethical (or unethical) associations with the communities represented by the three languages.

The libretto of *Survivor*, as an early example of Holocaust-themed art music, encourages reflection on memory, the representation of trauma, and the role of languages in that work of memory. The three languages used, whilst each serving different functions when taken on their own, also form a network in which each language unfolds its meaning in relation to the other two. Their main significance lies in destructions and constructions of community. As well as positing (and simultaneously questioning) the play of communities, Schoenberg's cantata also deals with the emergence and integration of the individual into those changing communities: here the individual is the witness and the victim, that exemplary protagonist of Holocaust narratives, who is afforded the authority and burden of bearing (and communicating) memory.

Musical Contexts

Schoenberg's combination of the *Shema Yisroel* with his own avowedly secular text maps on to long-established expectations of the cantata genre, especially in the German-speaking world. Indeed, the German baroque cantata tradition drew on religious or secular texts, or combined them. Schoenberg's piece compresses but preserves the hybrid textual nature of most German Lutheran cantatas, especially the so-called *Spruchodenkantate*, a hybrid of the *Odenkantate* (based around a religious song text in strophic form) and the so-called *Konzertmotette* (by the late seventeenth century a rarer form, drawing on older sacred traditions, and permissive in its use of instrumental and vocal resources). This hybrid form consisted of several stop-start sections, usually including at least two arias, a recitative, and at least one chorus. The textual and musical form of *Survivor* draws on Bach's *Kantaten* as a model, whilst also "through-composing" the contrasting sections into a continuous (but compacted) musical work.

Schoenberg's designation of *Survivor* as a cantata,[2] although included neither in the first published score of 1949 nor in the later 1979 revised score,[3] seems apt. And yet that designation also raises complex questions about Schoenberg's own relationship with both Judaism and German culture. Indeed, in 1933, as is well attested in the literature, Schoenberg re-entered the Jewish faith, and whilst the relation between this rediscovery of Judaism and his creative output can be demonstrated, the Christian musical traditions of Vienna persist in much of his oeuvre.[4] Although his unfinished oratorio *Die Jakobsleiter* (1917–22) could be said to address Judaism, it is probably better understood as belonging to a tradition of biblically-themed oratorios from the Christian tradition. In 1926, Schoenberg wrote his first consciously Jewish work, the play *Der biblische Weg*. The play is avowedly Zionist in its conception, and deals with the choice of the protagonists Asseino and Aruns between the way of Moses (the rule-giver) and the way of Aaron (the radical, the modern). The connection with his opera *Moses und Aron* (1927–32)[5] is clear, although the latter drops the explicit political tone of the former. Nonetheless, after the notorious Mattsee incident in 1921, when Schoenberg and his family were asked to leave the holiday resort because they were Jewish, Schoenberg's political reawakening as a Jew seemed unstoppable.[6] That both *Der biblische Weg* and *Moses und Aron* were written before his formal conversion to Judaism in Paris in 1933 is testament to the fact that Schoenberg's Jewish awakening occurred before he marked his formal return to the faith of his childhood.[7] Schoenberg was demonstrably aware of the political dimensions of his Jewish identity, as evidenced for instance in his famous letter to Kandinsky in 1924 where he wrote that he had been forced to learn that "ich nämlich kein Deutscher, kein Europäer, ja vielleicht kaum ein Mensch bin . . . sondern, dass ich Jude bin" (I am not a German, not a European, maybe not even a human, . . . but that I am a Jew).[8]

His next major explicitly Jewish-themed work was the *Kol Nidre* for speaker, mixed chorus, and orchestra (Op. 39, 1939), commissioned by Rabbi Jakob Sonderling, who later provided Schoenberg with the phonetic transcription of the *Shema Yisroel* for *Survivor*. The use of a speaking narrator here also clearly anticipates that used in *Survivor*. In several ways, the *Kol Nidre* works as a kind of early study for *Survivor*. The *Kol Nidre*'s conception is intimately connected to the plight of Jews in Nazi-occupied Europe, and the piece deals with the interrelationship of three languages: English, German (the original language of Schoenberg's first draft of the *Kol Nidre* libretto), and (missing, implied) Aramaic. The *Kol Nidre* was originally conceived, like *Survivor*, as a cantata, and, of course, it deals structurally, in a manner not unlike that of *Survivor*, with the juxtaposition of speech and song. However, the piece differs significantly in several important ways: it is largely tonal, whereas the cantata is written using curtailed hexachordal/serial procedures;[9] *Kol Nidre* does not stage any action or melodrama but is purely liturgical in conception; it attempts to set an existing *nigun* or melody (albeit extremely freely), whilst *Survivor* abandons liturgical musical traditions for the setting of the *Shema Yisroel*.

From Partisan Song to Cantata

The idea to compose a piece on the Holocaust originated in correspondence between Schoenberg and Corinne Chochem, a dancer from Russia who had by that time emigrated to New York. Chochem sent Schoenberg the English lyrics of a Partisan song from the Vilna ghetto,[10] wishing to commission a composition of six to nine minutes' length on a story heard by Chochem of Jews in the Warsaw ghetto who had started singing shortly before being killed. Schoenberg was willing to undertake the work, but the envisaged collaboration fell through because the composer's demand for a thousand dollars was too much for Chochem to pay. Schoenberg eventually wrote the piece for the Koussevitzky Music

Foundation.[11] Whilst the Partisan song Chochem supplied seems to have left no clear trace in *Survivor*, the idea of doomed Jews singing when facing death is central to the cantata's plot.

A Survivor from Warsaw was premiered by the Albuquerque Civic Orchestra at the University of New Mexico in November 1948, followed by its European première in Paris shortly after (December 1948); the score was published by Bomart in 1949.[12] Contemporary audiences were apparently both bewildered by and deeply impressed with the piece: at its original performance, the audience's reaction resulted in an *encore* of the performance, which apparently became the practice after the world première.[13] Indeed, as Calico states, the cantata has been "surprisingly popular," and the work "has had a significant, even disproportionate, influence on the composer's overall reception as well as on perceptions of his Jewishness."[14]

Schoenberg's Cantata and Early Postwar Responses to the Holocaust

Schoenberg's cantata is a relatively early instance of Holocaust memorialization in the art music canon.[15] It is one of three major works written in 1947 that deal with the Holocaust, the other two both hailing from the British Mandate of Palestine. Ödön Partós's *Yizkor* for viola and orchestra, was "dedicated to the memory of the victims in the war of extinction against the Jews in Central Europe during the Second World War." The solo viola stands for the *cantor* in a Jewish liturgical service, although the work does not cite any Jewish musical sources. Yitzhak Edel's suite *In Memoriam* for piano trio openly cites Jewish musical sources and deals similarly with the process of memorialization.

Schoenberg's cantata stands apart in that his is a work that comprises both words and music. It is important to note, however, that Schoenberg's work relates intimately to other early Holocaust representations, for example, Alfréd Radok's filmic portrayal of the transit camp Terezín in *Daleká cesta* (Distant Journey, Czechoslovakia, 1949). Similarly, the musical moment of repair or resistance embodied in the Hebrew prayer *Shema Yisroel* at the end of the cantata resonates with Natan Gross's uses of music as a kind of redemptive or reparative medium in his 1947 film *Undzere Kinder* (Our Children).

These two key early cinematic responses to the Holocaust deal explicitly with the question of memory and narrative. Ira Königsberg has suggested that *Undzere Kinder* can be understood as exploring "the possibilities of art as therapy for social trauma."[16] A key element of the film is the use of music as a kind of ritualization of memory: the children perform numerous musical works for onlookers, and the opening scene of the film is set in a theater in postwar Łódź. Unlike *Undzere Kinder,* which represents the Holocaust only in flashbacks, the narrative in Alfréd Radok's *Daleká cesta* is set during the Holocaust. This film is a melodrama that deals both with the buildup to deportations from Prague, the "ghetto without walls," and the lives of the inmates at the transit camp Terezín (Theresienstadt).[17] Jiří Sternwald's complex musical score for the film resonates with other European modernist musics from the time, not least Schoenberg's own (Sternwald was apparently an avid follower of Schoenberg's career). Perhaps most notable in the film is the strange expressionistic representation of the transit camp as a chaotic railway station, and the inmates' blocks as railway carriages.

The topsy-turvy confusion of places in the cantata (the sewers of Warsaw, concentration camps, gas chambers) shares with many early representations of the Holocaust a tendency to conflate various key sites of the atrocities. Avrom Sutzkever's Yiddish-language epic poem *Geheymshtot* (Secret City, 1945–47), for example, centers on the sewers of Vilnius, where the protagonists subsist in the damp and the dark: "These pipes, sewers, they are something quite different, / Like circuitous roads, dirt paths, trails . . . The city has sunk. The world has been turned on its head."[18] Similarly, Chaim Grade's 1945 poetry collections *Pleytim* (Refugees) and *Doyres* (Generations), and his 1947 *Farvoksene vegn* (Overgrown Paths) also deal with themes similar to those used by Schoenberg in the cantata: hiding underground, endless role calls, disturbed sleep, hunger, the frailty of the old, fractured communities, and so on.[19]

Staging Trauma

The title *A Survivor from Warsaw* is both apt and misleading: on the one hand, the narrator shares a traumatic memory that involves him being beaten savagely, narrowly escaping death, and hearing his fellow-sufferers erupt into song; on the other hand, this memory is not a historiographically reliable survivor testimony, because its location and timeframe are unclear. The initially specified Warsaw is revealed as a symbolic rather than a geographical space by the sergeant's reference to a gas chamber, which did not exist in Warsaw or the Warsaw ghetto; nor were there daily roll calls, as described in the libretto.[20] With its move beyond historically and locationally specific representation, the text encourages a more general and symbolic engagement with the legacies of the Holocaust, an engagement that, in turn, is informed by modernist cultural traditions.

The figure of the libretto's narrator emerges as a modern creature: aware of his own limitations but trying to overcome them through expression; juxtaposing different perspectives, locations, and time frames, thus testifying to the existential disorientation of the modern subject; desiring—but failing—to achieve clarity through rationality, while grappling instead with his unconscious; oscillating between foregrounding his subjectivity and seeking communion in a group. Right from the beginning, the narrator's unreliability is signposted: "I cannot remember ev'rything. I must have been unconscious most of the time."[21] The only memory he seems to have retained is that of the recitation of the *Shema Yisroel*: "the grandiose moment when they all started to sing . . . the old prayer." In these opening sentences, the libretto narrows down the scope of the narrator's recollection until it is delimited to the crucial moment of the sung prayer. And yet, the narrator protests too much: once he starts to unfold the events that led to the incantation, we are faced with a linear, chronological story, albeit one that provides a framework for exploring complexities surrounding traumatic memory, individuality, and community.

The narrator describes the day as starting like any other: "Reveille when it still was dark. Get out! Whether you slept or whether worries kept you awake the whole night." The introduction of sleep and its disturbance subtly connects with the opening lines, in that sleep, like unconsciousness, brings with it loss of control, helplessness, forgetting, and separation from others.[22] The positive functions of sleep—providing necessary rest for body and soul—are relativized by the more sinister associations pertaining to unconsciousness. Both the narrator's unconsciousness and the enforced pre-dawn reveille of the exhausted fit into this paradigm of the unnatural nature of the narrated concentrationary world. The perspective shifts from general reflections (daily routine, sleep or lack of it) and constant anxieties (the fate of absent loved ones) to more pressing worries brought about by the present situation of the roll call, conducted by a feared sergeant. The endeavors of the terrified to comply are futile, as barked orders and threats of violence turn into a vicious attack.

In the libretto, group identities are created, starting with a community built on worries and physical suffering, ending with them emerging in a twofold community of the dead on the one hand, and of surviving believers on the other. Before the abuse commences, the Jews are united in their fear; their responses to the Nazi threat atomize them into separate groups, which, however, are then indiscriminately subject to violence when the Nazis strike "everybody: young or old, quiet or nervous, guilty or innocent." The Jews are now united in their pain, voiced non-verbally: "it was painful to hear them groaning and moaning." This phrase shifts the sensation of pain from its source (the bodies of the sufferers) to auditory perception. The impersonal construction used here provides a transition to the narrator's first-person voice, which emerges for the first time in the actual story: "I heard it though I had been hit very hard." It is therefore at the moment of great pain that the suffering subject emerges linguistically, only to integrate himself expressly into the group of those felled by the Nazis' clubs. The narrator undergoes a near-death experience before regaining consciousness: "I lay aside—half-conscious. It had become very still—fear and pain." The sensations of fear and pain here echo the emotions experienced during the previous scene. As a survivor among the dead, the narrator is again isolated from the other Jews, and it is this isolation that turns him into a witness of the next events. This act of witnessing is once more channeled through the auditory: "Then I heard the sergeant shouting: 'Abzählen!'" (Count off!).

The roll call commences again, interrupted by the sergeant demanding a faster pace. Consequently, the speed picks up, becomes frenzied, and the counting-off turns into song: "They began again; first slowly: one, two, three, four, became faster and faster, so fast that it finally sounded like a stampede of wild horses, and all of a sudden, in the middle of it, they began singing the *Shema Yisroel.*" What started as a monotonous, bureaucratic exercise, endowing the individual victim with a specific (albeit merely numerical) identity of his own for the last time before annihilation, then, seems to get out of hand by virtue of the Jews' ever-faster counting-off. The metaphor of the "stampede of wild horses" suggests powerful, free, fast movement, but driven by panic and without orientation: neither controlled nor in control. What provides poise and dignity to the victims, as well as a sense of community, is their act of singing, giving them agency and voice.

Only the core section of the *Shema Yisroel* (Deuteronomy 6:4–7) has been included in the cantata (two other passages, Deuteronomy 11:13–21 and Numbers 15:37–41, are also often included as part of the *Shema*). As the declaration of Jewish faith, the *Shema* represents one of the most important prayers in the Jewish religion, recited twice daily by observant Jews. The words are sung in Hebrew. Ironically, as Barbara Barry has observed, the "rediscovery of identity is a doomed vision because it takes place only moments before they (the singers) are annihilated in the gas chambers, so the affirmation of identity is also, tragically, a lamentation of loss."[23] The choice of the *Shema Yisroel* befits this ambiguity, as it is the prayer Jews pray when they are about to die. In the scholarship, this final scene of the cantata has been interpreted as an instance of Jewish resistance to Nazi oppression (Argentino, for example, speaks of bravery, martyrdom, and heroism[24]): the singing Jews defy Nazi orders while at the same time demonstrating unity in faith, focusing on the Lord as their master, not the Nazis.

Language and Community

In Schoenberg's cantata, the two adversary groups (Nazis and Jews) are not only established through the plot's historical resonances (perpetrators and victims) but also through linguistic means. The most obvious of these is the use of different languages and their allocation to different speech

types: the narrator tells the story in English (recitative), the narrated figure of the Feldwebel is quoted in German (direct speech), the Hebrew
prayer is the chorus's part (song). It would be easy to say that German
is used here as the perpetrator language, but this description, while obviously correct, does not go far enough. The point is that the meaning of
German is generated in its relation to the other languages of the piece,
which form a network of languages.

This is remarkable, since Schoenberg lived in the United States when
he wrote the cantata, and, whilst he may not have had an exclusively
American, largely monolingual audience in mind, the effect of linguistic non-comprehension deserves consideration. As an émigré who had to
leave a German-speaking environment when he was already well advanced
in years, Schoenberg would not have been oblivious to language barriers.[25] Therefore, these barriers need to be regarded as intentional: not
erected in order to primarily confuse the audience but to evoke the Nazi
camps' multilingualism, which constituted a source of danger. Primo Levi
pointed out how vital a basic command of German was for prisoners:
"knowing or not knowing German was a watershed," he wrote, because a
command of German provided its speaker with a chance of being seen and
communicated to as a human being, at least to some extent, linguistically.
By contrast, the ignorant, in the eyes of the Nazis, ceased to be human,
and "as with cows and mules, there was no substantial difference between
a scream and a punch," as the "beast" would not have understood speech
anyway; apparently, in Mauthausen, the truncheon was referred to as
the "Dolmetscher" (translator, interpreter).[26] This mindset obviously
also characterizes the Feldwebel and his brutes, who beat the Jews with
their rifle butts when their commands are not immediately met. Since the
Feldwebel's orders are made in German, a connection is made between
the German language and violence, conjoining words and actions. It is
worth noting here that German makes up less than ten percent of the
libretto text. And yet, German is key to the narrated incident, because it is
the German commands that bring about the violence and hence structure
the episode. Therefore, German is constituted as doubled, both as a marginalized language (submerged in the flow of English) and as the central
language of instigation (initiating violence through barked commands).

The sergeant's German sentences consist, to a large extent, of one-
word injunctions: we hear his "Achtung! Stillgestanden!" at the beginning of the drill, hear him shouting "Abzählen!" after the attack, leading
to a repeated "Achtung!" followed by a staccato string of "Rascher!
Nochmal von vorn anfangen! In einer Minute will ich wissen wieviele
ich zur Gaskammer abliefere! Abzählen!" (Quicker! Start again from the
front! In a minute I want to know how many I'm sending to the gas
chamber. Count off!) This concentration of commands obviously illustrates the Feldwebel's authority over the Jews and the other soldiers;

Föllmi goes so far as to say that the very fact that the Feldwebel is quoted verbatim in German, whilst the soldier's words "They are all dead" are rendered in English, marks the latter figure out as a subordinate.[27] But the main point here is that the soldier's English words summarize a key point of the narrator's memory for the audience. English as the language of narration, which serves as the language in which Jewish suffering and commemoration are depicted, is eminently suitable for voicing information about the deaths inflicted.

What is also important about the use of German is that Schoenberg used a mix of *Hochdeutsch* and vernacular forms that invoke a Prussian dialect. In the autograph fair copy of the score of 1947, we read "stillgestann" and "jutt"; the typed text of the libretto that precedes this version of the score emphasizes the vernacular elements even more, as the Feldwebel here shouts "Stilljeshtann" and threatens to use his "Yewehr-Kolben."[28] For the 1949 published score, these vernacular forms were taken out and replaced with standard German, whereas the 1979 score re-introduces the vernacular letters J and Y throughout. Whilst vernacular forms in general tend to localize the speaker and can suggest *Gemütlichkeit*, homeliness, or an informal communication context, evoking Prussia linguistically in a military setting conjures up authoritarianism, unquestioning obedience, nationalism, and imperialist politics. Schoenberg was certainly aware of this fact, as his handwritten note in the 1947 score shows, where—underneath the words "Achtung! Stillgestann!"—he stipulates that the voice should be "imitating the manner of speaking and the shrill, breaking voice of the ~~Feldwebel~~ sergeant,"[29] thus linking the Prussian vernacular with aggressive, military authoritarianism. For Levi, key Nazi practices were built on Prussian legacies insofar as the cruelty of the roll call, that "very emblem of the Lager," "fits into the system, the tradition of the drill . . ., the ferocious military practice which was a Prussian inheritance."[30] The Prussian dialect therefore potentially suggests a historical dimension to Nazi Germany: a continuity of evil.

The aggressive *Feldwebelton* (military—or literally sergeant's—tone) has yet another function, which unfolds only in relation to the English narrative. As English is the main language, German stands out as alien, especially since it is not translated. All of the German lines are rendered in direct speech, and the only one speaking German is the sergeant. This marks him out as the central Other. The direct speech here functions as a distancing device for the narrator, who is relieved of the necessity to mediate the officer's commands using his own words, which would—linguistically speaking—have implied an appropriation on the narrator's part of the perpetrator's vantage point. The only other individual who speaks directly (apart from the narrator, of course) is the soldier who pronounces all the Jews dead—again, distance is signaled. However, the direct speech at the same time dramatizes words and scenes: the soldier's proclamation

marks a climax that leads to the surviving Jews singing the *Shema Yisroel*;
the sergeant's words underline the fact that he was present to the actions
of the narrative, whereas the narrator looks back in time.

At first sight, English seems to be reserved for the narrator's story
and reflections, marking English out as the language of the victims here.
However, a closer look reveals echoes of the German in the English, for
example when the words "Get out!" are used by the narrator not once
but twice, or when he declares: "In vain! Much too much noise, much too
much commotion! And not fast enough!" This negative verdict on the
Jews' efforts foreshadows the Nazis' judgment, feared and expected. The
short, abrupt sentences and exclamation marks in this section signal the
narrator's anxiety, as does the sudden shift into the present tense, which,
Camille Crittenden claims, is used "for the sense of immediate action."[31]
However, the present tense is soon abandoned after the description of
the commotion preceding the attack, despite the fact that much more
"immediate action" follows. What the present tense therefore rather constitutes is a passage written in interior monologue, which draws the audience into the thoughts of the narrator, encouraging identification.

The libretto blends several different temporal layers;[32] this is partly
reflected in the tenses chosen. The remembered scene, from daybreak
to the prayer, is represented in the past tense, the tense conventionally
employed in English for depicting events from the past. The narrated
scene gains its sense of immediacy from the Nazi soldiers' direct speech,
which is rendered in the present so that the text seems to shift from present to past tense. However, all direct speech is embedded in the narrative's preterit frame. By contrast, the opening lines, whilst not exclusively
written in the present tense, are nevertheless anchored in the present of
remembering, which is accentuated by the repetition of the verb "remember," and the noun "recollection." The difference between these two
English words is important, as a memory can come unbidden and may
not necessarily be shared, whereas a recollection usually implies a more
active searching of the past for a process or event that is then communicated. In the libretto, the narrator's statement that he had "no recollection" of his time in the Warsaw underground implicitly contrasts with
the dominant memory of the narrated atrocity in the camp: the traumatic
memory of savagery overshadows, even obliterates, the narrator's more
quotidian memories, even if those memories are of prolonged periods
spent avoiding and resisting persecution.

Why mention a period of time that has been forgotten and forms no
part of the narrated story to unfold? The answer to this question lies in
the image used: the "sewers" of Warsaw.[33] Whilst the sewage system was
certainly used by the Warsaw resistance, the term also conjures up associations with filth, waste, stench, in short: a nasty flipside of modern urban
civilization not intended for, even hostile to, human habitation. And of

course sewers *are* underground, their location resonating with the need of the resistance to hide. The only other image of the libretto is that of the "stampede" of wild horses, which contrasts sharply with that of the sewers. And yet, both expressions—"sewers" and "stampede"—serve to describe the Jews' collective acts of resistance, first when in hiding, then when captured and doomed; the alliteration emphasizes the connection between these two images. That this otherwise rather sober text, in which scarcely an adjective is used, should reserve these two powerful images for acts of the persecuted Jewish community underlines the importance attributed to these acts while at the same time betraying the narrator's strong emotional involvement in them.

The fact that the Jews, through the act of singing the *Shema Yisroel*, remember their "long forgotten creed" and emerge as a powerful group as a result, implicitly points to the power of remembrance, which can give agency and collective identity to the remembering subjects. Perhaps it could be argued that the time in the underground, the details of which remain, for the time being, forgotten and thus excluded in *this* narrative, might one day emerge, when somebody else does remember and share, like the narrator in the libretto: remembering and commemorating atrocity, whilst requiring an individual's voice, is grounded in community, which in turn is strengthened by its individuals.

That the act of remembering and communicating is undertaken in English has a resonance beyond the late 1940s when Schoenberg's cantata was conceived. It points to English as the language that was to gain in significance after the end of the war, especially for engagements with the Holocaust. Alan Rosen has pointed to the marginal role occupied by English in relation to the Holocaust at the time of its occurrence, which did not happen in English-speaking countries, nor was the language important for central and Eastern Europe at the time.[34] Yet English, albeit rare among primary sources, "did early on play a significant role in secondary ones," especially in early comprehensive histories of the Holocaust.[35] Schoenberg's libretto can therefore be seen to belong to a group of artistic responses to the Holocaust that form what has since become an extensive Anglophone tradition of writing about the Holocaust. Today, the English language assumes center-stage position when it comes to engagement with the Holocaust, primarily at the expense of Eastern European languages (most notably Polish and Yiddish), but also in comparison to Hebrew as a minority language.

The inclusion of the Hebrew prayer *Shema Yisroel* at the end of the cantata raises interesting questions not just about the relationship *between* languages in the immediate aftermath of the Holocaust, but also about contested versions of Judaism, and differing group affiliations. Modern ("standard") Hebrew, that version of the language developed by Eliezer Ben-Yehuda in the late nineteenth century, is based largely on so-called

Sephardic Hebrew pronunciation, whereas the majority of European Jews would have used so-called Ashkenazi pronunciation in their liturgy. It is worth noting, then, that there is a strong trace of Ashkenazi cultural practices in the use of that group's distinct pronunciation of Hebrew for liturgical purposes, for instance in the *Shema Yisroel.* One of the key markers of Ashkenazi pronunciation is a distinct predilection for the so-called darker vowels (u) and (oy) instead of Israeli Hebrew (o) and (ay): hence *Shema Yisroel* as opposed to modern Hebrew *Sh'ma Yisra'el* (the absence of the glottal stop—marked with an apostrophe—is also a key feature of this liturgical dialect).[36] That Schoenberg and Rabbi Sonderling should have chosen this liturgical dialect is understandable: the greater part of the Jewish community in Los Angeles was Ashkenazi in origin, and the Ashkenazi Jews carried the overwhelming burden of the Holocaust. Hence, this pronunciation tradition would have been profoundly resonant with the Los Angeles audience; it would also have been familiar to Schoenberg from his childhood. Indeed, in the context of Schoenberg and Sonderling's attempts to elicit sympathy and financial support for the plight of European Jewry in the 1938 setting of the *Kol Nidre*, the Ashkenazi articulation of the Hebrew prayer in *Survivor* is clearly more than a coincidence.

One language conspicuously absent in the cantata is that key language of the Jewish victims of the Holocaust, and a significant language of the camp and ghetto systems, Yiddish.[37] It would most likely also have been the language of the narrator, as a Jew incarcerated in the (admittedly fictitious) Warsaw concentration camp.[38] In the early phase of the cantata's gestation, Chochem seems to have tacitly suggested that Schoenberg might set Hirsh Glik's (originally Yiddish-language) Partisan song "Zog nit keynmol."[39] It is unclear from her letter to the composer dated April 2, 1947 whether she expected Schoenberg to set the original Yiddish or the English translation provided by Aaron Kramer.[40] Yiddish, already sidelined here, functioning as a silenced subaltern, is marked from the outset by a specific and consistent marginalization (even though the song in question was actually sung in Yiddish, not in Hebrew as Chochem seems to suggest). Indeed, German attitudes towards Yiddish, especially among the educated elite, and among the German-speaking Jewish elite to which Schoenberg undoubtedly belonged, were quite negative, and the language was routinely dismissed variously as a kind of broken German, a *Jargon*, or as a rootless *Mauscheln* (Yiddish babbling).[41] Schoenberg likely shared the dismissive attitude to Yiddish, common among assimilated German-speaking *Westjuden* (Western Jews) of Central Europe.

Conclusion

Using three languages in a piece little longer than six minutes might well seem, at first sight, somewhat extravagant. However, the juxtaposition of the three languages speaks to a need, not uncommon in early responses to the Holocaust, to restage the traumatic linguistic hybridity of the concentrationary universe and to mark the changes in the linguistic map of the post-Holocaust world. This urge to restage that world and its aftermath is particularly evident in Schoenberg's use of German: the German-speaking composer limits his German to the mimicry of Nazi commands, harsh words that stand out all the more sharply for having been embedded in an English narrative unfolded by a survivor of unknown national background. His choice of English points, perhaps, to the impossibility of speaking about the Holocaust in whatever his native tongue might have been: Polish, perhaps, as the reference to the Warsaw sewers suggests; Yiddish, as the lingua franca of vast swathes of East European Jews prior to their speakers' extinction; German, even, the language once thought to have been that of the "Dichter und Denker," now discredited as that of the "Richter und Henker," as Karl Kraus famously put it.[42]

Whilst Hebrew is confirmed as the language of Jewish religious ritual, English emerges here as the medium of remembrance and commemoration, but would also have been perceived, by Jews and non-Jews alike, as the new lingua franca of retribution and formal justice: the so-called "Subsequent" Nuremberg Trials had been in session since December 9, 1946 and, indeed, while Schoenberg was writing *Survivor*, the highly publicized "Judges' Trial" had been underway for some five months.[43] As the language of the US military authorities, then, especially during the second set of Nuremberg Trials, English was the language of the victors and the language of some notion (however compromised) of legal redress.[44]

That the narrator is the only primary witness, turning the audience into secondary witnesses, in a language not his own, poignantly illustrates the silent absence of those Jewish victims who did not survive (marked here, of course, by the absence, also, of Yiddish in the language matrix of the cantata). This further accentuates the loneliness of the narrator, whose former communities have vanished, and whose future affiliations are as of yet unclear. In traumatized communities after the Holocaust such as his, re-attachments to the old, pre-traumatic collective are blocked by trauma, thereby shaping the affective responses to the post-traumatic community. These blocked attachments re-emerge only as disassociated fragments and remnants of the community (like fetishized photographs, letters, diaries, half-remembered snatches of dialogue, and so on), promising, but always failing, to deliver a return to the plenitude of the originary collective. The fact that the narrator's subject position, like that of the composer's, is *translated*, underlines all the more his fragile, attenuated line to the community of the *Shema*.

The lines of the Hebrew prayer sung by the chorus at the end of the cantata serve both as a promise of attachment to the Law of the one true God and also as a traumatic eruption of the lost community into the narrator's consciousness, like a haunting. This doubled quality of the archaic materials of the *Shema* stages the structural incommensurability of thinking individual and collective together. The narrator in *Survivor* is looking for a modality of productive cultural work, which is invariably archaic: communities cohere around materials that have long since exhausted their logic, but which nonetheless remain as a kernel that persists, forming community's ground, its internal Other. The "forgotten creed," then, is just such an Other, erupting onto the scene like a terrible revelation: "Hear, O Israel, the Lord our God, The Lord is One." But it is an archaic core that no longer grounds a community, and that can only haunt the narrator as unattainable.

Notes

[1] See Joe R. Argentino, "Tripartite Structures in Schoenberg's *A Survivor from Warsaw*," *Music Theory Online* 19 no. 1 (2013): 26 pars.

[2] See Schoenberg's letter to Donald Gray, February 7, 1948, held at the Arnold Schoenberg Center, Satellite Collection, L10, rl.27, fr.261, 263.

[3] Bomart Music Publishers, 1949; revised J. L. Monod, 1979.

[4] Alexander Ringer, *Arnold Schoenberg: The Composer As Jew* (Oxford: Clarendon Press, 1990), 25; David Schiller, *Bloch, Schoenberg and Bernstein: Assimilating Jewish Music* (Oxford: Clarendon Press, 2003); Klára Móricz, *Jewish Identities: Nationalism, Racism, and Utopianism in Twentieth-Century Music* (Berkeley and Los Angeles: University of California Press, 2008).

[5] Moshe Lazar, "Arnold Schoenberg, and His Doubles, A Psychodramatic Journey to His Roots," *Journal of the Arnold Schoenberg Institute* 17, nos. 1–2 (1994): 8–150; Herbert Lindenberger, "Arnold Schoenberg's 'Der Biblische Weg' and 'Moses und Aron': On the Transactions of Aesthetics and Politics," *Modern Judaism* 9, no. 1 (1989): 55–70.

[6] Lazar, "Arnold Schoenberg and His Doubles," 143.

[7] See Naomi André, "Returning to a Homeland: Religion and Political Context in Schoenberg's *Dreimal Tausend Jahre*," in *Political and Religious Ideas in the Works of Arnold Schoenberg*, ed. Russell Berman and Charlotte Cross (New York: Garland, 2000), 259–88, here 265.

[8] Letter dated April 19, 1924, quoted in Nuria Schoenberg-Nono, *Arnold Schönberg, 1874–1951: Lebensgeschichte in Begegnungen* (Klagenfurt: Ritter Klagenfurt, 1992), 204.

[9] See in particular Argentino, "Tripartite Structures," par 1.

[10] The song is Hirsh Glik's famous "Zog nit keynmol az du gest dem letsten veg" (Never say you are on the final path). See Chochem's letter to Schoenberg, dated April 2, 1947, in which she enclosed a translation by Aaron Kramer of Glik's song: Arnold Schoenberg Center, Satellite Collection, L10, rl.24, fr.440–41. For the Yiddish original, see Shmerke Kaczerginski, *Dos gezang fun vilner geto* (Paris: Farband fun di Vilner in Frankraykh, 1947), 52.

[11] For further details, see Michael Strasser, "'A Survivor from Warsaw' as Personal Parable," *Music & Letters*, 76/1 (1995): 52–63, here 52–53. See also Barbara Barry, "Chronicles and Witnesses: *A Survivor from Warsaw* through Adorno's Broken Mirror," *International Review of the Aesthetics and Sociology of Music* 41, no. 2 (2010): 241–63, here 252.

[12] See Joy H. Calico, "Schoenberg's Symbolic Remigration: *A Survivor from Warsaw* in Postwar West Germany," *The Journal of Musicology* 26, no. 1 (2009): 17–43, here 22.

[13] See Strasser, "A Survivor from Warsaw," 56, and Calico, "Schoenberg's Symbolic Remigration," 23, note 17.

[14] Calico, "Schoenberg's Symbolic Remigration," 20.

[15] For a useful overview, and a comprehensive catalogue of Holocaust-themed compositions, see Ben Arnold, "Art Music and the Holocaust," *Holocaust and Genocide Studies* 6, no. 4 (1992): 335–49.

[16] Ira Konigsberg, "*Our Children* and the Limits of Cinema: Early Jewish Responses to the Holocaust," *Film Quarterly* 52, no. 1 (Autumn 1998): 7–19, here 14.

[17] For more on this film as a key statement in the emergence of an early Holocaust aesthetic, see Jiří Cieslar, "Daleká cesta (Distant Journey)," in *The Cinema of Central Europe*, ed. Peter Hames (London: Wallflower Press, 2004), 45–52.

[18] "Di rern, kanaln, zey zenen farsheydn / Geglikhn tsu umvegn, shliakhn un shteglekh . . . / Di shtot iz farzunkn. Di velt—farkapoyert." Avrom Sutzkever, *Geheymshtot* (Mexico City: Yidishe shul in Meksike, 1952), 13 and 18. Translation by Ian Biddle.

[19] Chaim Grade, *Pleytim* (Buenos Aires: Tsentral-farband fun poylishe yidn in Argentine, 1947); *Doyres* (New York: Ikuf farlag, 1945); *Farvoksene vegn* (Paris: Yidisher folks-farband in Frankraykh, 1947). For example, in Emanuel Ringelblum's Warsaw ghetto archive, known as Oyneg Shabes, for example, similar references abound in numerous poems, short stories, and diaries. See Peretz Opachinsky's "Herbstiger Ovnt" (Autumn Evening) and Khaim Semiatitski's "Varshe" (Warsaw); both unpublished, available at *Poetry in Hell*, accessed September 18, 2013, http://poetryinhell.org.

[20] Föllmi speaks of a "Vernebelung" (obfuscation) with regard to both time and location of the action. Beat A. Föllmi, "'I Cannot Remember Ev'rything.' Eine narratologische Analyse von Arnold Schönbergs Kantate 'A Survivor from Warsaw' op. 46," *Archiv für Musikwissenschaft* 55, no. 1 (1998): 28–56, here 30–33.

[21] Unless otherwise stated, quotations from the libretto follow the autograph fair copy, which is available electronically from the Arnold Schoenberg Center at http://www.schoenberg.at/compositions/allewerke.php (accessed September 9, 2014).

[22] There is a long tradition in art of exploring the link between death and sleep. Greek mythology sees sleep (Hypnos) as a brother of death (Thanatos). See Christiane Sourvinou-Inwood, "*Reading*" Greek Death: To the End of the Classical Period (Oxford: Oxford University Press, 1996), 326.

[23] Barry, "Chronicles and Witnesses," 250.

[24] Argentino, "Tripartite Structures," par 6.

[25] In his correspondence, Schoenberg repeatedly refers to the limitations of his command of English and to issues to do with translation. See, for example, letters held by the Arnold Schoenberg Center to: Mr. Herbert Askwith, November 28, 1933, Satellite Collection, L10, rl.1, fr.62; Mr. Willis Wagner, October 14, 1942, Satellite Collection, L10, rl.17, fr.893; Miss Dika Newlin, January 25, 1949, Satellite Collection, L10, rl.2, fr.164.

[26] Primo Levi, *The Drowned and the Saved* (London: Abacus, 2012), 70–71.

[27] Föllmi, "'I Cannot Remember Ev'rything,'" 25.

[28] "Rifle butt." For a facsimile of this score, see http://www.schoenberg.at/ (accessed September 12, 2013).

[29] Strikethrough in the original.

[30] Levi, *The Drowned and the Saved*, 92.

[31] Camille Crittenden, "Texts and Contexts: *A Survivor from Warsaw*, op. 46," in *Political and Religious Ideas in the Works of Arnold Schoenberg*, ed. Berman and Cross, 242.

[32] Föllmi, "'I Cannot Remember Ev'rything,'" 33.

[33] Barbara Barry claims that the "action is initially located in the sewers of Warsaw" (253), but this is not the case: the narrator simply mentions his time in Warsaw. It is also worth noting that Warsaw had, even in Schoenberg's days, already acquired the status of a symbol of Jewish resistance. Sven-Erik Rose refers to the Warsaw ghetto as a *lieu de mémoire*: "the memory of the Warsaw Ghetto as a universal symbol tended to unify and consolidate a wide spectrum of the Jewish community." Rose, "The Oyneg Shabes Archive and the Cold War: The Case of Yehoshue Perle's *Khurbn Varshe*," *New German Critique* 38, no. 1 (2011): 181–216, here 203–4.

[34] Alan Rosen, *Sounds of Defiance: The Holocaust, Multilingualism, and the Problem of English* (Lincoln: University of Nebraska Press, 2005), 7–11.

[35] Rosen, *Sounds of Defiance*, 10.

[36] Dovid Katz, "The Phonology of Ashkenazic," in *Hebrew in Ashkenaz: A Language in Exile*, ed. Lewis Glinert (Oxford: Oxford University Press, 1993), 46–87.

[37] Solomo Birnbaum suggests a figure somewhere in the region of 5,000,000 speakers: Birnbaum, *Grammatik der jiddischen Sprache* (4th enlarged edition, Hamburg: Buske, 1984), 3.

[38] Yiddish was certainly the majority language of Ringelblum's Oyneg Shabes archive.

[39] See Chochem's letter to Schoenberg, dated April 2, 1947 (see note 10). In the same letter, Chochem mentions the song "I believe the Messiah will come" ("ani ma'amin"), which might have been the kernel of the idea for Schoenberg's setting the *Shema Yisroel*.

[40] Ibid., recto.

[41] See, for example, Sander Gilman, *The Case of Sigmund Freud: Medicine and Identity at the Fin de Siècle* (Baltimore, MD, and London: Johns Hopkins University Press, 1993), 26–37.

[42] Karl Kraus, *Schriften*, vol. 12, ed. C. Wagenknecht (Frankfurt am Main: Suhrkamp, 1989), 41.

[43] The Judges' Trial was the third trial of the Nuremberg Military Tribunal and lasted seven months, from March 5 to December 4, 1947. For more on this, see Kevin John Heller, *The Nuremberg Military Tribunals and the Origins of International Criminal Law* (Oxford: Oxford University Press, 2011), 89–90.

[44] For a detailed analysis of the use of translation and the centrality of English in the Nuremberg Trials, see Francesca Gaiba, *The Origins of Simultaneous Interpretation: The Nuremberg Trial* (Ottawa: University of Ottawa Press, 1998), especially 73–74.

Translation

Understanding a Perpetrator in Translation: Presenting Rudolf Höß, Commandant of Auschwitz, to Readers of English

Peter Davies, University of Edinburgh

T HE MEMOIR OF RUDOLF HÖß, commandant of the Auschwitz concentration camp from May 1940 to November 1943, occupies a strange place on bookshop shelves in the German and English-speaking worlds.[1] It is rare for a major Nazi perpetrator to be present in this way, namely as author of a memoir sold under his own name and purporting to offer insight into his actions and motivation on his own terms: Albert Speer is another, but his memoir was an attempt at self-exculpation published while he was still alive, rather than being a text by an executed criminal. Although there has been a shift in scholarly interest away from the Nazi elite to the history of everyday life under the regime, the study of popular opinion and mentality, and the biographies of "ordinary people," interest in Höß's memoir does not seem to have diminished, though it may have affected the way it is read. In this essay, I will explore the changing status of Höß's text, in particular how developing interpretations have affected the way it has been translated. I will ask how the ways in which the text is translated and edited reflect the kinds of knowledge that the text is seen to convey, how different translations of the text position the reader in relation to Höß's narration, and what attitude towards the "Germanness" of the text is on display in each case.

The different editions that I discuss here make a variety of different claims to significance and relevance in order to justify their translation and editorial practices. I will be looking in detail at two English translations. The first, translated into British English by Constantine FitzGibbon, was published in 1959, a year after the first German edition, which was edited by the historian Martin Broszat, originally for the Institut für Zeitgeschichte, Munich; the second is a US English translation from 1992 by Andrew Pollinger, which forms part of a collection of materials on Höß and Auschwitz edited for young readers by Steven Paskuly.[2]

A key issue here is the status of the German language. These editions represent contrasting views about the relationship of the German language to National Socialism: the German edition stresses the linguistic uniqueness of the text, while the English editions work with ideas of universality. The present analysis will show that the editions discussed here place themselves within changing political and historical attitudes towards National Socialism, attitudes that one can characterize broadly as shifting from concern about German revanchism and revisionism to the priorities of Cold War theories of totalitarianism set against the idea of a German cultural "Sonderweg," and finally to a stance of ethical universalism in which Höß's story is seen as relevant for every potential reader.

The translators' task is to demonstrate the relevance of the text for the new readership, and to justify the re-publication of a text written by a mass murderer in a form accessible to an audience beyond scholarly specialists, making it useful for contemporary discourses of Holocaust memory. Specifically, this means emphasizing that the text in some way encapsulates a latent danger within the culture that needs to be counteracted by reflection on the lessons contained in the text.

This leads to a paradoxical situation in which, in order to nullify the danger of the text, it has to be made to feel relevant to the reader: even though Höß's dishonesty and the text's factual inaccuracies have long since been exposed by historians, the autobiographical narrative itself is still seen to tell us something important. The knowledge that the text is seen to convey is therefore of a different order than the facts of history, having to do with how Höß's life story is related and with a reader's tendency to identify with, or at least to seek common ground with, a story told according to the conventions of autobiography.

The Editions

Höß wrote his autobiographical text—the manuscript is entitled "Meine Psyche: Werden, Leben und Erleben"—in January/February 1947 while in prison in Poland. He had been encouraged by the Polish authorities to do so as a way of aiding the memory process while evidence was being gathered against him and other perpetrators. The text is carefully calibrated in order to explain his actions from his background, to stress his lack of personal responsibility, and to create the impression of an inner distance towards the mass murder that he organized: an image of the idealistic National Socialist who wanted the best for Germany, but who was traduced by both party leadership and sadistic underlings. For this reason one must be very alert when reading the text for rationalizations of his actions and motivations on the basis of his upbringing. If one reads carefully, one sees that the stories of trust (in his comrades in the army) and betrayal by authorities (by his father, the Church, the SS leadership, and his own subordinates) that structure the text are not evidence for hidden psychological structures of cause and effect, but were written with an eye to their author's needs at the time of writing.

The notion of "inner distance," the story of an authoritarian upbringing, and the emphasis on the individual's helplessness within the hierarchy of power diminishes Höß's personal responsibility while supporting a "Befehlsnotstand" defense. Thus, even the seemingly unpolitical sections of the text concerning the young Höß's love of nature should be read in the light of his self-defense: the manipulation of a language of nature that has a particular cultural prestige is part of an attempt to create a non-political space for an "I" that is not complicit in genocide. It is part of a postwar strategy to represent an innocent German cultural tradition that resisted Nazism. Paradoxically, the construction of such an "innocent" cultural space was very much part of the Nazi linguistic project, which had the consequence of also providing a ready-made postwar defense strategy. I would like to show that the different editions that I am discussing here provide specific shifts in perspective that are consistent with the development of discourse about the Holocaust in specific postwar contexts.

The first publication of Höß's memoir in any form was the Polish edition of 1956, including a complete translation of the text and accompanying material such as Höß's pen portraits of Himmler and other SS leaders, that had been produced for the Nuremberg prosecutions.[3] Since the manuscript was held in Polish archives, and Höß had been tried and executed in Poland for crimes committed on Polish soil, the new Polish state laid claim to "ownership" of the memoirs, and to the right to interpret them, and the publications were designed to confirm the justice of the verdict against Höß.

The Polish edition sets the text within a judicial context, making it bear a substantial weight of truth. This truth-claim is based on the authority of the Polish possession of the documents, on the role of Polish prosecutors in conducting the interrogation and gaining Höß's trust, and on the status of the text as evidence for Höß's guilt (as a confession) and as historical documentation: the editors take care not to comment on aspects of the narrative structure or on Höß's honesty, as this might undermine the truth-claim made for the text.

The first publication in German, edited by Martin Broszat, makes very different claims to authenticity, based not on its historical truth but on the voice that emerges from the text and on the authority provided by its publication in German. The edition does not include all the supplementary material that the Polish and English editions include, most importantly, Höß's letters to his wife, since these are interpreted as private documents rather than as part of Höß's effort to create a public image of familial decency. It also omits, on grounds of the identifiability of individuals, an episode describing male homosexuality in Auschwitz, which is included in the translated editions.

The truth-claim of the Broszat edition is based not on completeness, but on its Germanness. In order to establish this claim, Broszat begins by shifting the text away from a judicial towards a historiographical function. In his introduction, he describes the text as a "zeitgeschichtliches Dokument": Broszat suggests that this is the only justification for overcoming any scruples about publishing it.[4] The edition therefore requires a set of scholarly tools that make the text speak in a particular way, including careful source criticism and discussion of context. For Broszat, Höß is no longer an individual against whom a legal case is being made, but is a type with relevance beyond his individuality: Broszat intends to emphasize "den historischen Gehalt seines Lebensberichts und . . . das, was an der Person von Höß als typisch und repräsentativ festgehalten zu werden verdient" (*KiA*, 151).

Broszat's comments indicate that he was publishing Höß's text not simply as a historical document, but as an intervention in debates about the causes and contemporary significance of the Holocaust in the 1950s. In the light of theories of "totalitarianism" current in the 1950s, Höß is here seen as a man who sacrifices his individuality within a monolithic structure in which orders are passed from top to bottom, and in which the content of the ideology is less important than its function within the social structure:

> Eilfertig-eifrige Gewissenhaftigkeit eines Mannes, der immer nur im Dienst irgendwelcher Autoritäten steht, der stets seine Pflicht tut, als Henker wie als geständiger Delinquent, der fortgesetzt nur aus zweiter Hand lebt, immer auf ein eigenes Selbst verzichtet hat und deshalb auch bereitwillig sein eigenes Ich, ein erschreckend leeres Ich, dem Gericht in der Form einer Autobiographie übergibt, um *der Sache* zu dienen.[5]

As do all the editions of Höß's text, Broszat takes literally Höß's self-portrayal as a loyal, and largely ideology-free servant of the state, and does not ask why one should bother reading the autobiography of an "erschreckend leeres Ich." Factors such as anti-Semitism are not seen as a motivating force, and the individual initiative and independence of action that Höß shows throughout his career—an ideologically motivated dynamism that was a feature of the management structure of the SS—is downplayed.

Broszat's introduction shifts between defensiveness about accusations of German "barbarism"—"Am Beispiel Höß wird damit auch offenkundig, daß das Wesen der im Dritten Reich hervorgebrachten Unmenschlichkeit verkannt wird, wenn man die Gaskammern und Konzentrationslager allein auf eine besondere teutonische Grausamkeit zurückführt"[6]—and a view that stresses the uniqueness of the German cultural coordinates that produced National Socialism:

Hinzu kommt, daß der bezeichnende Sprachstil der Aufzeichnungen, dem als Zeugnis des Schreibers nicht unwesentliche Bedeutung zukommt, praktisch nur im deutschen Original faßbar wird. Die häufige Manieriertheit in Wortwahl und Ausdruck, durch die sich Höß als "Schöngeist" ausweisen will, seine dem Illustriertenklischee verhafteten "Selbstenthüllungen," schließlich auch der NS-Jargon, in den Höß vielfach unversehens verfällt, — all dies geht zwangsläufig bei einer Übersetzung weitgehend verloren.[7]

Broszat stakes a claim of ownership of the text for Germany based on its particular qualities of language: no translation is able to convey these features, and so genuine understanding is only available to those who are sensitive to particular nuances of German. We can detect here a desire to "repatriate" the text: the legacy of National Socialism is conceived as the Germans' business, and according to Broszat a translated edition can provide little insight into what is most significant about this text.

The first English edition, translated by Constantine FitzGibbon and with an introduction by Lord Russell of Liverpool, establishes itself explicitly as a rival publication to the German edition.[8] FitzGibbon notes in his translator's introduction that the two editions were being prepared simultaneously, making explicit the political link between the two, and making a claim to superiority: the English edition printed the text "exactly as Hoess [sic] wrote it," rather than, as the German edition did, dividing it into chapters and omitting some sections on homosexuality, "presumably for reasons of squeamishness."[9]

However, even FitzGibbon's edition still declined to publish Höß's final letters to his wife, treating them, as Höß himself requested, as personal documents. FitzGibbon's note suggests that he as a translator had an active role in guaranteeing the authenticity of the text: he discusses the source-critical issues connected with the manuscript's provenance, and establishes a connection with the original by discussing his correspondence with Martin Broszat while the latter was working on the German edition. Thus, this English edition authenticates itself by establishing a relation of intimacy with the contemporary German edition, while at the same time making certain claims to superiority. The translator's personal connection with Broszat, who had worked with Höß's Polish interrogators, seals the authenticity of the translation without commenting on the process of translation itself.

Russell's introduction takes the text beyond the simple historical documentation of past atrocity and relocates it within a Cold War paradigm in which Nazi crimes were still of current concern as an illustration of the functioning of "totalitarianism." The text is not relevant as a historical document, since the "horrors described by Hoess are now well known":[10] this is no piece of evidence against Holocaust denial. Instead, it is the style that is the key:

> Hoess's own account of his misdeeds is not only remarkable for what he has described but also for the way he has written it . . . I think that his story should be read for one very good reason. Hoess was a very ordinary little man. He would never have been heard of by the general public had not fate decreed that he was to be, perhaps, the greatest executioner of all time. Yet to read about it in his autobiography makes it all seem quite ordinary. He had a job to do and he carried it out efficiently.[11]

In emphasizing the "ordinariness" of Höß, Russell suggests that the text tells us something about what Hannah Arendt would later call the "banality of evil," namely that modern genocides are organized and carried out by ordinary bureaucrats who are convinced of their own fundamental decency. Here, Russell accepts Höß's self-portrait at face value, since it chimes with then-current thinking about totalitarianism, which tended to equate Nazi and Stalinist dictatorship, interpreting them as two expressions of the same kind of monolithic social structure, in which individuals are subordinated to a top-down force that reduces them to inhuman cogs in the machine: the content of the state ideology is less important than its function within the system.

This thinking has consequences for Russell's interpretation of the text he is introducing: instead of being seen as an account of how a particular upbringing and socialization led Höß towards National Socialism, Russell suggests that the text should be seen as "a reminder, never to be forgotten, of the appalling and disastrous effects of totalitarianism on men's minds."[12] In other words, Höß is seen as the passive tool of a monolithic political system, rather than as the active creator of his own fate, and his mindset is seen as the product of totalitarianism rather than as a contributing cause. The focus on Höß's "ordinariness" is designed to universalize the relevance of the text, taking it beyond a discussion about its specific "Germanness": questions of style are linked to the banality of his language rather than the German cultural roots of his self-expression.

FitzGibbon himself wrote more extensively about his translation and the political views connected with it in an essay published in *Encounter* in 1960, which he had originally offered as an introduction to his edition of Höß's memoirs. In his own account, the publisher had turned it down after the Auschwitz International Committee had objected to his equation of Nazi and Soviet crimes.[13] FitzGibbon writes that an honest appraisal of atrocities in China and the Soviet Union, or during the slave trade or the British occupation of Ireland, shows us that "Auschwitz was not a single or unique event."[14] His interest is therefore not in the Germanness of the text, but in aspects of Höß's personality that might be found in any country among a particular class of administrator: he is interested in Höß's "character or what he [Höß] calls, in his somewhat elevated style, his 'psyche.'"[15]

FitzGibbon finds this self-portrait as "conscientious administrator" credible, perhaps because it fits the "totalitarian" paradigm and the contemporary idea of the bureaucratic perpetrator as unimaginative cog in the machine, and because he rejects what he regards as a racist view of a peculiarly German barbarism.[16] Describing Höß's character as it is revealed in his style, FitzGibbon uses analogies that make Höß's character understandable for his British readers: "He has a somewhat flowery method of self-expression and a liking for what he must have regarded as fine phrases and high-class words. This, I am told, is not uncommon in the minutes of successful civil servants."[17] Höß is proud of his "bourgeois virtues," and "seems no more remarkable than the bore in the office or the country pub."[18]

As I will show, FitzGibbon's translation is a sophisticated attempt to make this style and attitude understandable to a British reader, while still showing concern for the stylistic features of the original. However, FitzGibbon's trust in the authentic revelation of character through style ensures that the vision of the perpetrator that emerges in this text is not substantially different from the image of the nonideological bureaucrat that supported the self-defense of men like Höß or Eichmann: the text is seen as trustworthy in this respect because it fits an explanatory paradigm ("the banality of evil") that has been constructed on the basis of just this kind of text.

A more recent edition of this translation dispenses with the introduction by Lord Russell in favor of Primo Levi's introduction to the Italian edition of the text, in a translation by Joachim Neugroschel.[19] This exchange of authorities in support of the text reflects shifting views about what voices are considered authoritative guides to the meaning of the Holocaust: the centrality of the victorious Allies and the Nuremberg prosecutions has given way to an emphasis on the authenticity and authority of the victim's voice, the judicial has given way to the biographical, and there is more emphasis on the motivating force of anti-Semitism, implying a view of the uniqueness of the Holocaust that FitzGibbon himself rejected.

The recent English edition edited by Stephen Paskuly and translated by Andrew Pollinger reflects a desire to make the biographical content of the memoir relevant to a particular target audience, namely young American readers: Paskuly was a high-school German teacher who taught courses on the Holocaust as part of a human rights curriculum. The text is a complex construction of supporting documentation designed to provide context, while at the same time emphasizing a direct connection between the reader and Höß's autobiographical narrative: the text is not seen as representing the danger of a specifically

German form of nationalism, nor of totalitarianism, but rather of ordinary people forgetting their duty of humanity in the face of dehumanizing media: "Because of the highly organized mass media of today and the orchestrated propaganda spewing forth, be it from the West or from the East, it will be the little men and women with their little hatreds who may once again be a tidal wave of destruction that will sweep humanity into another age of horror."[20]

Paskuly and Pollinger's edition treads a delicate line in encouraging an identificatory, autobiographical reading of Höß's text that emphasizes the danger inherent in familiar ordinariness. Pollinger makes his translation program clear: "to present Höß's words and thoughts in a readable form that today's young Americans could easily understand."[21] In doing so, translator and editor intervene in the style of the text in such a way that the intended readers can identify with the author, with the intention of showing how evil can arise in the most ordinary and familiar of circumstances: the style is contemporary and simplified in order to remove any barriers to comprehension. This has the effect of taking the text seriously as autobiography, taking Höß at his word in order to guard against the danger he represents, while at the same time presenting a personality that is very different from the one that Höß himself presents and to which FitzGibbon responded.

We can sum up the approaches of the four editions I have discussed here as follows. In the Polish edition, the text is a piece of evidence in the case against Höß; it is a document of German guilt, and is deliberately distanced from any universal moral relevance. The German edition, with Martin Broszat's apparatus, attempts to show the cultural specificity of National Socialism, and makes a double-edged claim to a form of German *Sonderweg*: Nazism is a uniquely German phenomenon, entailing profound self-critical scrutiny of cultural traditions and attitudes, but this also means that only those who possess the necessarily cultural understanding and linguistic competence can truly understand the text. The first English edition makes the opposite claim: that the Western Allies have sovereignty over the interpretation of National Socialism, which is a claim significant for what it says about totalitarianism in general, rather than about Germany itself. The second English edition stresses the universal ethical relevance of the text as a negative example, and positions it as a tool in the struggle against prejudice of all kinds in contemporary society.

The two English translations respond to Höß's style in different ways, reflecting their different aims. FitzGibbon explores ways of conveying the text's style in order to give a portrait of a functionary characterized by what Lord Russell refers to as "a schizophrenic capacity for sentiment and sadism."[22] By contrast, Pollinger's translation seeks ways of making a direct connection with the contemporary reader through the intensification of drama and linguistic simplification. It emphasizes Höß's ordinariness and plays down the cultural specificity of the text: it also shapes the text in ways that make clearer connections between Höß's upbringing and his later actions. All of the editions under consideration here make use of the text for present political concerns, encouraging readings that stress the text's immediate relevance in the current context.

Translation Strategies: Creating a Perpetrator in the Text

Where the Polish text is concerned with establishing the reliability and authenticity of the text as a factual source, and shows little interest in Höß's background or character, both of the English translations treat the text as an autobiography, attempting to create an impression of character through aspects of style, looking for explanations for Höß's actions in his background, as well as seeking to make the text relevant for their target audiences in different ways. Rather than looking at the way translators respond to his descriptions of his activities in the concentration camp system, I will instead look at how they set up his childhood and upbringing as a potential explanation for his later behavior as commandant of Auschwitz.

Höß opens his account as follows:

> Im Folgenden will ich versuchen, über mein innerstes Leben zu schreiben. Ich will versuchen, aus der Erinnerung wirklichkeitsgetreu alle wesentlichen Vorgänge, alle Höhen und Tiefen meines psychologischen Lebens und Erlebens wiederzugeben.
>
> Um das Gesamtbild möglichst vollständig zu umreißen, muß ich bis zu meinen frühesten Kindheitserlebnissen zurückgreifen.
>
> Bis zu meinem sechsten Lebensjahr wohnten wir ziemlich außerhalb der Stadt Baden-Baden. In der weiteren Umgebung unseres Hauses befanden sich nur einzelne Bauerngehöfte. (*KiA*, 31)

If we compare the FitzGibbon and Pollinger translations, we find quite different emphases:

> In the following pages I want to try and tell the story of my innermost being. I shall attempt to reconstruct from memory a true account of all the important events and occurrences in my life and of the psychological heights and depths through which I have passed.
>
> In order to give as complete a picture as possible, it is essential that I first return to the earliest experiences of my childhood.
>
> Until I was six years old, we lived in the remoter outskirts of Baden-Baden, in a neighbourhood consisting of scattered and isolated farmhouses. (*CoA*, 29)

> In the following narrative I will try to write about my deepest per-
> sonal thoughts and feelings. I will attempt to recall, to the best of
> my memory, all the important events, all the highs and lows of my
> psychological life, and the experiences which affected me. For the
> reader to completely understand the entire picture I will sketch, I
> must return to my earliest childhood memories.
>
> My family lived in an average home outside of Baden-Baden until
> I was six. In the surrounding area there were only isolated farm-
> houses. (*DD* 48)

FitzGibbon placed the emphasis on the "truthfulness" of the account and
on the attempt to give a complete picture: understandable when one of the
aims of the publication is to document historical facts. Characteristically for
his translation, he also tries to find ways of rendering Höß's attempts at a
cultivated style, for example, using "my innermost being" for "mein innerstes
Leben." By contrast, Pollinger employs a more contemporary colloquial register, and the emphasis is on the reader's understanding, rather than on the
truthfulness of the picture. His intention is to create an effect of immediacy
and personal relevance for his readers, and the key shift in this passage is the
statement that Höß grew up in an "average home," which is absent from the
original: the specifically German cultural context is less important here than
the connection that is made with contemporary readers.

Höß's childhood reminiscences are related in a drearily ingratiating
German style, combining a need to impress by using an awkward literary register with angling for sympathy with descriptions of his solitary
and romantic nature: "Dies behagte mir doch wenig, und ich versuchte,
mich wo es nur irgend angängig war, der Aufsicht zu entziehen und
allein auf eigene Entdeckungsfahrt zu ziehen. So hatte es mir der ganz
in der Nähe beginnende große Wald mit den hohen Schwarzwaldtannen
besonders angetan. Doch allzuweit drang ich nicht vor, meist nur so weit,
daß ich von den Berghängen unser Tal sehen konnte" (*KiA*, 31). Again,
FitzGibbon looks for stylistic equivalents, trying to convey what Broszat
referred to as Höß's "Manieriertheit," while Pollinger's version is concerned with immediacy:

> I derived little pleasure from this, and tried, wherever possible, to
> escape their supervision and go off on voyages of solitary explora-
> tion. I was fascinated by the immense woods with their tall, Black
> Forest pines, that began near our house. I never ventured to go far
> into them, however, never beyond a point where I was able, from
> the mountain slopes, to keep our own valley in sight. (*CoA*, 29)

> This wasn't much fun, and I always tried, whenever possible, to
> escape their supervision and go off exploring by myself. I was often
> lured into the nearby Black Forest by the tall pine trees. I never went

in very far and always kept sight of our valley from the mountain tops. (*DD*, 48)

A significant distinction between the translations is how they treat Höß's account of his upbringing as the root of his later career and attitudes. Pollinger, in particular, tends to look for explanations in Höß's early life: since the text is intended for young readers, these experiences gain an importance far beyond what they had been granted in the Polish edition, for example. It does, however, entail taking Höß at his word in his narration, so that the text can be read in order to discuss the effects of an authoritarian upbringing, rather than in terms of its narrative strategies.

For example, slight shifts in emphasis in translation and paragraph division give a very different impression of Höß's behavior as a child. Höß confesses that he was not especially well-behaved at school, but claims that he had a lot of friends and a pronounced sense of justice. He would always fight back against any slight: "Ich ließ mir nichts gefallen und setzte mich immer durch" (*KiA*, 36). FitzGibbon leaves this sentence in the middle of a paragraph, and translates it in a way that suggests standing up against injustice: "I stood no nonsense, and always held my own" (*CoA*, 33). By contrast, Pollinger emphasizes Höß's aggression and willpower, and presents the sentence as a separate paragraph: "I was always able to get my way" (*DD*, 51). While FitzGibbon uses language appropriate to the situation of children's games, Pollinger makes a comment on Höß's character that looks forward to his later crimes, separating it from its immediate context: Pollinger's Höß is active, subordinating others to his will, while FitzGibbon's defends himself and asserts his place in the group.

Pollinger and FitzGibbon deal with the contradictoriness of Höß's account of his relationship with his father in different ways. In Höß's account, it is hard to discern whether the child enjoyed freedom to do what he wanted or whether he was brought up according to strict military discipline. Höß seems to want to have it both ways, wanting to portray himself both as independent and as an individual who had been brought up to obey orders unquestioningly:

> Meine Eltern ließen mich gewähren.
> Durch das Gelübde meines Vaters, wonach ich Geistlicher werden sollte, stand mein Lebensberuf fest vorgezeichnet. Meine ganze Erziehung war darauf abgestellt. Ich wurde von meinem Vater nach strengen militärischen Grundsätzen erzogen. Dazu die tiefreligiöse Atmosphäre in unserer Familie. Mein Vater war fanatischer Katholik. (*KiA*, 33)

FitzGibbon squares the circle by separating the two ideas; he also softens Höß's description of his father:

My parents let me do more or less as I wished.
My father had taken a vow that I should be a priest, and my future
profession was therefore already firmly laid down. I was educated
entirely with this end in view. My father brought me up on strict
military principles. I was also influenced by the deeply religious
atmosphere that pervaded our family life, for my father was a devout
Catholic. (*CoA*, 31)

Pollinger takes up a more critical stance, employing the word "fanatic,"
which is unequivocally negative in English, without the echo of the positive connotations that it could have in Nazi discourse (for example, in
expressions like "fanatischer Glaube"):

My parents gave me the freedom to do as I wanted because my
father had made a vow that I would lead a religious life and become
a priest. The way I was raised was entirely affected by this. I was
raised in a strong military fashion because of my father. Because of
his faith, there was a strong religious atmosphere in our family. My
father was a fanatic Catholic. (*DD*, 49)

Pollinger creates a causal connection between the freedom that young
Höß claims he was granted and his father's plans for his career in the
priesthood. Although it is possible that this arises from a misunderstanding of the function of "durch" at the beginning of the sentence,
it strengthens the translation's critical stance towards Höß's account of
his upbringing, though at the cost of significant distortion in translation. Pollinger's Höß is therefore a child who responds to an oppressive
upbringing by asserting his willpower in other situations, and the text can
be made to fit a plea for tolerance and liberal values.

Höß's trivial Romanticism is an important aspect of his style, contributing to the portrait of a National Socialist functionary manipulating a culturally privileged language of *Innerlichkeit* in order to construct
an "innocent" inner life beyond politics and to establish his status as an
"Einzelgänger" (*KiA*, 32). This strategy begins early in the text, when
Höß uses language drawn from Romantic poetry to describe his visits
to the town reservoir: "Stundenlang konnte ich dem geheimnisvollen
Rauschen hinter den dicken Mauern lauschen" (*KiA*, 32). FitzGibbon
finds an appropriate poetic cliché—"For hours on end I would listen to
the mysterious whisper of the water" (*CoA*, 29)—while Pollinger is more
prosaic: "For hours on end I would listen in secret to the rushing water
behind its thick walls" (*DD*, 48).

The key to this pedantic manipulation of the language of
Romanticism—presumably part of his educational background and
perhaps remembered from *Wandervogel-* or *Freiluftdichtung* from his
youth—appears much later in the text, when Höß describes the scene

of victims going to their deaths in the first gas chambers at Auschwitz-Birkenau, which were housed in farmhouses converted in the spring of 1942: "Im Frühjahr 1942 gingen Hunderte von blühenden Menschen unter den blühenden Obstbäumen des Bauerngehöftes, meist nichts-ahnend, in die Gaskammern, in den Tod. Dies Bild vom Werden und Vergehen steht mir auch jetzt noch genau vor den Augen" (*KiA*, 194).

This passage encapsulates Höß's narrative stance in his text: an attempt to ingratiate himself with his reader and demonstrate his apolitical, sensitive nature only serves to reveal his self-centeredness and utter indifference to the fate of his victims; his manipulation of a poetic language of nature combined with trivial philosophizing treats the killings as a natural phenomenon, thus refusing personal responsibility and aligning himself with a supposedly non-political German tradition of nature lyric and *Innerlichkeit*.

Pollinger feels the need to clarify what is happening, introducing extra historical and technical words for aspects of the killing process: his translation exposes the reality behind Höß's euphemism, but pays no attention to the manner in which it is described: "In the spring of 1942 hundreds of people in the full bloom of life walked beneath the budding fruit trees of the farm into the gas chamber to their death, most of them without a hint of what was going to happen to them. To this day I can still see these pictures of the arrivals, the selections, and the procession to their death" (*DD*, 159). The irony is still there, but the translation lacks the pedantic attempt to underline the irony by repeating "blühend"; Pollinger's translation comments on Höß's text, lamenting the loss of the people "in the full bloom of life," instead of representing Höß's attitude towards them. The irony that arises from Pollinger's translation of Höß's text here is a humane irony, underlining the horror of the killing taking place in a bucolic scene, while Höß's is inhumane, commenting on an interesting incongruity in an attempt to display his sensitivity, depth, and *Bildung*. However, Pollinger's text does leave the possibility open that Höß is experiencing genuine repentance as the images parade before his eyes, while the German text makes very clear that he simply wishes to create a more sympathetic self-portrait.

FitzGibbon responds to this key passage in a very different way, one that supports his translation project: "During the spring of 1942 hundreds of vigorous men and women walked all unsuspecting to their death in the gas-chambers, under the blossom-laden trees of the 'Cottage' orchard. This picture of death in the midst of life remains with me to this day" (*CoA*, 100). If we bear in mind FitzGibbon's comment on Höß's style as reminiscent of the "successful civil servant" or the country pub bore, then this passage reveals a key to his strategy: the false-note poeticisms ("all unsuspecting," "blossom-laden") lead to a quotation from the Burial Service of the Book of Common Prayer

("In the midst of life we are in death"), which strikingly replaces Höß's attempt to place himself within the German cultural tradition with a phrase familiar amongst English-speaking Anglicans, and probably beyond. FitzGibbon has tried to reproduce a particular kind of British English speech, showing how the language of totalitarianism might work when spoken by an English-speaker: his own novel, *When the Kissing had to Stop* (1960), which portrayed a British Stalinist society, attempted to do much the same thing. Where the introduction by Lord Russell sets out the political purpose of the translation, FitzGibbon's text fleshes it out with a voice and personality.

Pollinger and FitzGibbon each create a voice tailored to the political project of their particular publication, and to their implied audience. Where FitzGibbon vocalizes a tweedy, conservative High Anglican English country-pub bore with an education beyond his intelligence, who is seen to be the kind of thoughtless administrator that a dictatorship requires, Pollinger portrays an "ordinary" child speaking in contemporary American colloquialisms, with a penchant for drama and excitement, and whose motivation for his crimes is found in his upbringing. FitzGibbon maintains an ironic distance to his subject, while Pollinger encourages the reader to identify with him, in order to show how easy it is for prejudice to take root in any society.

Conclusion

None of the editions I have discussed here are genuinely "resistant," in the sense of forcing the reader into a critical distance towards the text, undermining its assertions at every turn. Facts are corrected and falsehoods exposed in footnotes, but the deeper structures of the text, involving the conventions of autobiographical narrative and reader identification, are left untouched, or even emphasized. Neither English translation seeks to pin the blame for the crimes of National Socialism on a set of uniquely German historical or cultural characteristics (as had, for example, A. J. P. Taylor in 1945).[23] FitzGibbons's translation provides a Cold-War-era counterpoint to theories of a German *Sonderweg*, with "antitotalitarianism" assuming the mantle of ethical universalism, while Pollinger's is about the presence of prejudice in all societies and the dangers of particular kinds of upbringing: it takes a very different view to the theory of German exceptionalism put forward by Daniel Jonah Goldhagen a few years later.[24] Both translations develop a voice that is designed to speak to a particular target readership, suggesting that there is nothing uniquely German about a character like Höß.

Martin Broszat's insistence that the key to understanding Höß lies in a careful reading of particular features of his German suggests, by contrast, that National Socialism arose from uniquely German cultural coordinates expressed in features of the language that are untranslatable. The contrasting emphases amongst the editions under discussion here give us a clear view of the political subtext to the theories of translatability or untranslatability that underlie them: it is a question of ownership of the right to interpret the text and put it to use within a particular political context. If it is untranslatable, then only those with the right kind of knowledge—liberal Germans struggling with the legacy of National Socialism—are able to claim rights of interpretation; if it is translatable, then the text can be claimed for universalist values, while in the process making invisible cultural difference.

Notes

[1] *Kommandant in Auschwitz: Autobiographische Aufzeichnungen des Rudolf Höß,* ed. Martin Broszat (Munich: dtv, 22nd ed. 2004; original publication Stuttgart: Deutsche Verlags-Anstalt, 1958). This text will be referred to henceforth as *KiA.*

[2] *Commandant of Auschwitz,* trans. and ed. Constantine FitzGibbon (London: Phoenix Press, 2000; original publication London: Weidenfeld & Nicholson, 1959), henceforth *CoA; Death Dealer: the Memoirs of the SS Kommandant at Auschwitz,* ed. Steven Paskuly (Cambridge, MA: Da Capo Press, 1996; original publication Buffalo, NY: Prometheus Books, 1992), henceforth *DD.*

[3] *Wspomnienia Rudolfa Hoessa, komendanta obozu oświęcimskiego,* ed. Jan Sehn, trans. Jan Sehn and Eugenii Kocwy (Warsaw: Główna Komisja Badania Zbrodni Hitlerowskich w Polsce, 1956).

[4] Martin Broszat, "Einleitung," *Kommandant in Auschwitz,* 7–30, here 7.

[5] Broszat, "Einleitung,"13.

[6] Broszat, "Einleitung," 20.

[7] Broszat, "Einleitung," 15.

[8] Edward Russell had served as a legal advisor to the Nuremberg prosecution and was the best-selling author of *The Scourge of the Swastika: A Short History of Nazi War Crimes* (London: Cassell, 1954).

[9] Constantine FitzGibbon, "Translator's Note," *Commandant of Auschwitz,* 13–14, here 14.

[10] Lord Russell of Liverpool, "Introduction," *Commandant of Auschwitz* (1959), 15–29, here 25. This introduction is omitted from the 2000 edition.

[11] Russell, "Introduction," 25.

[12] Russell, "Introduction," 26.

[13] Constantine FitzGibbon, *Random Thoughts of a Fascist Hyena* (London: Cassell, 1963), 33–57, here 34. The re-publication of the essay also contains an account of FitzGibbon's trip to Auschwitz as translator for Henry Moore. FitzGibbon was a novelist and historian who had also translated a number of memoirs by former German officers, such as Heinz Guderian.

[14] FitzGibbon, *Random Thoughts,* 50.

[15] FitzGibbon, *Random Thoughts*, 54.

[16] FitzGibbon discusses the latter in his critical commentary on postwar Allied policy, *Denazification* (London: Joseph, 1969).

[17] FitzGibbon, *Random Thoughts*, 56.

[18] FitzGibbon, *Random Thoughts*, 55 and 56.

[19] Primo Levi, "Introduction," trans. Joachim Neugroschel, *CoA*, 19–25.

[20] Stephen Paskuly, "Preface," *DD*, 11–13, here 12.

[21] Andrew Pollinger, "Translator's Note," *DD*, 17.

[22] Russell, "Introduction," 25.

[23] A. J. P. Taylor, *The Course of German History* (London: Hamish Hamilton, 1945).

[24] Daniel Jonah Goldhagen, *Hitler's Willing Executioners: Ordinary Germans and the Holocaust* (New York: Knopf, 1996).

Translating Testimony: Jakob Littner's Typescript and the Versions of Wolfgang Koeppen and Kurt Nathan Grübler

Simon Ward, University of Durham

IN THIS ARTICLE, I will take up the question of how the Shoah inflected understandings of the German language through an examination of one particular and quite peculiar case study: how the unpublished typescript of Jakob Littner's testimony about life in a Jewish ghetto, "Mein Weg durch die Nacht," has been transformed into two distinct versions, firstly a fictionalized reworking by the German author, Wolfgang Koeppen, that for over forty years circulated as an authentic document under the name of Littner, and then, latterly, translated into English by a relative of Littner's, Kurt Nathan Grübler. That latter translation both relies upon and seeks to distance itself from Koeppen's text, by reclaiming an authenticity which it would appear Koeppen's fictional version occluded.

A key characteristic of testimony as it is conventionally conceived is its singularity, as a unique making of truth on the part of an irreplaceable witness. Testimony is always testifying to *a singular act*: "it does what it says at this very instant; it cannot essentially be reduced to narration."[1] For Derrida, testimony can only be testimony if it is radically incommensurable with an informational conception of truth. Yet the testimony (and its translations) under discussion in this essay has been marked, since its appearance in the public sphere, not by its singularity, but by its re-narration, its doubling through retelling via other acts of writing that are already "translations" of this preceding testimony and are frequently discussed in terms of the transmission of information.

The testimony in question, Jakob Littner's typescript (which is thus already at one remove from oral testimony, and may well not have been typed by Littner himself), was produced in 1945, only months after the end of his ordeal in, first, a Jewish ghetto in Zbaraz in what is now the Ukraine, and then in hiding in an unlit underground cellar. The history of the typescript is a complex but important story. It was completed in Munich (Littner's home town), on November 9, 1945, and was then (presumably) transported across to the United States when Littner emigrated from Europe in July 1947. The typescript must have been duplicated at certain times, for Kurt Grübler, who was researching the history of the Littner family, possessed two copies when he was contacted in the mid-1990s by Reinhard K. Zachau, the American academic. A copy of the typescript is now held in the Holocaust Memorial Museum in Washington, DC, an archive that will provide a photocopy on request.[2] It has also been translated into English by the same Kurt Nathan Grübler.[3]

This typescript also formed the basis for another text, *Jakob Littners Aufzeichnungen aus einem Erdloch*, that was published in 1948. That same text had been reprinted in a facsimile edition in 1985 by Kupfergraben Verlag in Berlin, and was then republished, to much literary debate, with the same title, but now under the authorship of the well-known West German writer, Wolfgang Koeppen, in 1992. While admitting that there had been some notes from which he had elaborated his text, Koeppen, however, did not mention the existence of the typescript in his preface to the 1992 publication. Reinhard Zachau encountered Kurt Grübler and the typescript as part of his quest to discover the "genuine" Jakob Littner,[4] whom he had sought to trace after it had become clear that Littner's biography and Holocaust experiences had, as Koeppen's preface suggested, been the basis for Koeppen's version. The belated surfacing of the typescript demonstrated how closely (and, one might say, faithfully), Koeppen had worked with the typescript in composing his own work.

The multifaceted ethical and documentary complexities of the Koeppen/Littner case have been described and analyzed on a number of occasions. The rights and wrongs of Koeppen's adaptation of Littner's text have produced two major lines of argument: one that condemns any "tampering" with a Holocaust memoir (the position of, e.g., McCombs, Klüger, and Zachau), and the other, less common, which more benevolently stresses the imaginative potential of literature and literary form. Ruth Franklin argues that Koeppen's work is "an artistically coherent text, one that rises above the specific circumstances of its narrator to present a vision of humanity in extremis."[5] In this article, I revisit in the specific context of translation the questions raised in my earlier reading of Koeppen's and Littner's texts, which focused on how Koeppen's text interrogates language as a specific tool of racial definition.[6] In doing so, I mean to open out questions of alterity that are implicated both in any work of translation, and any re-telling of testimony. My starting point is Walter Benjamin's citation from Rudolf Pannwitz in "Die Aufgabe des Übersetzers" (The Task of the Translator), where Pannwitz criticizes those translators who "have a far greater reverence for the usage of their own language than for the spirit of the foreign works . . . The basic error of the translator is that he preserves the state in which his own language happens to be instead of allowing his language to be powerfully affected by the foreign tongue."[7]

This essay argues that Koeppen's strategy is close to the spirit of translation that Pannwitz invokes, precisely through his attention to the foreignness of language in the postwar situation. Koeppen is attuned to the complexities of using the German language in the wake of its misuse by National Socialism, including the terminology of race and the Shoah, and thus his text is a re-imagining of Littner's experience through the lens of language. By contrast, Grübler's text, which is literally a translation, takes for granted the foundations on which it reworks and reshapes Littner's text for its own present linguistic context. It views the original and itself to a large extent, in Benjamin's terms, as simply "Mitteilung" (the communication of information), in which process language is a transparent medium, an assumption that Grübler's own translations ironically themselves demonstrate to be an illusion. There is indeed a point of contact between Derrida and Benjamin, in that what they view as inadequate in testimony and translation, respectively, is a method that privileges mere transmission of information.

In discussions of Littner's testimony, it is rarely, if ever described in terms of the value of its testimonial immediacy, but is almost always seen as in need of supplementation. The publication of Grübler's translation provides a striking example of this. Before the reader even arrives at the translation of Littner's text, she is confronted with a series of preliminary texts that mediate the encounter with Littner's testimony. The first of these is the frontispiece, which presents a facsimile of a *handwritten* dedication in German, presumably taken from one of the copies of the typescript in Grübler's possession (it does not appear in the typescript I obtained from the Holocaust Memorial Museum). Directly below this reproduction is a printed translation of the dedication, which indicates that it is dedicated to "Davis and his loved ones." In its doubled form, this frontispiece serves two rhetorical purposes: first, it establishes familial transference as the central function of the testimony; second, through the use of the handwriting, it gestures towards the authenticity and authorship of the testimony, but also of the translation that follows: that is, just as the English translation "matches" the authentic German text, so does the rest of the translation.

There follows a foreword, written by Reinhard Zachau, that establishes a set of premises for the encounter with the text. Zachau retells the search for the original source in order to argue, in a reiteration of his initial article from 1999, that Koeppen's account is a misrepresentation of Littner's "Urtext" (as Zachau terms it, reinforcing the sense of a primary originality which is crucial to his argument), and to assert that Grübler's version is more historically objective.

The first of these is significant in that Zachau claims that Koeppen only made use of episodes that "contained poetic power" in an attempt to render Littner's original "more literary," and that his use of symbolism and mythological frames of reference deprives "Littner's *suffering* [my emphasis—SW] of its singularity."[8] This is an odd claim, since, in Zachau's reading, Littner's testimony of suffering is of interest not for its singularity, but as part of the broader experience of the Holocaust. The singularity of his suffering was already undone in Koeppen's act of re-narration, not in any additional literary flourishes. In addition, Zachau claims Koeppen's mythologizing strategies enable "the SS butchers [to be] absolved of their guilt."[9] Neither Koeppen nor Littner use the German term for "butcher" ("Metzger") at any point, though Grübler does in his translation, thus constructing an odd doubling between the foreword and the translation that ultimately follows. At the same time, Zachau claims Koeppen over-represents "good Germans" in his work, whereas, as Ruth Franklin has shown, this would also have to be considered a "failing" of Littner's report, if one were to take it as a valid criterion.[10]

In contrast, Zachau subtly establishes the authority of Grübler's translation by quoting from it as if it were the original (in the form "Littner/Grübler"), thus erasing the question of translation as modification of the original at all. Such quotations are of course themselves always already selective and interpretative re-narrations of the testimony (and I shall discuss the nature of Grübler's translation below in more detail). Zachau's central claims for Grübler's "translation and edition"[11] are, first, that it enables Littner's text to appear in English for the first time, and that, second, through the addition of supplementary historic and personal documents, it provides Littner's text with "more historical significance." Zachau then however admits that these supplements "tend to slightly encroach upon the . . . usefulness . . . of Littner's report,"[12] presumably because they deflect from the "immediate experience" of the testimony, which Zachau sees as the report's usefulness. He is caught in a double-bind: he wants historical contextualization, but also the authentic impact of the "Urtext."

Zachau does not expand upon this point, but instead uses Grübler's translation as a way of returning to what he sees as the failings of Koeppen's text, which is "badly missing" "historical accuracy."[13] Zachau is now able to "classify" Koeppen's text as "an elaborate fictionalization of authentic events where the dividing line between truth and fantasy remains blurred (see Wilkomirski)."[14] Yet this attempt at "classification" is immediately undermined through Zachau's parenthetical comparison of Koeppen's reworking of Littner's typescript to the invented memoirs of Benjamin Wilkomirski, a comparison that does not do justice to the complexity of either case. In opposition thus to some dubious hybrid genre (fictionalized Holocaust testimony?), Zachau reinforces the status of Grübler's book as "more detailed" (in terms of Littner's biography as well as of "the bigger historical picture." Ultimately, the "host of documents . . . greatly enhances the historical objectivity of the book."

Zachau, who had argued that Koeppen had undone the "singular-ity" of Littner's suffering, seems to suggest that Littner's suffering was always in need of supplementation. That supplementation is understood in terms of the provision of information. Derrida is helpful in clarifying what is at stake here. As Derrida observes, in order to give testimony, I have to have had an experience that makes me *irreplaceable*. And yet my testimony has to be exemplary, that is, "anyone who *in my place*, at that instant, would have seen or heard or touched the same thing and could repeat exemplarily, universally, the truth of my testimony . . . The singu-lar must be universal."[15] Zachau's claim for the historical informativeness and objectivity of Grübler's text undermines the radical subjectivity of Littner's testimony.

Grübler makes quite different claims in the next preliminary, his preface to his translation of Littner's typescript. Grübler begins with an assertion of his authority to work on the text, which is grounded in his biography as a Viennese Jew related to Littner, born in 1925, who had himself gone into exile in the United States shortly after the *Anschluss* in 1938. He then writes not of translating the typescript, but of "compil-ing" the book, which again reinforces the idea of his book as a source of "information." The purpose of the book is to "enlighten future genera-tions of the terrible events that occurred during the supposedly advanced twentieth century."[16] While Grübler places his name at the end of this preface, the following "Editor's Note" is unsigned, and simply provides biographical detail about Jakob Littner himself. This apparently objective summary is striking for the fact that, although it re-narrates the events, contained in the memoir themselves, that precede Littner's arrival in the Zbaraz ghetto, it does not provide an account of "the harrowing events described in this memoir" but jumps directly to the details of Littner's life after the end of the war. This gives the reader the clear sense that the focus and indeed the importance of the memoir lies in the experience of reading directly about the events in the ghetto.

Whatever one may think of Koeppen's "fictionalization" or Grübler's translation, both texts are doublings of the original that seek to give it a wider significance through acts of supplementation. Neither work can be straightforwardly faithful to the original. In that sense, the concepts of "fidelity" and "freedom," which are for Walter Benjamin the "tradi-tional concepts" in every discussion of translation, do not provide a viable framework for reading the set of questions which these works provoke. Rather, a more viable question is posed through Pannwitz's question con-cerning the status of the translator: how does the translator reflect upon the language that they themselves use to appropriate a text (and experi-ence) that is foreign to them?

Grübler, as we have seen, claims to appropriate Littner's testimony in the service of a larger narrative about the history of the twentieth century, in other words, he sees himself as translating Littner's testimony into history. Koeppen goes down an altogether different route. In approaching Koeppen's text, we also have to see it as enveloped in a series of palimpsests. The most crucial of these is the foreword that Koeppen wrote for the re-publication of the work in 1992 (the 1948 edition, reprinted in 1985, had no foreword, just two epigraphs, presumably chosen by Koeppen.) In that foreword, Koeppen tells an abbreviated and ultimately false story about how he came to write his book:

> Zu dem neuen Verleger [Herbert Kluger] kam ein Mann aus der deutschen Hölle. Einst ein angesehener Bürger seiner Stadt, ein Briefmarkenhändler mit internationaler Reputation, dann ein Jude, der verschleppt wurde, in Ghettos und Vernichtungslagern gequält, vor der Tür des Todes gestanden und in Erschießungsgräben auf die schon Toten geblickt hatte. Das war noch nah.
> . . . Er wollte sprechen und blickte in Gesichter, die alles gebilligt hatten.
> Ich gehörte nicht zu den Leuten, die nichts gewußt haben. Die Hölle war überall. Ich war mir meiner Hilflosigkeit bewußt. Wer ging schon auf den Markt und schrie? Und hinter jedem stand der eigene Tod in jenen Jahren.
> . . . Der Verleger hörte zu, er notierte sich Orte und Daten. Der Entkommene suchte einen Schriftsteller. Der Verleger berichtete mir das Unglaubliche. Ich hatte es geträumt. Der Verleger fragte mich: "Willst du es schreiben?"
> Ich . . . schrieb die Leidensgeschichte eines deutschen Juden. Da wurde es meine Geschichte.[17]

In the light of what we now know about the production of Koeppen's work, this story is economical with the truth to say the least. There are, however, two key moments in this foreword that highlight Koeppen's approach in appropriating Littner's experiences. First, he claims that he "had dreamt" the unbelievable things that Littner reported; in other words, they were already present in his imagination. Second, the story of the suffering of a German Jew "became" Koeppen's story. Disregarding the potential play on story/history here ("Geschichte" means both), the phrase "German Jew" is striking, since, earlier in the foreword, Koeppen highlights the transition of Littner from a "respected citizen of his town" into a "Jew, who was deported." Koeppen's foreword demonstrates an awareness of the fluidity of classifications, something that is evident in his additions to Littner's typescript.

Koeppen's additions to the text demonstrate how his character's sense of collective identity is a process of narration and negotiation. This is one aspect where the difference in form between Littner's typescript and Koeppen's text makes itself profoundly evident. Littner's testimony is written after the event, and often looks forward to events that are to happen later.[18] Koeppen's text is written as a series of journal entries that retell or reflect on events that have just happened (with one exception, where the text slips into the present tense). It is a re-narration that not only lends his account immediacy and apparent authenticity, in that it reproduces the act of testimony "doing what it says at this very instant," but it also allows changes of consciousness in the narrative voice to be registered, something that was clearly not important to Littner, whose memoir was intended both to be a sign of his religious faith and "einen Gedenkstein" for those whom history would otherwise forget.[19] Thanks to the journal style of Koeppen's text, the shifts in the narrator's self-definition can be registered without any awkward self-consciousness. Indeed the freely-invented opening of Koeppen's book certainly appears to lack self-awareness: "Wir haben große Tage erlebt, und ich freue mich, daß es München war, wo der Welt, September 1938, der Frieden gegeben wurde."[20] Along with the dramatic irony of the protagonist's misplaced optimism regarding "peace in his time," the opening sentence also gives expression to his abstract sense of community in the first-person plural and to a fondness for Munich (which he shares with his real-life model). The second entry then discusses the lack of enthusiasm for war amongst "den Deutschen," a phrase that constructs "the Germans" as a group to which the observer Koeppen/Littner (as I shall henceforth refer to the narrator of Koeppen's text) does not belong; the entry also discusses his hope that the diplomatic solution will also ease "die Lage der Juden in Deutschland." This causes Koeppen/Littner to draw attention immediately to the way in which his language is not entirely his own.

> Ich habe über "die Lage der Juden in Deutschland" geschrieben, und so hingeschrieben finde ich den Ausdruck wieder fremd und künstlich. Was heißt das: Lage der Juden? Ich fühle mich nicht zugehörig einer besonderen und fremden Gruppe im deutschen Volk . . . Ich selbst aber sehe mich als Mensch wie alle anderen Menschen. Ich bin ein Bürger, ein Steuerzahler, ich liebe eine gewisse Behaglichkeit, ich bin kein Verbrecher. Diese ganze Propaganda . . . muß ein entsetzliches Mißverständnis sein.[21]

The first sentence of this passage demonstrates that writing is an activity that awakens the author to the fact that the language of self-definition he uses is in fact alien and artificial, although he has already adopted it as his own. Forced now to articulate the meaning of the book's opening "wir," he is ambivalently poised between two images: as "a human like all humans," and as a self-contented bourgeois taxpayer. The first image draws on a rhetoric of universal humanity that runs throughout Koeppen's text and is also present, though much less obtrusive, in Littner's typescript. That rhetoric can be read as a reaction to the destabilization of his bourgeois security, which he imagines in a threshold moment standing in the doorway of his (expressly symbolic) home.

> Ich klammerte mich an den Türgriff, und ich sah mich zufällig im Spiegel der Garderobe: einen dicken, keuchenden Mann in einem zu kurzen Hemd. Ich sah mich, wie ich mich nie gesehen hatte: gefährdet, heimatlos, krank. Meine Wohnung . . . zerplatzte gleichsam vor meinem Auge, und ein Sturm wehte mich hinaus in das Ungeschützte, vielleicht in das wahre Leben, und alles, was bisher war, ist nur Täuschung . . . Ich sah SA, SS, HJ, die geläufigen Abkürzungen für die Organisationen der Partei . . . und ich sah mich auf ihrer Straße liegen, unter ihren Marschstiefeln . . .[22]

The moment of identity crisis triggers off a projection, the premonition of a stripping away of not only of collective identity (he is "heimatlos") and personal identity. The passage suggests that bourgeois stability might have been an illusion, and that only now would he experience "das wahre Leben." Koeppen here presents National Socialism both as a (Benjaminian) natural phenomenon ("ein Sturm wehte mich hinaus") and as an existential experience.

Soon after this premonition, Koeppen/Littner is arrested. At this point, he describes himself as a "Jude polnischer Staatsangehörigkeit." His explanation makes clear that this is an accident of history for a man who had been living in Munich and feeling himself German well before the peace treaties of 1919 that remapped Europe.[23] He has great difficulties aligning himself with a sense of Polishness, but much less difficulty with his Jewishness—which he still sees at this stage as an accident of birth—and especially his religious feelings, which he describes as being awakened by his experiences. After almost being expelled from Germany following the so-called *Reichskristallnacht* of November 9/10, 1938, Koeppen/Littner is returned to Munich because the Polish authorities refuse to accept their citizens. At this point, Koeppen invents an episode that has no parallel whatsoever in Littner's typescript. Visiting Littner's home, a non-Jewish Bavarian expresses outrage at the methods and slogans of the National Socialists,

> während der jüdische Arzt, der einst in besseren Tagen sich zur deutsch-nationalen Partei gezählt hatte und jetzt vor dem Überschwang des Nationalismus aus seiner Wohnung geflohen war, nach Worten der Verteidigung für die Idee des Vaterlandes im losbrechenden Sturm des Pöbels suchte. Und während die beiden Meinung gegen Meinung stellten . . . brachte der Rundfunk Ausschnitte aus den Volkskundgebungen "gegen das jüdische Mörderpack," und aus dem Lautsprecher drangen die Stimmen wie ein Gebell tollwütiger Hunde.[24]

In the negotiating space of the no-man's land that is now Littner's home in Munich, these two characters demonstrate the ambivalence of collective identity within their individual subjectivities, and the complexity of conceptions such as "Vaterland" and "deutsch-national." These ambivalent human voices are contrasted not with each other, but with the loudspeaker. This machine brooks no argument or discussion, its performance of the state language is in no sense ambivalent, and it projects a notion of collective identity at the "*Volks*kundgebungen" [my italics—SW] through its construction of the Other, "das jüdische Mörderpack," while itself being presented as something bestial: "das Gebell tollwütiger Hunde." By staging such a clear opposition to the state-sanctioned designations, the passage illustrates that clear distinctions between German and Jewish identities are not that simple.

At this stage a change can also be registered in Koeppen/Littner's self-definition:

> Ich lebe in engerem Kontakt zur jüdischen Gemeinde in München . . .
> Not und Verfemung schließen zusammen. Die deutschen Juden, selber ihrer Existenz bedroht, haben uns polnischen Juden geholfen, soweit es möglich war.[25]

The first-person plural, such a sensitive indicator of imagined community in this text, has found a new site for identification in the "Polish Jews."[26] This is, of course, not a designation Koeppen/Littner has freely chosen. There is a three-way tension between the discourses that define him as Jew or German, his own religious feelings and tentative sense of belonging to a Jewish community, and the continued vision of a universal humanism, evident in another invented passage, which contains Koeppen/Littner's thoughts after his first experiences in Poland, when he encounters a nationalist Polish policeman who does not like the fact that Koeppen/Littner uses the German language: "Für den rassenstaatslosen Juden gäbe es dann nur ein Ziel und eine Rettung: den zionistischen Staat. Ich dachte einmal, wir hätten diese Entwicklung hinter uns, und über einen neuen, nun jüdischen Nationalismus nach Kanaan zu kommen, schien mir ein Rückschritt."[27]

The "wir" here might refer to a Jewish community, but not exclusively, since it still contains the dream of a "Menschheitsglauben" that is directed towards a universal humanism that has left an exclusionary nationalism behind. In a synagogue in Poland, Littner has, for the first time since his banishment from the German bourgeoisie, "ein Heimatgefühl," leading him to wonder whether the meaning of this experience, be it by fate or chance, will be his "Heimkehr" to true Judaism. The question remains open, however, and the longing for his old Munich home is still present, as becomes obvious when the Wehrmacht pass through Zbaraz, the town to which Littner and his fellow refugees have fled in the attempt to keep ahead of the advancing German troops.

This section describing the encounter with the German troops is particularly useful for highlighting the differences between Grübler's and Koeppen's modifications of Littner's typescript (as opposed to those "invented" passages that I have been discussing above; Koeppen seems to allow himself much more license to invent encounters prior to the experience of violence at the hands of the SS). Here is Littner's testimony from the typescript:

> Ich möchte betonen, daß die Soldaten der Wehrmacht uns gegenüber stets ja direct menschlich benommen haben. Unwillkürlich musste ich an den alten Münchner Spruch "leben und leben lassen!" denken. Wie konnte es nur kommen, dass sich diese Menschen, die alles andere als Untiere waren, für so grausame Ziele einsetzen liessen? Das wird wohl ein psychologisches Rätsel bleiben. Aus der nahegelegenen Brauerei wurden einige Fässer Bier geholt. Die Soldaten waren meistens Bayern und Oesterreicher, sie tranken mit uns, ja sie liessen uns beim Reihumgehen der gefüllten Feldbecher zuerst trinken. Für kurze Augenblicke versetzte ich mich nach München zurück. Ich konnte ja mit den Soldaten im bayerischen Dialekt plaudern; die Landser freuten sich heimatliche Laute zu hören.[28]

Here, then, is Koeppen's modified version of this section:

> In der Truppe sind Österreicher und Bayern. Sie wollen vorm Sterben eine ordentliche "Brotzeit" halten und handeln, für eine Stunde vom militärischen Kommando befreit, nach dem Münchener Spruch "Leben und leben lassen." Aus der nahe gelegenen Brauerei werden einige Fässer Bier geholt, und ich mache vor unserem Hause den Kellner. Bald muß ich mittrinken, bayerischen Dialekt reden und kann mich in Zbaraz wie im Hofbräuhaus fühlen.[29]

Koeppen cites and develops Littner's use of what he terms his "Spruch" (the addition of "Brotzeit"), to emphasize once more the role language plays in the performance of cultural identity. The soldiers are liberated from their uniform roles for an hour. This enables Koeppen/Littner to see the men not as soldiers, and to forget the principle they are serving and to place them within the locus of that community, the beer hall, an embellishment of Littner's original. The relationship between the soldiers and Koeppen/Littner is also marked by a transition enabled by language; he begins by taking on the subordinate role of "waiter," but is then incorporated by being socially required to speak in Bavarian dialect. This brief hour of community is immediately followed by a nocturnal opportunity for reflection "ohne Besatzung und ohne Regierung." Here Koeppen/Littner regains the first-person plural as he redefines himself within a community, but this free collectivity is only to be found *between* two situations in which his position is determined:[30] "Wir leben für eine kurze Spanne in großer Freiheit, losgetrennt von allem, außerhalb der Zivilisation."[31]

Here then is Grübler's translation of the Littner passage:

> The German soldiers acted generally in a correct manner toward us. How could it happen that these people would be used for such cruel purposes? The invading soldiers, many of whom came from Bavaria and Austria, discovered several barrels filled with beer at the local brewery. Since I was able to speak the Bavarian dialect, they invited me to join them. Momentarily I felt as if I had been magically conveyed back to Munich.[32]

It would be wrong to suggest that Grübler keeps to a pedantic fidelity to the letter of Littner's typescript. Grübler excises here all reference to language as a source of cultural identity. He also reframes Littner's description of the soldiers, diminishing the forcefulness of Littner's insistence on the soldiers as "always behaving towards us in a quite humane fashion," instead implying through his use of "generally" that there might have been exceptions to this "correct" behavior. He also adds the adjective "invading," which might be understood as providing historical detail, but nonetheless underscores an antagonistic reading of the Wehrmacht, which again goes against the "psychological puzzle" that Littner confronts (and which Koeppen solves through evoking the sense of impending death ('Sterben') that the soldiers apparently feel). This passage is a point of comparison that reveals the diverging intentions behind the works. Koeppen reworks Littner's text as a way of foregrounding questions about the way that language classifies, whereas Grübler is not attuned to Littner's sense of attachment to Munich, and uses his translation to draw clearer distinctions between all Germans and the exiled Jews.

With the arrival of the SS, the experiences of Koeppen/Littner become entirely defined by the condition of "otherness" which now designates him and his fellow ghetto inhabitants. Once the ghetto has been set up in Zbaraz, the designations "Jew" and "German" stand in clear opposition in Koeppen's version. The distinctions are now laid down by the orders barked through the loudspeakers.[33] Koeppen seems to find no space now for negotiation in this traumatic narrative, no room for the kind of reflections evident earlier in the book.

The arrival of the SS in Zbaraz is used by Grübler to reach for a metaphorical register that distorts the generally neutral tone of Littner's report: whereas Littner wrote "kam der 4. Juli 1941 . . . Die Soldaten des deutschen Heeres waren in den Weiten des Ostens und nun kam das Unheil,"[34] Grübler translates as follows: "Then came July 4, 1941. While this formidable war machine advanced swiftly into far-flung regions, a force of malevolent demons was on its way to torture us."[35] This kind of embellishment can be observed in Grübler's work on many occasions from this point on, but it is as important to recognize his ongoing depersonalizing description of the Wehrmacht as a "war machine" as it to observe the depersonalization of the SS, which he will use as a strategy in his depiction of the rest of the events in Zbaraz. This may well reflect the fact that Grübler produced his translation after the Wehrmacht exhibitions of the late 1990s, which made clear the involvement of the regular German army in the "war of extermination." It is ironic, however, to note that one passage from Grübler's translation that Zachau uses in his foreword as an example of Littner's "terse description" includes Grübler's addition of "furious" to the attributes of an SS officer that is not present in the original.[36]

When the ghetto is finally cleared, Koeppen/Littner marks this event with the following, curt sentences: "Zbaraz ist judenrein! Die Gewehre schweigen. Der Tod schweigt. Die Gräber schweigen. Deutschland schweigt. Die toten Juden sind still."[37] The reference to Germany, a word whose connotations have increasingly been unsettled through the course of the book, is important, but ambiguous. Is Germany silent in refusing to confront the reality of what is happening in the name of Germany in Eastern Europe?

By contrast, Littner's text does not address a collective: "Bis spat in die Nacht hinein hörten wir das Knattern des Maschinengewehres, bis auch dieses verstummte. Die letzte Aktion war beendet. Sie hatte gründliche Arbeit geleistet. Zbaraz war judenrein. Wir schrieben den 9. Juni 1943."[38] Grübler translates this as: "The carnage that took place within the ghetto perimeter did not end until late at night. The Nazi executioners performed their assigned task of rendering the district Judenrein in a remarkably efficient manner during June 9, 1943."[39] Grübler's translation again emotively emphasizes the violence and its mechanical perpetrators in a way that Littner's text does not.

The aim here is not to conduct a microscopic interrogation of Grübler's text, but to think more broadly, from the examples discussed here, of the implications of translating testimony. Ruth Franklin, for example, is most concerned when discussing Koeppen's and Grübler's texts to privilege the virtues of "creative ambition" in order to achieve a successful work of art.[40] For my part, Koeppen's fictionalization of Littner's report has an historical value in the way it pays attention to language. That attention to language is not overtly present in Littner's text, but it is very close to Viktor Klemperer's analysis in his *LTI: Notizbuch eines Philologen* (The Language of the Third Reich: A Philologist's Notebook), which was published in Germany in 1947.[41] Koeppen's version of Littner's testimony can be read as an attempt to interrogate the terms in which one can describe the experience of the Third Reich and its use and abuse of language. To be sure, as befits an encounter that predates much of the more mature reflection on the possibility of the transmission of Holocaust experience, it is perhaps too conciliatory in its universal humanistic conclusion,[42] in which Koeppen/Littner returns to Munich and reports that "als ich aus den Ruinen des Münchener Hauptbahnhofs kam . . . fand [ich] vernichtet, was mir einst teuer war, und das Bild, nach dem ich mich in der Verbannung gesehnt hatte . . . das Bild war für immer verschwunden."[43]

Already when in exile, Koeppen/Littner had envisaged returning to Munich not as a German, not as a Jew, but as a "Mensch." The passage highlights, however, the fact that it is his image of Munich that he had yearned for that has been destroyed. These are the ruins of an imagined community, which has been destroyed not only by the bombs, but perhaps also by his experiences. How can this "Mensch" locate himself in these ruins? Both Koeppen and the real Littner seek to find meaning in the ruins. For the real Littner, they represent a clean break with the past, while in his final sentences Koeppen/Littner tries to negotiate a position where Germans and Jews can find some kind of interconnection. It would appear that the inhabitants of Munich are no better off than Littner: "Da kommen sie, die ich kannte und den Krieg überlebt haben, aus ihren Kellern, aus ihren Verstecken, aus den Ruinen ihrer Häuser, stehen vor ihrer vernichteten Existenz und der schweren, ungewissen Zukunft und fragen mich: was hätten wir tun können, wie hätten wir uns wehren sollen?"[44]

Although they face similar questions as he does, Koeppen/Littner makes a clear and important distinction between this "großen Volk" and the "Häuflein verlorener Juden" who were very much at the mercy of the Germans. Koeppen/Littner's closing remarks are a dialogue with an "alte[n] Deutschland" that *could* have resisted out of "Einsicht, Klugheit, Charakterstärke und Christlichkeit."[45] Significantly, Littner does not suggest that he would have expected German resistance to the Nazis, but instead argues that if they had resisted, the Germans would not have experienced so much loss and destruction themselves: "die Städte würden dastehen in alter Pracht."[46] It is in this context that Littner makes an important use of the collective first-person: "wenn die Bewohner der Städte . . . geschrien hätten: nein, wir wollen das nicht erdulden, wir wollen leben—Wäre dann nicht die Macht des Dämons in sich zusammengefallen, ein Nichts geworden, und wir hätten über das Machtstäubchen lachen können, statt über den Staub der Städte weinen zu müssen."[47]

The first "wir" would have been enunciated by the Germans, but the second includes Littner himself as he joins in a collective mourning over the destruction. The common language of this "wir" is precisely not language, but tears of mourning for a destroyed collective tradition. This is the collective moment in the ruins that offers a zone for negotiation between Germans and Jews.[48] It is this collective moment, which concludes Koeppen's reflection on the destabilization of language through the experience of the Third Reich, that most sharply distinguishes Koeppen's text from Littner's, and not the rejection of "Haß" and the refusal to judge with which Koeppen's text concludes, which is already present in Littner's introduction.

Koeppen's imaginative interventions are not translations of something already present in Littner's typescript, but to insist, as Zachau does, on the primacy of the transmission of information is to misunderstand what it might mean to translate testimony. The lines of classification between testimony and fiction are always already blurred, as Derrida observes.[49] Koeppen's re-working of Littner's experiences exemplifies Derrida's conception of testimony as radically subjective in its use of a narration that appears to "do what it says at the moment of enunciation." At the same time, Koeppen universalizes that testimony by transforming it into a reflection on the abuse, and alienation, of the German language in the Third Reich. Grübler's translation may be more "informative," but its claim to objectivity is clearly undermined by its inability to pay attention to Littner's or its own language in writing about the experience of the Third Reich. Both texts are ultimately historical documents of how testimony is re-used into the context of its own period, and tell us about how language articulates contemporary versions of the experience of the Third Reich.

Notes

[1] Jacques Derrida, *Demeure: Fiction and Testimony*, translated by Elisabeth Rottenburg (Stanford, CA: Stanford University Press, 2000), 38.

[2] Jakob Littner, "Mein Weg durch die Nacht" (unpublished typescript, 1945).

[3] Kurt Nathan Grübler, *Journey through the Night: Jakob Littner's Holocaust Memoir* (New York: Continuum, 2000).

[4] Reinhard Zachau, "Foreword," in Grübler, *Journey through the Night*, ix–xvii; ix.

[5] Ruth Franklin, *A Thousand Darknesses: Lies and Truth in Holocaust Fiction* (Oxford: Oxford University Press, 2010), 179.

[6] Simon Ward, *Negotiating Positions: Literature, Identity, and Social Critique in the Works of Wolfgang Koeppen* (Amsterdam: Rodopi, 2001).

[7] Walter Benjamin, "The Task of the Translator," in *Illuminations*, ed. Harry Zohn (New York: Schocken, 1969), 81.

[8] Zachau, "Foreword," xvi.

[9] Zachau, "Foreword," xvi.

[10] Franklin, *A Thousand Darknesses*, 174–75.

[11] Zachau, "Foreword," xvii.

[12] Zachau, "Foreword," xvii.

[13] Zachau, "Foreword," xvii.

[14] Zachau, "Foreword," xvii.

[15] Derrida, *Demeure*, 41.

[16] Grübler, *Journey through the Night*, xx.

[17] Wolfgang Koeppen, *Jakob Littners Aufzeichnungen aus einem Erdloch* (Frankfurt am Main: Suhrkamp, 1994), ix.

[18] See, for example, Littner, "Mein Weg," 90.

[19] Littner, "Mein Weg,", 1.

[20] Koeppen, *Jakob Littners Aufzeichungen*, 9: there is no equivalent in the typescript.

[21] Koeppen, *Jakob Littners Aufzeichungen*, 10: no equivalent.

[22] Koeppen, *Jakob Littners Aufzeichungen*, 12: no equivalent.

[23] This is expressed more briefly in the typescript, with the exception that Littner notes that his father comes from Auschwitz, which causes Littner to reflect on how the name has taken on a terrible resonance in the meantime (Littner, "Mein Weg," 5).

[24] Koeppen, *Jakob Littners Aufzeichungen*, 24: no equivalent.

[25] Koeppen, *Jakob Littners Aufzeichungen*, 22: no equivalent.

[26] There is one comparable moment in Littner's text, where he reflects, when arrested on this occasion by the Gestapo, on the manner in which he and those he is arrested with are addressed only as "Du Jude." This is soon followed by Littner's use of the phrase "uns Juden," to indicate that he has internalized the categories of Goebbels's propaganda. (Littner, "Mein Weg," 11–12.)

[27] Koeppen, *Jakob Littners Aufzeichungen*, 38: no equivalent.

[28] Littner, "Mein Weg," 45–46.

[29] Koeppen, *Jakob Littners Aufzeichungen*, 55.

[30] Throughout Koeppen's work, the moment of freedom is only to be found between definitions. For further discussion of the freedom of being "between-states" in Koeppen's texts, see: Simon Ward, *Negotiating Positions: Literature, Identity and Social Critique in the Works of Wolfgang Koeppen* (Amsterdam: Rodopi, 2002).

[31] Koeppen, *Jakob Littners Aufzeichungen*, 55: no equivalent.

[32] Grübler, *Journey through the Night*, 23.

[33] Koeppen, *Jakob Littners Aufzeichungen*, 61–62.

[34] Littner, "Mein Weg," 47.

[35] Grübler, *Journey through the Night*, 24.

[36] Zachau, "Foreword," xiv; Grübler, *Journey through the Night*, 24–25; Littner, "Mein Weg," 47.

[37] Koeppen, *Jakob Littners Aufzeichungen*, 124.

[38] Littner, "Mein Weg," 145.

[39] Grübler, *Journey through the Night*, 85.

[40] Franklin, *A Thousand Darknesses*, 179.

[41] This is a suggestion of the broader cultural context in which Koeppen's work belongs. Citing Victor Gollancz (a quotation from whose 1947 book *Our Threatened Values* Koeppen uses for an epigraph), Roland Ulrich also attempts briefly to suggest the broader contemporary humanist context in which Koeppen's text has to be seen. Roland Ulrich, "Vom Report zum Roman: Zur Textwelt von Wolfgang Koeppens Roman *Jakob Littners Aufzeichnungen aus einem Erdloch*," *Colloquia Germanica* 32, no. 2 (1999): 135–50, here 150.

[42] Although Klüger condemns Koeppen for his rhetoric of universal humanism in the concluding passages of the book (Ruth Klüger, "Zeugensprache: Koeppen und Andersch," in *Deutsche Nachkriegsliteratur und der Holocaust*, edited by Stephan Braese, Holger Gehle, Doron Kiesel, and Hanno Loewy [Frankfurt am Main: Campus, 1998], 171–83; 177), there is also a basis for this in Littner's typescript: "Nicht nur einzelne Menschen oder Völker machten einen solchen Weg durch die Nacht. Die ganze Menschheit wanderte ihn" (Littner, "Mein Weg," 181).

[43] Koeppen, *Jakob Littners Aufzeichungen*, 148. The comparable sections from the typescript run as follows: "Wehmütig war das Wiedersehen mit dieser einst so behaglich schönen Stadt. Sie war kaum wiederzuerkennen" (Littner, "Mein Weg," 180). "Als ich nach meiner Rückkehr in München die ruinenumsäumten Strassen durchwanderte und fast alles vernichtet fand, was mir dereinst teuer und Erinnerung war, erkannte ich in dieser Symphone der Zerstörung den Willen Gottes, auf solche Weise die Brücken abzubrechen zu jenem Zeitalter der Entfremdung von ihm, ein neues anbrechen zu lassen aus Schutt und Trümmern und Asche" (Littner, "Mein Weg," 181–82).

[44] Koeppen, *Jakob Littners Aufzeichungen*, 148: no equivalent.

[45] Koeppen, *Jakob Littners Aufzeichungen*, 149: no equivalent.

[46] Koeppen, *Jakob Littners Aufzeichungen*, 149: no equivalent.

[47] Koeppen, *Jakob Littners Aufzeichungen*, 149: no equivalent.

[48] This is the first version of such a "contact zone" in Koeppen's postwar work, but it would become a dominant trope of his oeuvre. See Ward, *Negotiating Positions*, 99–130.

[49] Derrida, *Demeure*, 29.

Lightning Source UK Ltd.
Milton Keynes UK
UKOW04n1904271114

242278UK00004B/57/P